The ProgramLive Companion

Paul Gries

University of Toronto

Petra Hall

University of Toronto

David Gries

Universities of Georgia and Cornell

John Wiley & Sons, Inc.

New York   Chichester   Weinheim   Brisbane   Singapore   Toronto

ACQUISITIONS EDITOR   Paul Crockett

SENIOR MARKETING MANAGER   Katherine Hepburn

SENIOR PRODUCTION EDITOR   Ken Santor

SENIOR DESIGNER   Harold Nolan

This book was set in LaTeX by the authors and printed and bound by Malloy Lithographing.

The cover was printed by Phoenix Color Corporation.

This book is printed on acid-free paper. ∞

The paper in this book was manufactured by a mill whose forest management programs include sustained yield harvesting of its timberlands. Sustained yield harvesting principles ensure that the numbers of trees cut each year does not exceed the amount of new growth.

ISBN 0-471-20804-3 (pbk)

Printed in the United States of America

10 9 8 7 6 5 4 3 2 1

The
ProgramLive Companion

Preface

Traditional textbooks provide an excellent medium for presenting facts. But programming is *not* fact-based! Instead, it is almost entirely problem-solving. There are many solutions to *every* programming problem, and *how* solutions are developed is more important than the solutions themselves, especially when first learning to program.

A paper-based presentation of the development of a program is difficult to do well, because that development is dynamic. Programs are written in little pieces, and discussion of the development of these pieces is necessarily interwoven with the pieces themselves, leading to a disjointed and overly long —and often boring— presentation.

Our dissatisfaction with paper as a medium for programming course materials led us to multimedia and finally to our livetext, *ProgramLive*, which is bundled with this *ProgramLive Companion*. *ProgramLive* contains over 250 recorded lectures, with synched animation. *ProgramLive* enhances the traditional course, but it also makes long-distance learning and self learning more viable, because students can repeat the lectures over and over, even when an instructor is not present.

The one drawback to multimedia is that it cannot be studied away from a computer. Many people —colleagues, instructors, and students alike— felt the need for something they could read and study when not bound to a desk. Therefore, we decided to write this *Companion*.

However, the presence of *ProgramLive* meant that we could write a different kind of text. There was no need for the traditional lengthy explanations, exercises, and so on, for all these things were already on *ProgramLive*, and we could explore other avenues. Thus, this *Companion* contains three new components.

First, it can be used as a "workbook". As students listen to *ProgramLive* lectures, they answer simple questions in this book itself, making them more active participants and helping them to assimilate the material. A teacher can require that they bring their *Companion* to class, or a lab, with certain questions answered. By the end of a course, the students will have written definitions of almost all programming terms that are used in *ProgramLive* and have solved many problems, and their completed workbook serves as their own personal reference for study.

Second, there are three detailed lesson plans, making it easier for an instructor to use *ProgramLive* not only as a text by itself but also as a supplementary when using Horstmann's *Computing Concepts with Java Essentials* and Niño and Hosch's *Programming and Object-Oriented Design using Java.*

Third, this is one of the first Java texts with a substantial collection of Java API specifications. The 80-page Appendix D should make it easier for instructors and students alike to use the classes that come with Java. We cover most of the basic packages, including the graphical user interface package called *Swing.*

The John Wiley website

Another aid for both the instructor and the student is a website:

www.wiley.com/college/gries

The instructors' part of the website can be accessed only with a password (speak to your Wiley rep about obtaining access). The website provides Powerpoint lecture slides for an introductory programming course using *Program-Live* and its *Companion*, answers for all questions in the *Companion*, and examples of midterms and finals. As time goes on, it will contain more programming projects.

The students' website contains answers to selected exercises from both *ProgramLive* and its *Companion.*

We hope that *ProgramLive*, its *Companion*, and this website will help to raise the level of teaching in all kinds of introductory programming courses —traditional courses, long-distance courses, and self-paced courses.

About the authors

Paul Gries, Petra's husband, received his B.A. in 1992 and M.Eng. in 1994 at Cornell University. A lecturer in Computer Science at the University of Toronto since 1999, Paul has been experimenting with teaching introductory programming in a self-paced course, using, naturally, *ProgramLive.* Paul has already received four awards for his teaching, from Cornell and Toronto.

Petra Hall, David's daughter-in-law, has been a teaching assistant for first-year courses at the University of Toronto and was extensively involved with a pilot project using *ProgramLive.* She is finishing her undergraduate degree part time at the University of Toronto. She is one of the few people in the world whose text (this *Companion*) is being used in the department in which she is an undergraduate.

David Gries, Paul's father, received his B.S. in 1960 from Queens College, his M.S. in 1962 from the University of Illinois, and his Dr. rer. nat. in 1966 from the Munich Institute of Technology. He taught for three years at Stanford and thirty years at Cornell and has been at the University of Georgia since July 1999. Known for his contributions to compiler writing and programming methodology, he has received four international computer science education awards, from the AFIPS, the ACM SIGCSE, the ACM, and the IEEE Computer Society.

Acknowledgments

The Computer Science Departments at Cornell, Toronto, and UGA have been extremely supportive of our work. Each, in its own way, has contributed greatly to this project. For example, the entire class in the self-paced pilot project at Toronto in summer 2000 deserves thanks for their feedback on (and patience with) the beta version of *ProgramLive*, especially Marc Lubin and Jay Fallah.

The people at Data Description are great! Matt Clark wrote the software to produce the first livetext, *Activstats*. As we wrote *ProgramLive*, he responded quickly to our calls for changes and additions to fit our needs, and in a thoroughly professional manner. John Sammis, the business manager, has been our constant companion and "encourager" for several years, as *ProgramLive* and then this *Companion* neared completion. Paul Vellemen, the author of *Activstats*, was instrumental in getting us started with *ProgramLive*. And a cadre of other people at Data Description —Michell Lamarre, Mike Prentice, Tracy Stewart, Steve Wampler, David Vellemen, Aaron Lowenkron, Peter Nix, and Tianyu Xie— have been supporting the project in many ways, like producing the icons for each activity, cleaning audio files, synching animations to audios, and translating *ProgramLive* from its Macintosh author-base to the Windows environment. The amount of work that has to be done to produce a livetext continues to amaze us.

Several publishers refused to take a chance with our nontraditional product. But he who wants the best apple must go out on a limb! Paul Crocket of Wiley & Sons saw the possibilities at once and worked with us and Data Description to bring this *Companion* to fruition in quite a short time. His suggestions and encouragement were invaluable. Also, the reviewers of the *Companion* did a marvelous job, providing us with many inciteful comments. Thanks also to the Wiley copyeditor and the production manager, Ken Santor.

The text was written using LaTeX. Thanks go to Don Knuth for creating TeX and to Leslie Lamport for building LaTeX on top of it.

The API Java specs in the appendix were produced by a doclet, which is a (greatly) modified doclet written by Gregg Wonderly of C2 Technologies Inc.

Sage, Paul and Petra's daughter (6 months old when this was written), is much too young to read this, but she has been a wonderful stimulus and enormous distraction. To counteract the kid distraction, a bevy of babysitters have been at our beck and call. Many thanks go to Petra's parents Helena Frei and Mike Hall; to the entire 280 crew (Mike, Helena, Kersti Wain-Bantin, and Elizabeth Reid) for plentiful dinners; to babysitter Anna; to Matt Adams and Sally Miller for "The West Wing" Wednesday evenings; and to Susan and James Doukas for hours upon hours of walking Sage all over Toronto while we slaved away at the *Companion*.

Last —and certainly not least— we thank Elaine Gries, our mother, mother-in-law, and wife, for all that she has put up with during the writing of *ProgramLive* and its *Companion*. She has been supportive in countless ways and patient in many more during the long, drawn-out months and years of this project.

Contents

CONTENTS

CONTENTS

CONTENTS

Chapter 0

The *Companion*: three lesson plans

0.1 How to use the *ProgramLive Companion*

Welcome to *ProgramLive*! Or, rather, welcome to this paper companion to the livetext *ProgramLive*. This companion will help you in learning to program, although you will spend most of your time working with the livetext itself. *ProgramLive* contains the bulk of the teaching material: over 250 lectures with synchronized narration and animation, along with an index, a glossary that is unmatched in any other programming text, exercises, labs, homeworks, and programming projects. This *Companion* will help you find your way through *ProgramLive*.

The Organization of this *Companion*

This *Companion* consists of three parts:

1. Chapter 0, the chapter you are now reading, contains a discussion of how to study and three lesson plans.

   The lesson plan for *ProgramLive* (p. 4) provides an ordering of the material in *ProgramLive* and a checklist that you can use to mark your progress. It includes all the material that is usually covered in a one-semester freshman-level course, as well as additional optional material for those who want to go further. It introduces objects and classes early.

   The lesson plan for Horstmann's *Computing Concepts with Java 2 Essentials*, John Wiley & Sons, Inc., New York, 2000 (p. 14) provides a similar checklist for Horstmann's text, indicating with each section corresponding material in *ProgramLive*. This facilitates the use of *ProgramLive* as a supplement to Horstmann's text.

   The lesson plan for Niño and Hosch's *Programming and Object Oriented Design using Java*, John Wiley & Sons, Inc., New York, 2001 (p. 27) provides a checklist for this text, indicating with each section corresponding material in *ProgramLive*. This facilitates the use of *ProgramLive* as a supplement to Niño-Hosch, as we call it.

2. The "workbook": chapters 1–17 correspond to lessons 1–17 of *Program-Live* —Chap. 1 to lesson 1, etc. For each activity of a lesson, we have

included charts to fill in, questions to answer, places to write definitions, and areas to take notes, as well as summaries and short explanations. Use this part of the *Companion* in conjunction with *ProgramLive*. Write on the pages, and use them later for review and reference.

3. The appendices provide reference material. All this material can be found in one form or another on *ProgramLive* or on the web. However, the appendices can be used when your computer is not available. Also, in some situations, it is easier to use reference material that appears on paper.

0.1.1   Executional versus organizational aspects of programming

There are two aspects to a program, which we might term *executional* and *organizational*. The first refers to the statements of the program, which are executed or performed by the computer; the second, to the way the program is structured and organized. Before the 1990's, the executional aspect was emphasized, and the major organizational techniques were actually a reflection of the executional aspect. For example, the major organizational unit was the *procedure*, or *subroutine*, which was tied to the statement named the *procedure call*. Execution of a procedure call caused the procedure to be executed, or performed. Think of a procedure as a recipe in a cookbook; the cook (the computer) follows the instructions (statements) in the recipe (procedure). Having the cook "Make the chocolate cake on page 250" is executing a procedure call.

From the beginnings of the computing age, the executional aspect was emphasized, mainly because organizational tools not tied to the executional aspect weren't available. Just as a cookbook is organized as a set of recipes, a program consisted of a set of procedures, whose bodies consisted of sequences of instructions to be executed.

Object orientation, or object-oriented programming, provides a new set of organizational tools. (Object orientation was born in the late 1960's, did not become viable for 20 years, and finally reached full acceptance in the 1990's.) Object-oriented concepts are aimed not at indicating how a program is to be executed but how it is organized. Object orientation provides the mechanisms that make the development, maintenance, and reuse of large programs possible, and it helps with small programs, too. It is fair to say that without object orientation, a lot of the programming that goes on would be much harder, if not impossible. Most modern languages are object oriented (e.g. Java), and some older languages have had object orientation grafted on to them.

Introductory programming is usually taught in one of two ways. The traditional course emphasizes the executional aspect and teaches object orientation only near the end of the course (if at all). Therefore, students get little chance to digest and use object-oriented concepts. Object orientation seems more like an add-on, and not that useful, since the first ten weeks or so of the course don't use it. This makes it harder for students to switch to object-oriented thinking later on.

The second approach introduces object orientation as soon as possible and uses it as a matter of course throughout the course. Taught suitably, and early in the course, object orientation is digested fairly easily by students.

Particularly with Java, we feel that object orientation is best taught early, because almost every program fragment has something to do with objects. With the traditional approach, too much of a Java program remains a mystery for too long.

We do think that one needs some idea of the executional aspect before learning about object orientation. After all, the purpose of executing a program is to get some task done, and a basic familiarity with the executional aspect is needed. Our object-oriented lesson plan reflects this.

Those who want to get all the executional aspects of programming out of the way before tackling the object-oriented stuff can place Units 5, 6, and 7 (on iteration and arrays) of the *ProgramLive* lesson plan before Unit 3 (Classes).

0.1.2   Some ideas on studying

There are two *absolutely* necessary tasks that you must do when learning to program. They are:

- **Take notes.** When listening to an activity in *ProgramLive*, pause it often, relisten to it where necessary, and *take notes*. This *Companion* will help you with that. When you are done with the livetext, most pages of this supplementary book should be covered with your handwriting. Use the margins as well as the outlined areas; write as much as you need to remember the material. *ProgramLive* is the only place where you can have the lecturer repeat something as often as you like!

- **Write programs.** As soon and as often as you can, write programs and run them. Just as you can't learn to write poetry by reading the works of Robert Frost, you can't learn to program just by reading our programs. This *Companion* provides many exercises for you to reinforce what you have just learned.

Beginning a whole new area of study almost always calls for learning new phrases and terms, and the area of programming is no different. We encourage you to use whatever means necessary to master the new terminology immediately, because you will use it over and over again in later work. If you don't understand the terminology, you won't understand later material.

When a new term is defined, write it down in a list, or put it on a flashcard along with its definition, or rehearse saying the term and its precise meaning —do whatever it takes to make the term part of your working vocabulary. This means *studying*, and not just reading and listening. Reading and listening do little good if they are not followed by real study and practice. When you see a term that you don't understand, look it up in the glossary and learn what it means. Don't put off looking up a word; do it immediately.

All this requires more work on your part, but you will find that you will learn the material far more effectively, and in less time, than if you just read and listen.

0.2   Lesson plan for Gries and Gries's *ProgramLive*

This lesson plan divides a course into six units, each of which requires about two weeks of work, more or less. There are five optional units, on multidimensional arrays, exception handling, interfaces, recursion, and applets, each of which takes about a week to cover.

Below, we give an overview of each unit followed by a checklist for the activities in it. Check off each item as you complete it.

Unit 1. Introduction

This first part of this unit introduces the mechanics of a livetext. Do spend half an hour on lesson 0 of *ProgramLive*, learning about the features of the livetext. In addition to the activities, it offers a plethora of learning tools such as the glossary, index, exercises and labs.

The second part of this unit provides a look at the programming language Java. This may be your first contact with a programming language, and you will see lots of new terminology and concepts. Don't expect to remember everything from this first look at Java. You will also learn how to run Java programs on the computer, using either an IDE (Interactive Development Environment) or a UNIX or PC command-line environment.

In learning to run Java programs, use material that is appropriate to the system you are using —perhaps lesson 18 (for IDE Visual Cafe), lesson 19 (for IDE CodeWarrior), Appendix B (for a command-line system), or whatever else is provided with your IDE.

☐ Introduction to livetexts   *PL* Lesson 0-1

☐ Activities   *PL* Lesson 0-2

☐ The lesson book page   *PL* Lesson 0-3

☐ Global features   *PL* Lesson 0-4

☐ Page controls   *PL* Lesson 0-5

☐ Dealing with Java programs   *PL* Lesson 0-6

☐ Learning effectively   *PL* Lesson 0-7

☐ Hardware and software   *PL* Lesson 1-1, page 41

☐ Some simple Java programs   *PL* Lesson 1-2, page 43
Pay attention to the filing cabinet metaphor, for it is a good analogy for understanding just what a class is. We use it throughout *ProgramLive*.

☐ Components of a Java program   *PL* Lesson 1-3, page 47
The sooner you learn the terminology introduced on this page, the better off you
will be. The notions of *variable* and *expression* will probably not be new to you;
you just have to learn how they are used in Java.

☐ Three statements   *PL* Lesson 1-4, page 51
This is your first hard look at what it means to execute a statement, using three
of Java's most common statements. Memorize what it means to execute these
statements, and also become familiar with the statement-comment.

☐ Conventions for indentation   *PL* Lesson 13-3, page 189
You need not listen to the activities now. Just read the lesson page and the two
footnotes concerning the if-statement and the if-else-statement.

☐ Input/Output   *PL* Lesson 1-5, page 56
Definitely listen to the first activity on output. Skip the second activity unless
your instructor requires it; there is no need to know about it now. But the activity
on `JLiveWindow` is important, because `JLiveWindow` will be used often, You will
also want to listen to the activities on drawing lines, circles, etc., because that
stuff is fun.

☐ Do Lab PGL-1 (assignment) of this lesson.   *PL* Lesson 1

☐ Do Lab PGL-2 (if-statement) of this lesson.   *PL* Lesson 1

☐ Do Lab PGL-3 (if-else-statement) of this lesson.   *PL* Lesson 1

☐ Types   *PL* Lessons 6-1, page 117, and 6-2, page 118
You already know that a type defines a set of values and operations on them.
You can declare variables of type `int` and write simple expressions, and you can
also write simple `String` expressions. At some point, you will want to study all of
lesson 6 carefully, to get a more precise understanding of Java's primitive types.
For now, just read these two lesson pages, and you can skip casting for now.

☐ Introduction to your IDE. Use whatever materials are available for your method
of running Java programs.

Unit 2. Methods

This unit introduces you to a basic building block of programs, the method.
A method is like a recipe: a sequence of instructions to be executed to get
something done. You will be writing methods as well as reading them, so we

want to give you some insight into how to write them and test them. In this unit, then, we introduce you to five things:

1. The "assertion" as a way of understanding methods,

2. The definition of methods,

3. Statements that call a method in order to get its task performed,

4. Top-down programming: a strategy for developing methods, and

5. How to test a method.

We also ask you to look at a few activities in *ProgramLive* on programming style, which, for organizational purposes, are in lesson 13.

☐ Good programming practices   *PL* Lesson 13-1, page 185
This is just a short essay for your reading enjoyment.

☐ Assertions in programs   *PL* Lesson 1-6, page 58

☐ Methods   *PL* Lesson 2-1, page 61
A method is just a recipe for doing something. Here, you learn the "user's" view of a method, i.e. the view of someone who wants to have a method executed.

☐ Method bodies and method calls   *PL* Lesson 2-2, page 64
We now look more closely at procedure bodies, and we also define precisely how a procedure call is executed. Memorize the steps!

☐ Two components of method bodies   *PL* Lesson 2-3, page 67
The local variable and the return statement can ease the task of writing a procedure.

☐ Functions   *PL* Lesson 2-4, page 70
The *function* is another kind of method. A procedure call is a statement; a function call is an expression.

☐ Testing and debugging   *PL* Lesson 14-1, page 193
This lesson page introduces terminology concerning testing and debugging and gives you some guidelines that, if followed, will reduce the chance of your programs having errors. The single activity on this page uses an example that contains a loop, which you don't need to know about yet. Skip the example.

☐ Testing strategies   *PL* Lesson 14-2, page 194
Listen only to activities 1 and 2 and concentrate mainly on the first one, unless your instructor tells you to concentrate on the second one.

☐ Debugging   *PL* Lesson 14-4, page 196
The two activities will give you some idea about how to track down bugs.

☐ Do Lab PGL-4 (writing simple functions) of this lesson.   *PL* Lesson 2

☐ Naming conventions   *PL* Lesson 13-2, page 185
Read the lesson page and listen to only the first activity on naming parameters, the second activity on naming local variables, and the second-last activity on naming methods.

☐ Conventions for indentation   *PL* Lesson 13-3, page 189
Listen to the two activities and read the footnote for indenting a method body.

☐ Guidelines for writing methods   *PL* Lesson 13-4, page 190
The first two activities try to convince you of the importance of method specifications. Get in the habit of writing a spec first! The last three activities provide insight on how to structure method bodies when they get long.

☐ Do Lab PGL-1 (Statement-comments) of this lesson.   *PL* Lesson 2

☐ Top-down programming   *PL* Lesson 2-5, page 72

Unit 3. Classes

This unit introduces you to some fundamental concepts of object-oriented programming and their realization in Java. As mentioned earlier, the *class* is a basic building block in Java. In our examples, a class corresponds to a drawer of a filing cabinet. The class is used to describe two things:

1. Class variables and methods, which go into the drawer, and

2. Objects, which also go into the drawer when they are created.

You will see how to create and use objects.

☐ Classes   *PL* Lesson 3-1, page 75
This lesson page introduces the first use of a class. There is a description of class methods and variables, which go in its file-cabinet drawer.

☐ Class `Math`   *PL* Lesson 3-2, page 77
Class `Math` contains useful static methods (i.e. class methods) and static fields (i.e. class fields). There's nothing to "memorize" here; just become familiar with the items in class `Math`, so that you can find and use them when you need them.

☐ Classes and objects   *PL* Lesson 3-3, page 79
This lesson page begins the discussion of the second use of a class: as a description of or template for objects of the class.

☐ Creating and initializing objects.   *PL* Lesson 3-4, page 82
Static methods and field are in the class drawer when execution of a program begins. Objects are created (and stored in the drawer) during execution of the program.

☐ Class `String`   *PL* Lesson 5-3, page 106
Lesson page 3-4 has an activity on creating objects of class `String`. This is a good time to become thoroughly familiar with this class, by studying Lesson page 5-3.

☐ Scope boxes and constructors   *PL* Lesson 3-5, page 85
The introduction of classes forces us to introduce scope boxes into the model of execution. The constructor, a special kind of method, is used to initialize the fields of objects.

☐ Do Lab PGL-1 (Writing constructors) of this lesson.   *PL* Lesson 3

☐ Nonstatic methods   *PL* Lesson 3-6, page 87
Static methods go in the class drawer; nonstatic methods, or *instance methods*, belong in each instance of the class.

☐ Do Lab PGL-2 (Drawing objects) of this lesson.   *PL* Lesson 3

☐ Consequences of using objects   *PL* Lesson 3-7, page 90
We (1) extend the model of execution to include calls on instance methods, (2) talk about equality of object names, as opposed to equality of objects, and (3) introduce, as a convention, method `toString`.

☐ Do Lab PGL-3 (Drawing frames) of this lesson.   *PL* Lesson 3

☐ Style considerations concerning classes   *PL* Lesson 13-2, page 185
Listen only to the third activity (p. 187) on naming instance variables and class variables; the last activity (p. 188) on naming classes; and the footnote on lesson page 13-3 (p. 189) on indenting components of a class.

☐ Describing variables   *PL* Lesson 13-5, page 191

☐ Testing strategies   *PL* Lesson 14-2, page 194
Listen only to the activity on using assertions (p. 195), and read the footnote at the bottom of the page.

☐ Numerical wrapper classes   *PL* Lesson 5-1, page 105
Now that you know about classes, you can learn about the "wrapper classes" for the primitive types. This lesson page describes wrapper class **Integer**, which wraps an **int**. The wrapper classes for the other numerical types are similar; refer to the footnotes for them when you need them. Lesson page 5-2 describes wrapper classes **Boolean** and **Character**. You don't have to look at them now, but remember their existence and look at them when you need them.

☐ Object-oriented design   *PL* Lesson 3-8, page 93

Unit 4. Subclasses

This unit introduces subclasses and superclasses, inherited methods, overriding methods, and casting an object. This will require some preparatory study of primitive types and casting. After studying this unit, you will know all the basics of object-oriented programming in Java (except for interfaces) and will be able to understand just about all parts of Java programs —finally!

This material requires the idea of casting, so some material in lesson 6 on types is included here. If you have already covered this material, skip it.

☐ The integral types   *PL* Lesson 6-2, page 118
The important part here is the conversion (casting) from one type to another. Study mainly the activities on promoting values to a wider type (p. 119) and casting integer values (p. 119).

☐ Do Lab PGL-2 (Casting among integral types) of this lesson.   *PL* Lesson 6

☐ Subclasses   *PL* Lesson 4-1, page 97
The subclass is an important tool in object-oriented programming. Without it, our tools for organizing programs would be very limited.

☐ Do Lab PGL-1 (Drawing objects II) of this lesson.   *PL* Lesson 4

☐ Constructors and inherited methods   *PL* Lesson 4-2, page 99
This lesson page introduces a variety of concepts that stem from having subclasses. The final activity tells you about the important class `Object`, the "superest" class of them all.

☐ Do Lab PGL-2 (Writing constructors II) of this lesson.   *PL* Lesson 4

☐ Casting and method calls   *PL* Lesson 4-3, page 101
The idea of "casting" an object of a subclass to a superclass but still having the overriding methods of the subclass be used is extremely important for object-oriented programming. Be sure you understand it. At this point, we can give the final model of execution.

☐ Do Lab PGL-3 (Drawing frames II) of this lesson.   *PL* Lesson 4

☐ Selecting test cases and checking them   *PL* Lesson 14-3, page 195
We finish the lesson on testing and debugging with a study of different kinds of testing.

☐ (Optional) Do Lab PGL-3 (Formatting in locales) of this lesson.   *PL* Lesson 6

☐ Object-oriented design with subclasses   *PL* Lesson 4-4, page 103

☐ (Optional) Abstract classes   *PL* Lesson 4-5, page 104
Although this lesson page is optional, it is short, and we recommend that you study it.

☐ (Optional) Do Lab PGL-4 (Practice with shapes) of this lesson.   *PL* Lesson 4

Unit 5. Loops

To iterate means to repeat over and over again. Well, then, to reiterate should mean to do it again, that means, to again repeat over and over again. So it goes, with English.

In Java (and other programming languages), execution of a "loop" causes a statement, called its "repetend" or "body", to be executed over and over again. The loop is an extremely useful statement, but it is much harder to understand then the statements that you have learned already. That's why a complete unit is devoted to it.

☐ Iteration (only the first activity)   *PL* Lesson 7-1, page 127
This activity takes you through one execution of a **while** loop. It introduces some
terminology, and it shows you a flow chart that describes how a loop is executed.
Memorize this material before proceeding!

☐ Do Lab PGL-1 (Executing a while loop) of this lesson.   *PL* Lesson 7

☐ Iteration (all but the first activity)   *PL* Lesson 7-1, page 127
Knowing how a loop is executed is not enough; you have to know how to understand what happens within a loop, and you have to be able to explain a loop to
others. This requires the notion of a loop invariant. Study this material carefully.

☐ Several examples of loops   *PL* Lesson 7-2, page 132
The first activity discusses the development loop invariants. The rest of them develop three algorithms. Study them with an eye to understanding the development
process. You may want to obtain the spiral program and play with it.

☐ Do Lab PGL-2 (Developing loops from invariants) of this lesson.   *PL* Lesson 7

☐ (Optional) Do Lab PGL-3 (Developing loops ... II) of this lesson.   *PL* Lesson 7

☐ Conventions for indentation   *PL* Lesson 13-3, page 189
Read the footnote on indenting loops, near the bottom of the lesson page.

☐ Loop schemata   *PL* Lesson 7-3, page 134
Rather than write each loop from scratch, learn to use loop schemata.

☐ Do Lab PGL-4 (Using loop schemata) of this lesson.   *PL* Lesson 7

☐ The **for** loop   *PL* Lesson 7-4, page 136
The **for** loop is an abbreviation of a **while** loop that uses a "loop counter". It
is extremely useful when the number of iterations to perform is known before
execution of the loop. You'll see lots of **for** loops in Java programs.

☐ (Optional) Do Lab PGL-4 (Translating **while**s into **for**s).   *PL* Lesson 7

☐ Making progress and stopping   *PL* Lesson 7-5, page 138
Many people will get by without studying this lesson page. However, you will
have a much better understanding of loops if you study it carefully.

☐ Miscellaneous points about loops   *PL* Lesson 7-6, page 140
Do read the warning note at the top of the page. It will take only a few seconds.

The first two activities illustrate an important use of the statement-comment:
abstraction helps us say that we *never* think of nested loops (well, ...).

You need *not* study the information about the do-while loop, the **continue** statement, and the **break** statement. In general, these constructs are not needed at
this point of your programming career. If you see them in a program and want to
find out about them, look in the *ProgramLive* glossary or index.

Unit 6. Arrays

An array is a collection of elements of the same (primitive or class) type —int, String, JLiveWindow, etc. Arrays are used in many situations; for example, to hold a list of courses offered by a college.

☐ Introduction to arrays   *PL* Lesson 8-1, page 143
This lesson page introduces all the technical details concerning arrays.

☐ Talking about array segments   *PL* Lesson 8-2, page 146
The notation described here, including pictures, makes it easier to discuss algorithms that manipulate arrays.

☐ Some programs that use arrays   *PL* Lesson 8-3, page 148
Activities 1 and 2 develop two useful schemata for processing arrays. You will use them often. The next five activities develop algorithms that manipulate arrays. Study them all! Particularly important are the last two; they show you how to test for array equality and show you that a function can return an array.

☐ Do Lab PGL-1 (Using arrays) of this lesson.   *PL* Lesson 8

☐ Arrays and classes —a student report   *PL* Lesson 8-4, page 153
The first two activities develop a first application of arrays, showing how arrays are actually used.

☐ (Optional) Arrays and classes —dynamic arrays   *PL* Lesson 8-4, page 153
You may also want to look at class **Vector** on lesson page 5-5 (p. 111).

☐ Some basic array algorithms   *PL* Lesson 8-5, page 156
Eight basic algorithms on arrays are developed on this page. You need not study them all at this point. At a minimum, though, study the first activity on finding the first value, the activities on finding the minimum value, partitioning an array segment, and the important activity on binary search.

☐ Selection sort and Insertion sort   *PL* Lesson 8-6, page 161
Do study the two activities on Selection sort. Insertion sort is optional.

☐ (Optional) Do Lab PGL-2 (Timing execution) of this lesson.   *PL* Lesson 8

Unit 7. Multidimensional Arrays (optional)

This unit, which is optional, shows you how you can have two- and three-dimensional (and more) arrays in Java. You can live without this material in your first exposure to programming and Java.

☐ Multidimensional arrays   *PL* Lesson 9-1, page 163
This lesson page presents the technical details you need to work with two- and three-dimensional arrays. It also presents a non-Java notation that makes talking about multidimensional arrays easier.

☐ Programs that use two-dimensional arrays   *PL* Lesson 9-2, page 165
Don't skip the second activity on the page, which develops a surprisingly simple algorithm. Finding a loop invariant first and following the methodology for developing loops that was explained in lesson 7 leads to an algorithm that otherwise is extremely difficult to discover.

☐ Do Lab PGL-1 (Rectangular arrays) of this lesson.   *PL* Lesson 9

☐ The Java concept of a multidimensional array   *PL* Lesson 9-3, page 168
You will discover that we didn't give the whole story on lesson page 9-1. For example, you will see that a two-dimenssional array is really an array whose elements are arrays —which can be of different lengths!

☐ Programs that use ragged arrays   *PL* Lesson 9-4, page 170

Unit 8. Exception handling (optional)

This material is optional.

☐ Output of thrown Exceptions and Errors   *PL* Lesson 10-1, page 173
Explains some basic error messages.

☐ The throwable object.   *PL* Lesson 10-2, page 173
Shows how to pass an error message out of a nested method call without crashing the program.

☐ Catching a thrown exception   *PL* Lesson 10-3, page 174
Deals with exceptions within your own code.

☐ The throw-statement   *PL* Lesson 10-4, page 175
Tell what to do when your program encounters some problems and how to tell the user which problem occurred.

☐ Checked exceptions and the throws clause   *PL* Lesson 10-5, page 176

☐ Hints on using exceptions   *PL* Lesson 10-5, page 176

Unit 9. Interfaces (optional)

This material is optional.

☐ Interfaces   *PL* Lesson 12-1, page 179
Introduces the interface and its implementation.

☐ The interface as a type   *PL* Lesson 12-2, page 180
Classes can implement more than one interface, and interfaces can be extended to cover more methods.

☐ Interface `Comparable`   *PL* Lesson 12-3, page 182

☐ Interfaces `Enumeration` and `Iterator`   *PL* Lesson 12-4, page 183
An advanced topic.

Unit 10. Recursion (optional)

Anything you can do with iteration you can do with recursion (methods that can call themselves), and in many cases recursion will be the simpler tool to use. You already have all the technical tools you need to understand recursion; there is really nothing new about it.

☐ Recursion   *PL* Lesson 15-1, page 197
This lesson page discusses what it means for a method to call itself, develops three recursive methods, and talks about the "recursive pattern". Understand this pattern, and you understand recursion.

☐ Execution of calls on recursive methods (optional)   *PL* Lesson 15-2, page 200
Do only the first activity. You will see that you already know how to execute recursive calls by hand. The model of execution already discussed needs no changing.

☐ Execution of calls on recursive methods   *PL* Lesson 15-2, page 200
Java doesn't execute recursive methods as efficiently as they might be —Java wastes space. The activities after the first one are optional. They tell you about tail recursion and show you how to change a method to eliminate tail-recursive calls, thus saving the space that they require for frames. It's neat stuff, but not necessary at this point.

☐ Interesting recursive methods   *PL* Lesson 15-3, page 202
Of the three algorithms developed here, "Tiling Elaine's kitchen" is the most impressive. Recursion can make a seemingly impossible problem appear relatively simple.

☐ Quicksort   *PL* Lesson 15-4, page 202
Quicksort is the most famous and most widely used sorting algorithm. Every computer scientist and professional programmer should know it. The first version is relatively simple. In order to save space and make it more efficient, the first method has to be manipulated a bit.

Unit 11. Applets (optional)

An *application* is a Java program whose execution starts when the system calls method `main` of some class. An *applet* is a Java program whose execution starts when a browser (e.g. Netscape or Internet Explorer) loads an html page that contains a command to start the applet.

Some instructors prefer to use applications in their course; others, applets. For those who prefer applets, this Unit may be placed earlier in the lesson plan, perhaps after Unit 2 (Methods). This Unit on applets is short and should take only one lecture.

☐ Applets   *PL* Lesson 16-1, page 205
Here, we show only what an applet looks like, not how it is called.

☐ HTML and applet commands   *PL* Lesson 16-2, page 206
Html is the language in which files that appear in a browser are written. This is a brief introduction to html.

☐ Examples of applets   *PL* Lesson 16-3, page 208

0.3   Lesson plan for Horstmann's
Computing Concepts with Java 2 Essentials

This lesson plan matches the chapters of *Computing Concepts with Java 2 Essentials* (second edition), by Cay Horstmann, with activities in *ProgramLive*. Each unit of the lesson plan corresponds to a chapter. Different authors of programming texts introduce material in different orders and emphasize different concepts, so the match between Horstmann and *ProgramLive* is not exact.

Below, we give an overview of each unit together with a checklist for the activities in it. Check each one off as you complete it. But first:

- An activity or lab that is labeled "optional" is in *ProgramLive* but not in *Computing Concepts*.

- Instead of using Horstmann's class `Console` for input and output, *ProgramLive* uses `JLiveRead`. The classes are similar.

- It is possible to skip the lesson in *ProgramLive* on how to use the livetext, but you will save time if you spend half an hour on lesson 0 of *ProgramLive*, learning about the features of a livetext. In addition to the activities, there are a plethora of instructional tools such as the glossary, index, exercises, and labs.

☐ Introduction to livetexts   *PL* Lesson 0-1

☐ Activities   *PL* Lesson 0-2

☐ The lesson book page   *PL* Lesson 0-3

☐ Global features   *PL* Lesson 0-4

☐ Page controls   *PL* Lesson 0-5

☐ Dealing with Java programs   *PL* Lesson 0-6

☐ Learning effectively   *PL* Lesson 0-7

Unit 1. Introduction

This may be your first contact with a programming language, and you will see lots of new terminology and concepts. Don't expect to remember everything from this first look at Java. You will also learn how to run Java programs on the computer, using either an IDE (Interactive Development Environment) or a UNIX or PC command-line environment.

In learning to run Java programs, use material that is appropriate to the system you are using. *ProgramLive* covers the Interactive Development Environments Visual Cafe (lesson 18), CodeWarrior (lesson 19), and the UNIX command-line system (Appendix B of this text).

☐ **Horstmann, Secs. 1.1-1.7, p. 2. Hardware and software**

☐ Hardware and software   *PL* Lesson 1-1, page 41
Horstmann does a more thorough job of discussing hardware and software.

☐ **Horstmann, Sec. 1.8-1.10, p. 21. Compiling and errors**

☐ Some simple Java programs   *PL* Lesson 1-2, page 43
This lesson page introduces *ProgramLive*'s filing cabinet metaphor to help you understand what a class is. The `import` statement is mentioned, which Horstmann does much later.

☐ Introduction to your IDE. Use whatever materials are available for your method of running Java programs. Visual Cafe is covered in *ProgramLive* lesson 18; Code-Warrior, in lesson 19. There is an introduction to the UNIX command-line system in Appendix B.

☐ Type `char` (advanced) (first activity)   *PL* Lesson 6-5, page 121
Horstmann, Sec. 1.8, provides an advanced topic: escape sequences. Look at the footnote for a synopsis of Java escape sequences. One difference: Horstmann does not introduce primitive type `char` until much later, preferring instead to do everything in terms of class `String`.

☐ Components of a Java program (only activities 1–3)   *PL* Lesson 1-3, page 47

☐ Good programming practices   *PL* Lesson 13-1, page 185

☐ Syntax errors   *PL* Lesson 19-5

☐ **Horstmann, Sec. 1.11, p. 31. A first look at objects and classes**

☐ Class and objects   *PL* Lesson 3-3, page 79
The class as a way of collecting related pieces of information, and how classes and objects are related.

Unit 2. Fundamental data types

A *type* defines a set of values and operations on them. A *variable* is a named box into which a value can be stored for later use. Chapter 2 explores the use of numerical and `String` types.

☐ **Horstmann, Sec. 2.1, p. 48. Number types (int and double)**

☐ Overview of primitive types   *PL* Lesson 6-1, page 117
This lesson page lists all primitive types and shows their ranges and precision (advanced).

☐ The integral types   *PL* Lesson 6-2, page 118
Covers integral constants (literals), and operations on types **int** and **long**. Also covers casting (optional).

☐ A minimalist view of floating point   *PL* Lesson 6-3, page 120

☐ Remarks about floating point (advanced)   *PL* Lesson 6-4, page 121

☐ **Horstmann, Sec. 2.2, p. 56. Assignment**

☐ Components of a Java program   *PL* Lesson 1-3, page 47
Do the last activities, on variables, types, and expressions.

☐ Assignment (only activities 1 and 2)   *PL* Lesson 1-4, page 51

☐ Do Lab PGL-1 (Assignment) of this lesson.   *PL* Lesson 1

☐ **Horstmann, Sec. 2.3. Type conversion, p. 59**

☐ The integral types   *PL* Lesson 6-2, page 118
Do all the activities and read the discussion at the bottom of lesson page 6-3.

☐ Naming conventions   *PL* Lesson 13-2, page 185
Read the lesson page and listen to only activity 1, on naming parameters; activity 2, on naming local variables; and activity 4, on naming constants.

☐ **Horstmann, Sec. 2.4-2.5, p. 66. Constants and arithmetic**

☐ Class **Math**   *PL* Lesson 3-2, page 77
Arithmetic expressions were covered already in lesson 1-3, activity 5, and lesson page 6-2. This lesson page covers constants and the methods in class **Math**.

☐ **Horstmann, Sec. 2.6, p. 75. Strings**

☐ Strings   *PL* Lesson 5-3, page 106

☐ **Horstmann, Sec. 2.7, p. 81 Reading input**

☐ Input/output (activities 1 and 2)   *PL* Lesson 1-5, page 56
ProgramLive's class `JLiveRead` is similar to Horstmann's `ConsoleReader`.

☐ **Horstmann, Sec. 2.8, p. 83. Reading input (advanced)**

☐ Reading from the keyboard and files   *PL* Lesson 5-7, page 113

Unit 3. An introduction to classes

The study of classes requires you to learn about the interplay between (a) objects and (b) the methods that objects contain. A method is like a recipe; when the recipe (method) is to be carried out, the chef (the computer) follows its instructions. *ProgramLive* and Horstmann introduce objects and methods in different ways. *ProgramLive* first provides a thorough discussion of methods and then proceeds to study objects; Horstmann mingles the study of the two. Therefore, matching this Horstmann chapter to *ProgramLive* is a bit tricky. Further, *ProgramLive* provides a model of memory, along with detailed instructions on executing method calls, which is not covered in Horstmann.

☐ **Horstmann, Sec. 3.1-3.4, p. 104. The basics of classes**

☐ Classes (only the first activity)   *PL* Lesson 3-1, page 75
Also, read about the placement of classes in a Java program.

☐ Method   *PL* Lesson 2-1, page 61
This lesson page studies executing method calls, but in a simpler, non-object-oriented context.

☐ Method bodies and method calls   *PL* Lesson 2-2, page 64
This lesson page provides, in more detail, the material in Horstmann's Sec. 3.2 and 3.4. The model of execution provides understanding on how method calls are carried out.

☐ Functions (only activities 1 and 2)   *PL* Lesson 2-4, page 70

☐ Classes and objects   *PL* Lesson 3-3, page 79
This lesson page discusses the reason for objects and shows how to write a class. It introduces instance variables (Horstmann, Sec. 3.3).

☐ Creating and initializing objects.   *PL* Lesson 3-4, page 82
Objects are created (and stored in the file drawer) during execution.

☐ Nonstatic methods   *PL* Lesson 3-6, page 87
Static methods go in the class drawer, nonstatic methods, or *instance methods*, belong in each instance of the class.

☐ **Horstmann, Sec. 3.5, p. 112. Constructors**

☐ Scope boxes and constructors   *PL* Lesson 3-5, page 85
Do the first activity, on scope boxes, only if *ProgramLive*'s model of memory is being taught.

☐ Do Lab PGL-1 (Writing constructors) of this lesson.   *PL* Lesson 3

☐ Do Lab PGL-2 (Drawing objects) of this lesson.   *PL* Lesson 3

☐ Consequences of using objects   *PL* Lesson 3-7, page 90
Listen to the first activity only if *ProgramLive*'s model of memory is being taught. Listen to the rest of this page only if method `toString` is being emphasized.

☐ Do Lab PGL-3 (Drawing frames) of this lesson.   *PL* Lesson 3

☐ Describing variables   *PL* Lesson 13-5, page 191

☐ Style considerations concerning classes (optional)   *PL* Lesson 13-2, page 185
Listen only to the third activity (p. 187) on naming instance variables and class
variables, the last activity (p. 188) on naming classes, and the footnote on lesson
page 13-3 (p. 189) on indenting components of a class.

☐ **Horstmann, Sec. 3.7, p. 120. Discovering classes**

☐ Object-oriented design   *PL* Lesson 3-8, page 93

☐ **Horstmann, Sec. 3.9, p. 127. The null reference**

☐ Classes and objects (last activity)   *PL* Lesson 3-3, page 79

Unit 4. Applets and graphics

An *application* is a Java program whose execution starts when the system
calls method **main** of some class. An *applet* is a Java program whose execution
starts when a browser (e.g. Netscape or Internet Explorer) loads an html page
that contains a command to start the applet.

Both applications and applets can be used as graphics programs —i.e. programs that draw graphics (line, rectangles, circles, etc.) in graphics windows.

☐ **Horstmann, Secs. 4.1-4.3, p. 141. Applets**

☐ Applets   *PL* Lesson 16-1, page 205

☐ Examples of applets   *PL* Lesson 16-3, page 208

☐ HTML and applet commands   *PL* Lesson 16-2, page 206

☐ **Horstmann, Secs. 4.4-4.7, p. 150. Graphics**

☐ Input/Output   *PL* Lesson 1-5, page 56
The material in these sections of Horstmann is not covered in *ProgramLive*. The
closest the livetext comes is activity 5 and activity 6 on page 1-5.

☐ **Horstmann, Sec. 4.8, p. 161. Reading text input**

☐ Examples of applets   *PL* Lesson 16-3, page 208
Listen to activity 2 for a discussion of class **JOptionPane**. Look in the index of
this *Companion* to get to a specification of this class.

Unit 5. Decisions

This section discusses conditional statements and the boolean expressions that are used as conditions of such statements.

☐ **Horstmann, Sec. 5.1, p. 184. The if statement**

☐ Three statements ... (activities 3, 4, 6, and 7)   *PL* Lesson 1-4, page 51

☐ Conventions for indentation   *PL* Lesson 13-3, page 189
  Do activity 1 and read the footnotes on indenting the if- and if-else-statements.

☐ Do Lab PGL-2 (if-statement) of this lesson.   *PL* Lesson 1

☐ Do Lab PGL-3 (if-else-statement) of this lesson.   *PL* Lesson 1

☐ **Horstmann, Sec. 5.2, p. 189. Comparing values**

☐ Three statements ... (only activity 5)   *PL* Lesson 1-4, page 51
  For comparisons of floating-point numbers, read lesson page 6-4.

☐ Strings (comparing)   *PL* Lesson 5-3, page 106
  Listen to activity 6 and peruse the third footnote.

☐ Objects (comparing)   *PL* Lesson 3-7, page 90
  Read the section on equality and aliasing, including the footnotes.

☐ **Horstmann, Sec. 5.3, p. 195. Multiple alternatives**

☐ Three statements ... (only activity 5)   *PL* Lesson 1-4, page 51

☐ Occasionally useful statements   *PL* Lesson 1-7, page 60
  Read the section on the **switch** statement, including the footnotes.

☐ **Horstmann, Sec. 5.4, p. 207. Boolean expressions**

☐ Type **boolean**   *PL* Lesson 6-6, page 123

☐ Assertions in programs   *PL* Lesson 1-6, page 58
  This material is covered more briefly in Horstmann.

Unit 6. Iteration

The loop is the most difficult statement to understand, and the best way to understand a loop is in terms of a "loop invariant". *ProgramLive* introduces the loop invariant almost immediately, and just about every loop studied is presented in terms of a loop invariant. Horstmann, on the other hand, treats the loop invariant as an advanced topic (on p. 256).

☐ **Horstmann, Sec. 6.1, p. 224. while loops**

☐ Iteration   *PL* Lesson 7-1, page 127

☐ Do Lab PGL-1 (Executing a `while` loop) of this lesson.   *PL* Lesson 7

☐ Several examples of loops   *PL* Lesson 7-2, page 132
This lesson page discusses the development of loop invariants and then gives three
examples of the development of loops.

☐ Do Lab PGL-2 (Developing loops from invariants) of this lesson.   *PL* Lesson 7

☐ (Optional) Do Lab PGL-3 (Developing loops ... II) of this lesson.   *PL* Lesson 7

☐ Conventions for indentation   *PL* Lesson 13-3, page 189
Read the footnote on conventions for indenting loops.

☐ Loop schemata   *PL* Lesson 7-3, page 134
Rather than write each loop from scratch, learn to use loop schemata.

☐ Do Lab PGL-4 (Using loop schemata) of this lesson.   *PL* Lesson 7

☐ **Horstmann, Sec. 6.2. For-loops**

☐ The for-loop   *PL* Lesson 7-4, page 136
The for-loop is an abbreviation of a while-loop that uses a "loop counter". It
is extremely useful when the number of iterations to perform is known before
execution of the loop.

☐ Do Lab PGL-4 (Translating whiles into fors) of this lesson.   *PL* Lesson 7

☐ **Horstmann, Sec. 6.3, 227, p. 231. Do loops**

☐ Miscellaneous points (the do-while loop)   *PL* Lesson 7-6, page 140
Read the section on the do-while loop, including the footnote.

☐ Making progress and stopping (activity 1)   *PL* Lesson 7-5, page 138

☐ **Horstmann, Common errors 6.2-6.4, p. 232**

☐ Making progress and stopping   *PL* Lesson 7-5, page 138
For "off-by-one errors", do activity 4.

☐ Miscellaneous points   *PL* Lesson 7-6, page 140
For "a semicolon too many", read the warning at the top of the lesson page.

☐ **Horstmann, Quality tip 6.2, p. 234**   *PL* Lesson 7-5, page 138
Activity 2 deals with the use of `!=` in the loop condition and comes to the opposite
conclusion of Quality tip 6.2. This sort of disagreement is very common in the
programming world. Think about both sides of the argument and use whichever
convention your instructor prefers.

☐ **Horstmann, Sec. 6.4, p. 237. Nested loops**

☐ Miscellaneous points (nested loops)   *PL* Lesson 7-6, page 140
Activities 1 and 2 make the point that you should not think in terms of nested
loops, even if they are in the program. The third activity shows how not to develop
a loop. There is no need to read the rest of the page.

☐ **Horstmann, Sec. 6.5. Processing input, p. 239**

☐ Loop schemata (activities 1 and 2)   *PL* Lesson 7-3, page 134

☐ **Horstmann, Advanced topic. 6.3, p. 239**

☐ Miscellaneous points   *PL* Lesson 7-6, page 140
The **break** and **continue** statements are discussed at the bottom of this lesson page.

Unit 7. Methods

In this chapter, Horstmann provides a more in-depth overview of methods in reference to classes. *ProgramLive* studies methods thoroughly in isolation before introducing classes. This is why the match of Horstmann and *Program-Live* is not clean.

☐ **Horstmann, Sec. 7.1, p. 270. Method parameters**

☐ Methods (activities 2, 4, and 5)   *PL* Lesson 2-1, page 61
A parameter is initialized to the value of the corresponding argument when the method in which it is declared is called. A parameter can also be assigned other values within the method body.

☐ Naming conventions   *PL* Lesson 13-2, page 185
Read the general guidelines and listen to the activity on naming parameters.

☐ Method bodies and method calls   *PL* Lesson 2-2, page 64
At this point, this material should be a review.

☐ Guidelines for writing methods   *PL* Lesson 13-4, page 190
The first two activities try to convince you of the importance of method specifications. The last three activities provide insight on how to structure method bodies when they get long.

☐ **Horstmann, Sec. 7.2, p. 273. Accessor methods, mutator methods, and side effects**

☐ Nonstatic methods   *PL* Lesson 3-6, page 87
This lesson page reviews instance methods. The fourth activity talks about "getter" and "setter" methods, *ProgramLive*'s terminology for Horstmann's accessor and mutator methods.

☐ **Horstmann, Sec. 7.3, p. 276. Static methods**

☐ Classes   *PL* Lesson 3-1, page 75

☐ **Horstmann, Sec. 7.4, p. 281. The return statement**

☐ Two components of method bodies (last activity)   *PL* Lesson 2-3, page 67

☐ Form of a function call (activity 1)   *PL* Lesson 2-4, page 70

☐ Do Lab PGL-4 (writing simple functions) of this lesson.   *PL* Lesson 2

☐ **Horstmann, Sec. 7.5, p. 283. Static variables**

☐ Class `Math` (activity 2)   *PL* Lesson 3-2, page 77

☐ Naming conventions (activity 2)   *PL* Lesson 13-2, page 185

☐ **Horstmann, Sec. 7.6, p. 287. Variable lifetime, initialization, and scope**
These terms are introduced and discussed at various places within *ProgramLive*. For a summary of "lifetime" and "scope" of variables, look the words up in *ProgramLive*'s glossary.

For the default initial values of static and instance variables, look up "default" values in the *ProgramLive* glossary. A parameter is initialized to the value of the corresponding argument. A local variable is not initialized.

☐ **Horstmann, Sec. 7.7, p. 291. Comments**

☐ Guidelines for writing methods   *PL* Lesson 13-4, page 190
This lesson page describes (in detail) specifications of methods, as well as the use of statement-comments.

☐ Describing variables   *PL* Lesson 13-5, page 191

☐ Javadoc   *PL* Lesson 13-1, page 185
Javadoc is described in a footnote at the bottom of this lesson page and in more detail on p. 245 of this *Companion*.

☐ **Horstmann, Sec. 7.8, p. 296. Preconditions**

☐ Assertions in programs (last activity)   *PL* Lesson 1-6, page 58

☐ **Horstmann, Sec. 7.9, p. 298. Recursion**

☐ Recursion   *PL* Lesson 15-1, page 197
Lesson 15-1 of *ProgramLive* provides a more thorough study of recursion than Horstmann.

Unit 8. Testing and debugging

☐ **Horstmann, Sec. 8.1-8.5, p. 314. Introduction to testing**

☐ Introduction to testing and debugging   *PL* Lesson 14-1, page 193

☐ Testing strategies (second activity)   *PL* Lesson 14-2, page 194
Class `JLiveRead` is similar to Horstmann's class `ConsoleReader`.

☐ Selecting test cases and checking them . . .   *PL* Lesson 14-3, page 195

☐ **Horstmann, Sec. 8.6, p. 323. The debugger**

☐ Debugging   *PL* Lesson 14-4, page 196

☐ The CodeWarrior debugger   *PL* Lesson 19-1

☐ Breakpoints and expression in the IDE   *PL* Lesson 19-2

☐ **Horstmann, Sec. 8.7, p. 332. Debugging strategies**

☐ Debugging   *PL* Lesson 14-4, page 196

Unit 9. Inheritance and interfaces

☐ **Horstmann, Sec. 9.1, p. 342. Introduction to inheritance**

☐ Subclasses   *PL* Lesson 4-1, page 97

☐ Do Lab PGL-1 (Drawing objects II) of this lesson.   *PL* Lesson 4

☐ **Horstmann, Sec. 9.1, p. 345. Converting between class types**

☐ Casting and a new model of execution   *PL* Lesson 4-3, page 101
This lesson page introduces *ProgramLive*'s final method of execution. Don't listen to the last activity yet.

☐ **Horstmann, Sec. 9.3, p. 348. Inheritance hierarchies**

☐ Constructors and inherited methods (last activity)   *PL* Lesson 4-2, page 99

☐ **Horstmann, Sec. 9.4- 9.5, p. 351. More about subclasses**

☐ Constructors and inherited methods   *PL* Lesson 4-2, page 99

☐ A last look at classes `Employee` ... (last activity)   *PL* Lesson 4-3, page 101

☐ Do Lab PGL-2 (Writing constructors II) of this lesson.   *PL* Lesson 4

☐ Do Lab PGL-3 (Drawing frames II) of this lesson.   *PL* Lesson 4

☐ Object-oriented design   *PL* Lesson 4-4, page 103

☐ **Horstmann, Sec. 9.6, p. 359. Polymorphism**

☐ Classes (overloading method names, last activity)   *PL* Lesson 3-1, page 75
This activity treats polymorphism, under the title "overloading method names".

☐ **Horstmann, Sec. 9.7, p. 362. Interfaces**

☐ Interfaces   *PL* Lesson 12-1, page 179

☐ The interface as a type   *PL* Lesson 12-2, page 180

☐ Interface `Comparable`   *PL* Lesson 12-3, page 182

☐ **Horstmann, Advanced topic 9.2, p. 366. Abstract classes**

☐ Abstract classes   *PL* Lesson 4-5, page 104

☐ (Optional) Do Lab PGL-4 (Practice with shapes) of this lesson.   *PL* Lesson 4

☐ **Horstmann, Sec. 9.8, p. 368. Access control**

☐ Constructors and inherited methods (last activity)   *PL* Lesson 4-2, page 99
  Look at item *access modifier* in *ProgramLive*'s glossary for a short summary.

☐ **Horstmann, Sec. 9.9, p. 371. The cosmic superclass**

☐ Constructors and inherited methods (last activity)   *PL* Lesson 4-2, page 99

☐ Consequences of using objects   *PL* Lesson 3-7, page 90
  Look at the activities on method `toString` and read about equality testing.

☐ **Horstmann, Sec. 9.10, p. 380. Packages**

☐ Packages   *PL* Lesson 11-1, page 177

Unit 10. Event handling

This chapter is about GUIs and the events that occur within them.

☐ GUIs and event-driven programming   *PL* Lesson 17-1, page 209

☐ Components and container   *PL* Lesson 17-2, page 210

☐ Layout managers   *PL* Lesson 17-3, page 211

☐ Listening to a GUI   *PL* Lesson 17-4, page 212

☐ Interfaces —ActionListener (last activity) *PL* Lesson 12-1, page 179

Unit 11. Arrays and vectors

An "array" is a collection of elements of the same (primitive or class) type —`int`, `String`, `JLiveWindow`, etc. With arrays we can discuss algorithms such as searching arrays and sorting arrays into ascending order.

☐ **Horstmann, Sec. 11.1, p. 432. Using arrays**

☐ Introduction to arrays.   *PL* Lesson 8-1, page 143
  This lesson page introduces all the technical details concerning arrays.

☐ Talking about array segments   *PL* Lesson 8-2, page 146
  The notation makes it easier to discuss algorithms that manipulate arrays.

☐ About array schemas (activities 1 and 2) *PL* Lesson 8-3, page 148

☐ **Horstmann, Sec. 11.2, p 443. Array parameters and return values**

☐ Some programs that use arrays (last two activities)   *PL* Lesson 8-3, page 148

☐ **Horstmann, Sec. 11.3, p. 444. Simple array algorithms**

☐ Some programs that use arrays (activities 4 and 5)   *PL* Lesson 8-3, page 148

☐ Some basic array algorithms   *PL* Lesson 8-5, page 156

☐ Do Lab PGL-1 (Using arrays) of this lesson.   *PL* Lesson 11

☐ **Horstmann, Sec. 11.5, p. 455. Arrays as object data**

☐ Arrays and classes (first three activities)   *PL* Lesson 8-4, page 153

☐ **Horstmann, Sec. 11.6, p. 461. Vectors**

☐ Arrays and classes   *PL* Lesson 8-4, page 153
Do the last three activities; they introduce the concept of a dynamic array using
a class that is slightly different from class `Vector`.

☐ Class `Vector`   *PL* Lesson 5-5, page 111

☐ **Horstmann, Sec. 11.7, 465. Two-dimensional arrays**

☐ Multidimensional arrays   *PL* Lesson 9-1, page 163

☐ Programs that use two-dimensional arrays   *PL* Lesson 9-2, page 165

☐ Do Lab PGL-1 (Rectangular arrays) of this lesson.   *PL* Lesson 9

☐ The Java concept of a multidim. array (optional)   *PL* Lesson 9-3, page 168
You will see that a two-dimenssional array is really an array whose elements are
arrays, whose elements can be different lengths!

☐ Programs that use ragged arrays (advanced)   *PL* Lesson 9-4, page 170

Unit 12. Graphical user interfaces

This topic is covered in a cursory manner in *ProgramLive*.

☐ GUIs and event-driven programming   *PL* Lesson 17-1, page 209

☐ Components and container   *PL* Lesson 17-2, page 210

☐ Layout managers   *PL* Lesson 17-3, page 211

☐ Listening to a GUI   *PL* Lesson 17-4, page 212

Unit 13. Streams and exceptions

☐ **Horstmann, Sec. 13.1-13.2, p. 516. Reading and writing streams**

☐ Reading from the keyboard and files   *PL* Lesson 5-7, page 113

☐ Writing to the Java console and files   *PL* Lesson 5-8, page 116

☐ **Horstmann, Sec. 13.3-13.4, p. 522. Exception handling**

☐ Output of thrown exceptions and errors   *PL* Lesson 10-1, page 173

☐ The throwable object   *PL* Lesson 10-2, page 173

☐ Catching a thrown exception   *PL* Lesson 10-3, page 174

☐ The throw-statement   *PL* Lesson 10-4, page 175

☐ Checked exceptions and the throws clause   *PL* Lesson 10-5, page 176

☐ Hints on using exceptions   *PL* Lesson 10-6, page 176

Unit 14. Object-oriented design

The material on designing and developing programs, including object-oriented design, is covered in several different lessons in *ProgramLive*. For this chapter of Horstmann, we list those lesson pages.

☐ Top-down programming   *PL* Lesson 2-5, page 72
This may be a review.

☐ Object-oriented design   *PL* Lesson 3-8, page 93
How to develop a program in an object-oriented framework.

☐ Object-oriented design with subclasses   *PL* Lesson 4-4, page 103

Unit 15. Algorithms

☐ **Horstmann, Secs. 15.1-15.3, p. 614. Selection sort**

☐ Selection sort and insertion sort   *PL* Lesson 8-6, page 161

☐ **Horstmann, Sec. 15.4-15.5, p. 622. Merge sort**

☐ Some interesting recursive methods (last activity)   *PL* Lesson 15-3, page 202

☐ Quicksort   *PL* Lesson 15-4, page 202
This sorting algorithm, which is perhaps the most famous and most widely used sorting algorithm, is not covered in Horstmann.

☐ **Horstmann, Sec. 15.6, p. 630. Linear search**

☐ Some basic array algorithms (first two activities)   *PL* Lesson 8-5, page 156

☐ **Horstmann, Sec. 15.7, p. 632. Binary search**

☐ Some basic array algorithms (last activity)   *PL* Lesson 8-5, page 156

0.4 Lesson plan for Niño and Hosch's
Programming & Object Oriented Design using Java

This lesson plan matches the chapters of *Programming & Object Oriented Design using Java*, by Jaime Niño and Frederick A. Hosch, with activities in *ProgramLive*. Each unit of the lesson plan corresponds to a chapter. Different authors of programming texts introduce material in different orders and emphasize different concepts, so the match between Niño-Hosch and *ProgramLive* is not exact.

Below, we give an overview of each unit together with a checklist for the activities in it. Check each one off as you complete it. But first:

- An activity or lab that is labeled "optional" is in *ProgramLive* but not in Niño-Hosch.

- Niño-Hosch do not discuss the running of Java programs on a computer, leaving that detail to an instructor. *ProgramLive* has tutorials on the Interactive Development Environments Visual Cafe (lesson 18) and CodeWarrior (lesson 19), and Appendix B of this *Companion* discusses the use of the UNIX command-line system for compiling and running Java programs.

- It is possible to skip lesson 0 of *ProgramLive* on how to use the livetext, but you will save time if you spend half an hour on it. In addition to the activities, there are a plethora of instructional tools such as the glossary, index, exercises, and labs.

☐ Introduction to livetexts   *PL* Lesson 0-1

☐ Activities   *PL* Lesson 0-2

☐ The lesson book page   *PL* Lesson 0-3

☐ Global features   *PL* Lesson 0-4

☐ Page controls   *PL* Lesson 0-5

☐ Dealing With Java programs   *PL* Lesson 0-6

☐ Learning effectively   *PL* Lesson 0-7

Unit 1. Introduction

This chapter of Niño-Hosch goes into great detail on some issues that are only moderately covered, or not at all, in *ProgramLive*'s introduction. Object-oriented systems, for example, are not covered in the introduction of *Program-Live*.

☐ **Niño-Hosch, Secs. 1.1–1.7, p. 1–22. What is computer science, what is a software system, object-oriented systems, a model of a computer system, software tools, errors in the programming process**

☐ Hardware and software   *PL* Lesson 1-1, page 41
This provides a brief look at hardware and software, a more indepth treatment of the computer and memory, and a brief introduction to software tools such as programming languages and compilers or interpreters for them.

Unit 2. Data abstraction: introductory concepts

☐ **Niño-Hosch, Sec. 2.1, p. 27. Values and types**

☐ Variables and types (activity 3)   *PL* Lesson 1-3, page 47
Values, types, variables, and assignments to them are discussed.

☐ **Niño-Hosch, Sec. 2.2, p. 28. Primitive types in Java**

☐ Overview of primitive types   *PL* Lesson 6-1, page 117
Use lesson pages 6-2–6-6 as a reference for information on primitive types.

☐ **Niño-Hosch, Secs. 2.3–2.4, p. 30–39. Objects and Classes**
Niño-Hosch introduces objects and classes in an abstract way, without reference to corresponding constructs of Java, while *ProgramLive* introduces objects and classes and the corresponding Java features at the same time. Because of these fundamentally different approaches, it does not make sense to list *ProgramLive* activities corresponding to these sections.

Unit 3. Basic Java structural components

☐ **Niño-Hosch, Sec. 3.1, p. 47. Syntactic structure of a system definition in Java**

☐ A do-nothing Java program (activity 1)   *PL* Lesson 1-2, page 43
Pay special attention to *ProgramLive*'s filing cabinet metaphor to help you understand what a class is.

☐ Packages   *PL* Lesson 11-1, page 177

☐ **Niño-Hosch, Sec. 3.2, p. 49. Identifiers**

☐ Components of a Java program (activities 3 and 4)   *PL* Lesson 1-3, page 47

☐ Naming conventions (last activity)   *PL* Lesson 13-2, page 185
   Also, read the basic guidelines and at the top of the page.

☐ **Niño-Hosch, Sec. 3.3, p. 53. Literals**

☐ Do the first activity of these Lesson pages: 6-2 (Integral types), 118
                                          6-3 (A minimalist view of floating-point), 120
                                                    6-5 (Type **char**), 121
                                                  6-6 (Type **boolean**), 123
                                                    5-3 (Strings), 106

☐ **Niño-Hosch, Sec. 3.4, p. 55. Lexical structure**

☐ Components of a Java program (activities 1 and 2)   *PL* Lesson 1-3, page 47

Unit 4. Specification of a simple class

This chapter of Niño-Hosch provides an overview of the process of specifying a class, using three examples. The process results in a Java class in which the bodies of methods have not yet been written. Along the way, Java syntax for instance variables, instance methods (constructors, functions, and procedures), and method calls is introduced, but not in full detail.

ProgramLive uses a different order: (1) methods and their specification are studied in full, (2) classes are thoroughly explored, and (3) an example of class specification is given. This difference in approach results in some problems in matching *ProgramLive* to Niño-Hosch.

There is a difference in terminology. *ProgramLive* considers three kinds of methods, the latter two being traditional in mathematics and older programming languages:

- constructor: a method for initializing fields of a class;

- function: a function call is an expression, and the call produces a result;

- procedure: a procedure call is a statement (or command), and the call does not produce a result.

Niño-Hosch uses *method* and *function* interchangeably and uses *query* for a function call and *command* for a procedure call.

☐ **Niño-Hosch, Sec. 4.1–4.4, p. 59–84. Object specifications and Specifying a class**

☐ Classes and objects (first three activities)   *PL* Lesson 3-3, page 79

☐ Methods (first three activities)   *PL* Lesson 2-1, page 61
   These activities relate methods to recipes and view a method as a black box
   —only its specification can be seen.

☐ Do Lab PGL-2 (Understanding method calls) of this lesson.   *PL* Lesson 2

☐ Do Lab PGL-2 (Drawing objects) of this lesson.   *PL* Lesson 3

☐ Functions versus procedures (only the first activity)   *PL* Lesson 2-4, page 70
A function must return a result; a procedure cannot.

☐ Constructors   *PL* Lesson 3-5, page 85
Skip the part on scope boxes for now, and concentrate on constructors.

☐ The new expression (only the first activity)   *PL* Lesson 3-4, page 82
The new expression creates an object and yields its name.

☐ Invoking a method: activities 4, 5 on procedure calls, Lesson page 2-1, page 61
                               activity 2 on function calls, Lesson page 2-4, page 70
                    activities 1–3 on nonstatic methods, Lesson page 3-6, page 87

☐ Object-oriented design   *PL* Lesson 3-8, page 93
Skip activities 5, 7, and 8 on implementing the design.

☐ A program to print a student report   *PL* Lesson 8-4, page 153
Activities 1–3 illustrates another class design, along with part of its implementation.

☐ Static methods (activities 1, 2, and 4)   *PL* Lesson 3-1, page 75
Niño-Hosch covers static methods and variables elsewhere, but this is a good place
to introduce them.

Unit 5. Implementing a simple class

We now look at the implementations of methods. This requires us to introduce
decarations of variables and to discuss certain *statements* and *expressions*.

☐ **Niño-Hosch, Sec. 5.1, p. 91. Implementing data descriptions**

☐ Variables and types (only activity 5)   *PL* Lesson 1-3, page 47

☐ A class as a type (only the last activity)   *PL* Lesson 3-3, page 79

☐ Hiding instance variables (only the last three activities)   *PL* Lesson 3-6, page 87

☐ Constants (only the second activity)   *PL* Lesson 3-2, page 77

☐ Naming conventions (only activities 3 and 4)   *PL* Lesson 13-2, page 185

☐ Describing instance variables (only the first activity)   *PL* Lesson 13-5, page 191

☐ **Niño-Hosch, Sec. 5.2.1, p. 97. Method implementation: simple queries**
This section defines "statement", says that the body of a method is a sequence of
statements, and illustrates the use of a return statement in a function body, with
the value of a simple variable being returned. *ProgramLive* introduces all these
notions in different places, and we cannot point to any place that would make
sense at this time.

☐ **Niño-Hosch, Sec. 5.2.2, p. 100. Arithmetic expressions**

☐ Expressions (only activities 5 and 6)   *PL* Lesson 1-3, page 47

☐ Operations on type **int** (only activity 2)   *PL* Lesson 6-2, page 118

☐ Do Lab PGL-1 (Integral types) of this lesson.   *PL* Lesson 6

☐ Operations on type **double** (only activity 2)   *PL* Lesson 6-3, page 120

☐ Casting (only activities 3 and 4)   *PL* Lesson 6-2, page 118

☐ Casting (read only the end of the page)   *PL* Lesson 6-3, page 120

☐ Do Lab PGL-2 (Casting among integral types) of this lesson.   *PL* Lesson 6

☐ Look in the *ProgramLive* Glossary under *precedence* for information about operator precedence.

☐ Catenation of `Strings` (only activity 3)   *PL* Lesson 5-3, page 106

☐ **Niño-Hosch, Sec. 5.2.3, p. 105. Method implementation: simple commands**
Niño-Hosch discusses only the assignment statement in this section.

☐ The assignment statement (activities 1 and 2)   *PL* Lesson 1-4, page 51
Read also the discussion of the statement-comment after these two activities.

☐ Do Lab PGL-1 (The assignment statement) of this lesson.   *PL* Lesson 1

☐ **Niño-Hosch, Sec. 5.2.4, p. 107. Using parameters**

☐ The method body (only the first activity)   *PL* Lesson 2-2, page 64

☐ **Niño-Hosch, Sec. 5.2.5, p. 112. Invoking a method**

☐ Invoking a method: activities 4, 5 on procedure calls, Lesson page 2-1, 61
                                  activity 2 on function calls, Lesson page 2-4, 70
                            activities 1–3 on nonstatic methods, Lesson page 3-6, 87

☐ **Niño-Hosch, Sec. 5.2.6, p. 121–124. Local variables**

☐ Local variables (only the first activity)   *PL* Lesson 2-3, page 67

☐ Statement-comments (only activities 3–5)   *PL* Lesson 13-4, page 190
The "statement-comment" is not a Java construct but a convention for allowing more "abstraction" in the documentation of a program. It is not discussed in Niño-Hosch. These activities explain why the statement-comment is so useful.

☐ **Niño-Hosch, Sec. 5.3, p. 121. Testing an implementation**

☐ Introduction to testing and debugging   *PL* Lesson 14-1, page 193
In addition, you might want to look at GUI `JLiveWIndow`, which is discussed in activity 3 of Lesson page 1-5 (see *Companion* page 56), as a driver to test some programs.

Unit 6. Conditions

A *conditional statement* is used to choose one of two alternatives. The choice depends on the value of a *condition*, which is a *boolean expression* (an expression that yields **true** or **false**). Boolean expressions are also used also in making assertions about a program.

☐ **Niño-Hosch, Sec. 6.1, p. 131. Conditional statements**

☐ Assertions in programs   *PL* Lesson 1-6, page 58

☐ Do Lab PGL-6 (Relations) of this lesson.   *PL* Lesson 1

☐ Do Lab PGL-1 (Assertions) of this lesson.   *PL* Lesson 1

☐ Conditional statements (only activities 3 and 4)   *PL* Lesson 1-4, page 51

☐ Blocks, or compound statements (only activity 6)   *PL* Lesson 1-4, page 51

☐ Do Lab PGL-2 (The if-statement) of this lesson.   *PL* Lesson 1

☐ Do Lab PGL-1 (The if-else-statement) of this lesson.   *PL* Lesson 1

☐ **Niño-Hosch, Sec. 6.2, p. 141. Boolean expressions**

☐ Boolean expressions (only activity 5)   *PL* Lesson 1-4, page 51

☐ Boolean expressions   *PL* Lesson 6-6, page 123

☐ Do Lab PGL-4 (Boolean expressions) of this lesson.   *PL* Lesson 6

☐ String equality   *PL* Lesson 5-3, page 106

Unit 7. Programming by contract

This chapter discusses a programming style in which "the invocation of a method is viewed as a contract between a client and server, with each having explicitly stated responsibilities". *ProgramLive* also takes this view, but it doesn't devote a lesson specifically to it. Instead, the view pervades *Program-Live*, and almost no method is given without providing a precise specification as a comment. Here are the activities that deal with this topic.

☐ Assertions (only activity 3)   *PL* Lesson 1-6, page 58

☐ Guidelines for writing methods (only activities 1–2)   *PL* Lesson 13-4, page 190

☐ Top-down programming   *PL* Lesson 2-5, page 72

Unit 8. Testing a class

☐ **Niño-Hosch, Sec. 8.1, pp. 183. Testing**

☐ Introduction to testing and debugging   *PL* Lesson 14-1, page 193

☐ **Niño-Hosch, Sec. 8.2–8.3, pp. 185–187. Testing a class implementation and Building a test system**

☐ Testing strategies   *PL* Lesson 14-2, page 194

☐ Selecting tests cases and checking them   *PL* Lesson 14-3, page 195

☐ Debugging   *PL* Lesson 14-4, page 196

Unit 9. Relations

This material is not covered in *ProgramLive*.

Unit 10. Putting a system together

☐ Top-down programming   *PL* Lesson 2-5, page 72
This lesson page introduces the notion of stepwise refinement, or top-down programming, as an aid to writing a method (or set of methods).

☐ Object-oriented design   *PL* Lesson 3-8, page 93
This lesson page discusses the design of an object-oriented program, using an example of a simple clock game.

Unit 11. Software quality

☐ Good programming paractices   *PL* Lesson 13-1, page 185
ProgramLive has no equivalent discussion of software quality. Lesson 13, "Programming style", provides some of these thoughts.

Unit 12. Lists and iteration

Niño-Hosch first specifies a class `StudentList` and then discusses loops in terms of this class, using as examples only loops that process a list; *Program-Live* provides a more thorough study of loops with more varied examples. Niño-Hosch delays discussion of loop invariants until a later chapter but never uses them; *ProgramLive* uses loop invariants right from the start and develops and presents all loops in terms of loop invariants.

Finally, all the algorithms that Niño-Hosch discusses in this chapter, like searching a list for a value, are discussed in *ProgramLive*'s Lesson 8 on arrays.

Therefore, it is impossible to give a useful correspondence between sections of this chapter of Niño-Hosch and activities in *ProgramLive*. In place of this, we give below a checklist for *ProgramLive*'s lesson on iteration.

☐ Iteration (first activity)   *PL* Lesson 7-1, page 127

☐ Do Lab PGL-1 (Executing a while loop) of this lesson.   *PL* Lesson 7

☐ Iteration (all except the first activity)   *PL* Lesson 7-1, page 127
Knowing how a loop is executed is not enough; you have to know how to understand what happens within a loop, and you have to be able to explain a loop to
others. This requires the notion of a loop invariant. Study this material carefully.

☐ Several examples of loops   *PL* Lesson 7-2, page 132

☐ Do Lab PGL-2 (Developing loops from invariants) of this lesson.   *PL* Lesson 7

☐ (Optional) Do Lab PGL-3 (Developing loops . . . II) of this lesson.   *PL* Lesson 7

☐ Conventions for indentation   *PL* Lesson 13-3, page 189
Read the footnote near the bottom of the lesson page on conventions for indentation and for loop invariants.

☐ Loop schemata   *PL* Lesson 7-3, page 134

☐ Do Lab PGL-4 (Using loop schemata) of this lesson.   *PL* Lesson 7

☐ The **for** loop   *PL* Lesson 7-4, page 136

☐ (Optional) Do Lab PGL-4 (Translating **whiles** . . .) of this lesson.   *PL* Lesson 7

☐ Making progress and stopping   *PL* Lesson 7-5, page 138

☐ Miscellaneous points about loops   *PL* Lesson 7-6, page 140
The first two activities illustrate an important use of the statement-comment.

You need *not* study the information about the do-while loop, the **continue** statement, and the **break** statement. In general, these constructs are not needed at
this point of your programming career. If you see them in a program and want to
find out about them, look in the *ProgramLive* glossary or index.

Unit 13. Sorting and searching

The corresponding lesson pages of *ProgramLive* treat arrays and not lists.

☐ **Niño-Hosch, Secs. 13.1–13.2, pp. 302–303. Orderings and Simple sorts**

☐ Finding the minimum value (activity 3)   *PL* Lesson 8-5, page 156
This algorithm is used within selection sort.

☐ Inserting into a sorted segment (activity 4)   *PL* Lesson 8-5, page 156
This algorithm is used within insertion sort.

☐ Selection sort and insertion sort   *PL* Lesson 8-6, page 161
(*ProgramLive* does not do bubble sort.)

☐ **Niño-Hosch, Sec. 13.3, pp. 314. Binary search**

☐ Binary search (last activity)   *PL* Lesson 8-5, page 156

☐ Linear search (first two activities)   *PL* Lesson 8-5, page 156

☐ **Niño-Hosch, Sec. 13.4, pp. 320. Verifying correctness: using a loop invariant**

☐ Loop invariants (activities 2-3)   *PL* Lesson 7-1, page 127

☐ Developing loop invariants (activity 1)   *PL* Lesson 7-2, page 132

☐ Making progress and stopping   *PL* Lesson 7-5, page 138

Unit 14. Abstraction and inheritance

This chapter introduces the subclass and all the features that go with it. Object-oriented programming without subclasses would be possible, but not half as useful as with subclasses.

☐ **Niño-Hosch, Secs. 14.1–14.2, pp. 329–331. Abstraction and Extension and inheritance**

☐ Subclasses   *PL* Lesson 4-1, page 97

☐ Do Lab PGL-1 (Drawing objects) of this lesson.   *PL* Lesson 4

☐ Object-oriented design with subclasses   *PL* Lesson 4-4, page 103
Skip the details about implementing the methods.

☐ **Niño-Hosch, Sec. 14.2.2, pp. 336. Abstract classes and abstract methods**

☐ Abstract classes   *PL* Lesson 4-5, page 104

☐ **Niño-Hosch, Sec. 14.2.3, pp. 338. Constructors and subclasses**

☐ Writing a constructor for a subclass (activity 1)   *PL* Lesson 4-2, page 99

☐ Do Lab PGL-2 (Writing constructors) of this lesson.   *PL* Lesson 4

☐ **Niño-Hosch, Sec. 14.3, pp. 340. Overriding and polymorphism**

☐ Overriding an inherited method (activity 2)   *PL* Lesson 4-2, page 99

☐ Overloading method names (activity 4)   *PL* Lesson 3-1, page 75

☐ **Niño-Hosch, Sec. 14.4, pp. 344. Subclasses and contract**
No specific activity in *ProgramLive* corresponds to this section.

☐ **Niño-Hosch, Sec. 14.5, pp. 346. Using inheritance**
No specific activity in *ProgramLive* corresponds to this section.

☐ **Niño-Hosch, Sec. 14.6, pp. 350. Feature accessibility**
No specific activity in *ProgramLive* corresponds to this section.

☐ Calling an overridden method (activity 3)   *PL* Lesson 4-2, page 99

☐ Keywords **this** and **super** (activity 4)   *PL* Lesson 4-2, page 99

☐ Modifier **protected** (activity 6)   *PL* Lesson 4-2, page 99

☐ The class hierarchy (activity 7)   *PL* Lesson 4-2, page 99

☐ **Niño-Hosch, Sec. 14.7, pp. 358. Java scoping rules**

> In *ProgramLive*, the scope rules for each kind of variable or method are treated at the place where the variable or method is defined. Look up "scope" in *ProgramLive*'s Glossary for a summary and in *ProgramLive*'s Index in order to get to the activities where more detail is given.

Unit 15. Modeling with abstraction

This chapter introduces the *interface*, which is a Java construct.

☐ **Niño-Hosch, Sec. 15.1, pp. 371. Abstract classes and interfaces**

☐ Abstract classes   *PL* Lesson 4-5, page 104

☐ Interfaces   *PL* Lesson 12-1, page 179

☐ The interface as a type   *PL* Lesson 12-2, page 180

☐ Interface **Comparable** (as an example)   *PL* Lesson 12-3, page 182

☐ **Niño-Hosch, Sec. 15.2, pp. 380. Extension and composition**
This material is not discussed in *ProgramLive*.

☐ **Niño-Hosch, Sec. 15.3, pp. 386. Extension and state**
This material is not discussed in *ProgramLive*.

Unit 16. Organizing lists

No part of *ProgramLive* corresponds to this chapter.

Unit 17. Recursion

What can be done with iteration can be done with recursion, and vice versa. Recursion may be a bit slower (in execution), but its use allows many programs to be expressed more simply. Some extremely beautiful *functional* rely solely on recursion —they don't have iteration, or even an assignment statement.

☐ **Niño-Hosch, Sec. 17.1, pp. 407. Recursion and iteration**

☐ Recursion   *PL* Lesson 15-1, page 197

☐ Execution of calls on recursive methods   *PL* Lesson 15-2, page 200
ProgramLive goes into more detail on how recursive calls are executed. *Program-Live* also shows how to eliminate tail recursion.

☐ Do Lab PGL-1 (Writing recursive String methods) of this lesson.   *PL* Lesson 15

☐ Do Lab PGL-2 (Writing recursive integer methods) of this lesson. *PL* Lesson 15

☐ **Niño-Hosch, Sec. 17.2, pp. 416. Example: the towers puzzle**

☐ Some interesting recursive methods   *PL* Lesson 15-3, page 202
Instead of towers of Hanoi, *ProgramLive* gives three other examples.

☐ **Niño-Hosch, Sec. 17.3, pp. 422. Quicksort**

☐ Partitioning an array segment (activity 5)   *PL* Lesson 8-5, page 156

☐ Quicksort   *PL* Lesson 15-4, page 202
The basic algorithm may require n^2 space; *ProgramLive* shows how to reduce this to logarithmic space.

☐ **Niño-Hosch, Sec. 17.4, pp. 430. An inefficient algorithm**
This example is not covered in *ProgramLive*.

☐ **Niño-Hosch, Sec. 17.5, pp. 431. Indirect recursion**
This topic is not covered in *ProgramLive*.

☐ **Niño-Hosch, Sec. 17.6, pp. 433. Object recursion**
This topic is not covered in *ProgramLive*.

Unit 18. Failures and exceptions

☐ **Niño-Hosch, Secs. 18.1–18.2, pp. 443-444. Failures and the Java exception mechanism**

☐ Output of thrown Exceptions and Errors   *PL* Lesson 10-1, page 173

☐ **Niño-Hosch, Sec. 18.2.1, pp. 445. Exceptions as objects**

☐ The throwable object   *PL* Lesson 10-2, page 173

☐ **Niño-Hosch, Sec. 18.2.2, pp. 446. Catching exceptions**

☐ Catching a thrown Exception (activities 1–3)   *PL* Lesson 10-3, page 174

☐ **Niño-Hosch, Sec. 18.2.3, p. 449. Propagated exceptions**

☐ Propagation of a thrown object (activity 4)   *PL* Lesson 10-3, page 174

☐ The throw statement   *PL* Lesson 10-4, page 175

☐ **Niño-Hosch, Sec. 18.2.4, pp. 449. Checked and unchecked exceptions**

☐ Checked exceptions and the throws clause   *PL* Lesson 10-5, page 176

☐ **Niño-Hosch, Sec. 18.3, pp. 450. Dealing with failure: using exceptions**

☐ Hints on using exceptions   *PL* Lesson 10-6, page 176

Unit 19. Building the user interface

☐ **Niño-Hosch, Sec. 19.1, pp. 464. The system interface**

☐ GUIs and event-driven programming   *PL* Lesson 17-1, page 209

☐ **Niño-Hosch, Sec. 19.2, pp. 468. An introduction to Swing**
ProgramLive does not concentrate on the Swing classes but also briefly discusses the awt classes.

☐ Components and containers   *PL* Lesson 17-2, page 210

☐ **Niño-Hosch, Sec. 19.3, pp. 475. Creating components**

☐ Layout managers   *PL* Lesson 17-3, page 211

☐ **Niño-Hosch, Sec. 19.4, pp. 482. Events: programming the user interface**

☐ Listening to a GUI   *PL* Lesson 17-4, page 212

☐ **Niño-Hosch, Sec. 19.5, pp. 491. Some class features**
Appendix D of this *Companion* contains the specifications of many methods of many of the Swing and awt classes. Reference this appendix often when writing Java programs that deal with GUIs.

☐ Listening to a GUI   *PL* Lesson 17-4, page 212

☐ Components and containers   *PL* Lesson 17-2, page 210

☐ Windows and frames   *PL* Lesson 17-1, page 209

Unit 20. Designing the GUI front end

This material is not covered in *ProgramLive*.

Unit 21. Computational complexity

This material is generally not covered in a first course. There are a few instances in *ProgramLive* where analysis of execution time is discussed — e.g. with binary search, linear search, and quicksort— but *ProgramLive* does not contain a full discussion of analysis of execution time.

Unit 22. Implementing lists: array implementations

☐ **Niño-Hosch, Sec. 22.1, p. 557. Arrays**
Niño-Hosch covers arrays mainly to show how to implement their `Lists` of Sec. 12.1. For example, they do not discuss array initializers and uses of arrays for other than `Lists`. *ProgramLive* gives a more thorough, traditional coverage of arrays.

☐ Introduction to arrays   *PL* Lesson 8-1, page 143

☐ Talking about array segments   *PL* Lesson 8-2, page 146

☐ Do Lab PGL-1 Using arrays) of this lesson.   *PL* Lesson 8

☐ Some programs that use arrays   *PL* Lesson 8-3, page 148

☐ Arrays and classes (activities 1–3)   *PL* Lesson 8-4, page 153

☐ Some basic array algorithms   *PL* Lesson 8-5, page 156

☐ **Niño-Hosch, Sec. 22.2, p. 562. An array-based list implementation**

☐ Class `StudentReport` (activities 2)   *PL* Lesson 8-4, page 153
Activity 2 implements the list of students in an array.

☐ **Niño-Hosch, Sec. 22.3, p. 573. Dynamic arrays**

☐ A class that implements dynamic arrays (activities 5–6) *PL* Lesson 8-4, page 153

☐ Class `Vector`   *PL* Lesson 5-4, page 110

Unit 23. Implementing lists: linked implementations

This topic is not covered in *ProgramLive*.

Unit 24. Organizing list implementations

☐ **Niño-Hosch, Sec. 24.1, p. 603. A library structure**
This example is specific to Niño-Hosch.

☐ **Niño-Hosch, Sec. 24.2, p. 608. Iterators**

☐ Interfaces `Enumeration` and `Iterator`   *PL* Lesson 12-4, page 183

☐ **Niño-Hosch, Sec. 24.3–24.4, p. 617–625. Iterators as arguments and Comparing implementations**
This material is specific to Niño-Hosch.

☐ **Niño-Hosch, Sec. 24.5, p. 625. The java.util Collection hierarchy**
This material is not covered in in *ProgramLive*.

Unit 25. Dispensers and dictionaries

This material is not covered in *ProgramLive*.

Unit 26. Appendix A: Stream I/O

☐ **Niño-Hosch, Sec. a.1, p. 654. OOJ library classes**

☐ Input/output (activities 2 and 3)   *PL* Lesson 1-5, page 56
Activity 2 introduces a class `JLiveRead` for reading values from the keyboard, which provides the functionality of Niño-Hosch's class `BasicFileReader`. This is basically what is needed in the beginning of an introductory course. Activity 3 discusses a simple GUI, `JLiveWindow`, for small amounts of I/O.

☐ **Niño-Hosch, Sec. a.2, p. 657. The java.io library**

☐ Reading from the keyboard and files   *PL* Lesson 5-7, page 113

☐ Writing to the Java console and files   *PL* Lesson 5-8, page 116

Unit 27. Appendix B: Applets

☐ Applets   *PL* Lesson 16-1, page 205

☐ Html and applet commands   *PL* Lesson 16-2, page 206

☐ Examples of applets   *PL* Lesson 16-3, page 208

Chapter 1

Introduction
to Java

Lesson page 0-1. Introduction to Livetexts

We provide only one question. You will find it easier to use the *ProgramLive* after studying this lesson.

Question 1. Define *livetext*.

Lesson page 1-1. Hardware and software

Lesson page 1-1 provides a general introduction to computers. Its two activities use many phrases with which you are probably already familiar. The important ones to learn are:

> hardware, software, program, CPU, I/O (input/output), memory, memory location, address of a memory location, byte, and bit.

It is useful to know that the bits in a memory location can be used to represent many things, like integers, characters, and computer instructions. Also, there are different representations of integers —e.g. decimal, binary, and octal. You don't have to master these ideas right now —you can learn a lot about programming without them— but they are fundamental concepts that every programmer knows.

Question 1. Define *program* (as used in computer programming).

Question 2. Define *programming language*.

Question 3. Define *machine language*.

Question 4. Define *assembly language*.

Activity 1-1-1 Hardware versus software

We don't provide questions for this activity.

Activity 1-1-2 Computer memory

Question 5. Define *memory*.

Question 6. Define *address*.

Question 7. Define *bit*.

Question 8. Define *byte*.

Question 9. List the symbols (or signs) that are used in writing nonnegative integers in decimal notation.

Question 10. List the symbols (or signs) that are used in writing nonnegative integers in binary notation.

Question 11. Write the binary equivalent of the following decimal integers:

0:	5:	10:	15:
1:	6:	11:	16:
2:	7:	12:	17:
3:	8:	13:	18:
4:	9:	14:	19:

Lesson page 1-2. Some simple Java programs

Lesson page 1-2 gives an overview of Java programs and their execution. The details will be explained in later lessons, so don't expect to or try to remember everything you see and hear about Java programs on this lesson page. Pay attention to the filing-cabinet metaphor for illustrating the notion of a class, because we use it throughout *ProgramLive*.

Activity 1-2-1 A do-nothing Java program

We use this program to introduce the basic structure of a simple program.

Question 1. Define *keyword*.

Question 2. Define *method*.

Question 3. Execution of a program starts by calling:

Question 4. Every program has a method called:

Question 5. The _____ is the basic building block in Java.

Question 6. The body of every class begins with this symbol: _____ and ends with this symbol: _____.

Question 7. In programming, the terms *instruction* and *statement* mean the same thing. ☐ true ☐ false

Question 8. Programming task: Circle the parts of this Java program that you think are wrong.

```
// This program won't even compile.
public class Garble (
    public static void start(String[] args) {
    }
)
```

1. Type it in exactly as shown and see what happens when you compile it. You will get an *error message*, which indicates that the computer couldn't understand something about your program while trying to compile. Read the error message carefully, review your notes from this section, and fix the two errors. When you try to compile again, it will work.
2. Now try to run it. You will get another error message; if you read it carefully it will seem to have something to do with method **main** being missing. And it is —the method in this program is called **start**, not **main**. Change the name, recompile, and run it again. This time, nothing will happen: 0 statements were executed. Nothing was printed, so there is no output.

Activity 1-2-2 A program that prints

Question 9. What is the *Java console*?

Question 10. What is the difference between `print` and `println`?

Question 11. What happens when the following statement is executed?

```
System.out.print("Hello, everyone");
```

Question 12. Programming task: Write a program that prints your name on the first line, then prints a blank line, and then prints your address. Hint: use the following code to print a blank line: `System.out.println();`

Activity 1-2-3 A program that creates a window

The major point is not for you to learn and remember how to create a window but to see how one uses programs that others have written, using the import statement, and to learn a bit about packages.

Question 13. What does API stand for?

Question 14. What does GUI stand for?

Question 15. What is a package?

Question 16. Name the package that deals with input and output.

Question 17. Name the package that deals with graphical user interface components.

Question 18. What must you put at the top of a class to announce that you want to use the graphical user interface package?

Question 19. Which class deals with windows?

Question 20. Programming task: Write a program that creates and shows three windows. Hint: you will need three statements inside method `main`, instead of one.

Activity 1-2-4 A program that draws

Question 21. Write the two `import` statements that are shown in the code window:

Question 22. What is the name of the method that redraws the graphics window?

Question 23. When does method `paint` get called?

Question 24. Where is the origin (pixel (0,0)) for drawing?

Question 25. What statement sets the drawing color?

Question 26. When talking about pixel (a,b), which coordinate comes first, the horizontal one or the vertical one?

Question 27. Pixel (10,10) is closer to the bottom of the drawing window than pixel (40,10). ☐ true ☐ false

Question 28. Pixel (10,10) is closer to the bottom of the drawing window than pixel (10,40). ☐ true ☐ false

Question 29. What statement would you use to draw the `String` `"Wahoo!"` at pixel (40,60)?

Question 30. Programming task: Make a copy of the program of this activity. (Look on the lesson page for instructions on how to find it on the livetext, and be sure to get both of the files.) Modify method `paint` in class

`Draw1` to draw a face: add `setColor`, `drawRect` and `drawOval` statements to the end of method `paint` to draw an oval face with blue eyes, a red rectangular nose, and a red, wide and thin oval mouth.

You will find it useful to sketch the face on paper first, in order to figure out roughly which pixel values to use for the various pieces of the face. For now, don't worry about drawing your face on top of the circles and rectangles that we drew: just get your face on the screen.

Activity 1-2-5 Simple Java program exercises

The last activity on lesson page 1-2, an interactive exercise, will help you check whether you have digested the terminology that was introduced on this page. Be sure to take part in this activity!

Lesson page 1-3. Components of a Java program

Lesson page 1-3 begins a detailed explanation of Java. This is the time to begin learning terminology in earnest. When you finish this page, check to make sure that you understand fully the terms that are discussed below.

Activity 1-3-1 Comments and whitespace

Question 1. Describe the purpose of comments.

Question 2. The form of comment that can span several lines begins with this: _____ and ends with this: _____.

Question 3. Write an example of a one-line comment:

Question 4. Write down the five forms of whitespace:

   1.

   2.

   3.

   4.

   5.

Question 5. Comments are not a form of whitespace. ☐ true ☐ false

Question 6. Where can whitespace appear?

Question 7. Where can't whitespace appear?

Question 8. **Programming task:** Go back to the programming task on drawing faces (activity 1-2-4, p. 46) and "comment out" the lines of code that produce the rectangle and oval and the two `String`s. Add comments above the lines of code you added to describe what the code you added does. Use both types of comments. Compile and run the program to make sure that your face is still being drawn correctly.

Activity 1-3-2 Exercises on comments and whitespace

Don't forget to do these exercises!

Activity 1-3-3 Keywords and identifiers

Question 9. Define *keyword*.

Question 10. Write the six keywords used in this activity.

Question 11. Define *identifier*. Make sure you give the precise rules for forming identifiers.

Question 12. What is another word for *alphameric* (look in *ProgramLive*'s glossary).

Question 13. What two non-alphanumeric characters (characters that are not letters or numbers) can appear in identifiers?

Question 14. The identifiers `Dingbat` and `dingbat` are really the same, because Java ignores capitalization. □ `true` □ `false`

Question 15. Write the two conflicting guidelines for choosing identifiers:

    1.

    2.

Activity 1-3-4 Exercises on keywords and identifiers

Don't forget to do these exercises!

Activity 1-3-5 Variables and types

The notion of a type is particularly important. Make sure you know that a type defines a set of values and operations on them. However, you don't have to memorize every little aspect of each type that you run across, because references are just a few mouse clicks away. Lesson 6 contains all the details of the primitive types of Java; use it as a reference.

Question 16. Define *variable*.

Question 17. Any keyword can be used as the name of a variable. □ `true` □ `false`

Question 18. Define *type*.

Question 19. Define *variable declaration*.

Question 20. Describe the three parts of a variable declaration:

1.

2.

3.

Question 21. The range of an **int** variable is _____ to _____ inclusive.

Question 22. The range of a `byte` variable is _____ to _____ inclusive.
   You don't have to memorize the previous two items, but you should recognize that an **int** can hold a much wider range of values than a **byte**.

Question 23. How is type `String` different from **char**, **int**, and **byte**?

Activity 1-3-6 Expressions

Question 24. What is weird about division when both operands are of type int?

Question 25. Calculate the values of the following Java expressions. Assume all numbers are of type **int**:

1. 5 + 2 * 3 =

2. 5 + (2 * 3) =

3. (5 + 2) * 3 =

4. 5 / 2 =

5. 7 / 2 * 4 =

6. 7 / (3 * - 2) =

Write (and run) a program that prints the value of each of these to verify your answers.

Question 26. For each line below, execute it, showing what is in z upon termination. Assume that x is 5, y is 2, and z is 3 for each line:

1. z= 4;

2. z= y;

3. z= 22 / x;

4. z= x + z;

5. z= x + (z * y);

6. z= y + z * x;

7. z= (3 * (- (z)));

Write a program that prints the value of each of these to verify your answers.

Activity 1-3-7 Exercises on variables and expressions

Be sure to do these exercises!

Lesson page 1-4. Three statements: assignment, conditional and block statements

The three statements discussed on this lesson page are used in just about every program we write. There are basic building blocks.

Activity 1-4-1 The assignment statement

The assignment statement is used to give a variable a new value.

Question 1. Write the form of an *assignment* (look in *ProgramLive*'s glossary).

Question 2. Write the form of a *variable declaration.*

Question 3. Write the steps in executing an assignment statement:

1.

2.

Question 4. A variable may be assigned a value only once during execution of a program. ☐ true ☐ false

Question 5. Programming task: The statement

```
int numberOfFeet= 2;
```

stores the value 2 in variable `numberOfFeet`, and the statement

```
System.out.println(numberOfFeet);
```

prints the value stored in `numberOfFeet`.

You probably recognize the pythagorean formula $a^2 + b^2 = c^2$ for calculating the length of a hypotenuse of a right triangle. Write a program that declares an `int` variable named `cSquared` and stores in it the square of the length of the hypotenuse of a triangle with side a of length 3 and side b of length 5. The last statement of the program should print the value of `cSquared`.

Activity 1-4-2 Swapping two variables

Question 6. **Programming task:** Write (and run) a program that: (1) Declares three variables, a, b, and c; (2) assigns them the values 1, 2, and 3; rotates their values, so that a has b's initial value, b has c's, and c has a's. Write a statement-comment for this code and make sure its implementation is indented. Hint: you will need to use a temporary variable.

Activity 1-4-3 Conditional statements: if

Question 7. Write the form of an if-statement:

Question 8. What possible values can a boolean expression evaluate to?

Question 9. What happens if the condition of an if-statement evaluates to true?

Question 10. What happens if the condition evaluates to false?

Activity 1-4-4 Conditional statements: if-else

Question 11. Write the form of an if-else-statement:

Question 12. What happens if the condition of an if-else-statement evaluates to true?

Question 13. What happens if the condition evaluates to false?

Activity 1-4-5 Boolean expressions

Activity 1-4-5 introduces boolean expressions. If you need more help with them at this time, read lesson page 6-6.

Question 14. List all the elements in the set of `boolean` values.

Question 15. Define *boolean expression.*

Question 16. Define *proposition.*

Question 17. List six mathematical expressions that produce a boolean value.

Question 18. List three boolean operators.

Question 19. Programming task: Write (and run) a program that prints the values of the following expressions. (Make sure you understand the output!)

```
true && false
true || false
false || false
false && false
false && true
false || true
false && !true
!false
!true
```

Activity 1-4-6 Blocks

Question 20. Define *aggregate.*

Question 21. Write the form of a block:

Question 22. Because all the statements in a block get executed, it doesn't matter what order they are in. ☐ `true` ☐ `false`

Question 23. Write the indentation rule for a block:

Question 24. Programming task: There are errors (both with the uses of blocks and with indentation) in this program. Fix them.

```
public class ErrorRiddled {
public static void main(String[] args) {
}}
```

Activity 1-4-7 Exercises on assignments, conditionals, and blocks

Question 25. Programming task: Save the following code in a file:

```
public class IfX {
    public static void main(String[] args) {


    }
}
```

Add statements to the body of `main` that do the following (in this order):

1. Declare an **int** variable `y` and give it the value 3.

2. Declare an **int** variable `x` and give it the value 4 (for now).

3. If `x` is less than `y`, store the value `y + x` in `x`.

4. Print `"Now x >= y."`

Run your program. Run it again changing the value of x to be less than y, and again after changing x to be equal to y. Is the print statement always executed?

Finally, change the print statement to read "Now x < y." and move it into the then-part of the if-statement. Change the value of x to test the change in the program.

Lesson page 1-5. Input/Output

Activity 1-5-1 Using the Java Console for output

Question 1. What is the output of the following program fragment?

```
System.out.print("Once more un");
System.out.print("to the breach, dear friends,");
System.out.println(" once more;\nOr close the wall up...");
System.out.print("    -Shakespeare, King Henry V, Act ");
System.out.println(3 + ", Scene " + 1);
```

Activity 1-5-2 Using the Java Console for input

Question 2. Define *prompt*.

Question 3. Programming task:
Type the following code into a file named Test.java:

```
public class Test {
    public static void main(String[] args) {
        System.out.println("Hi" + "Phred.");
    }
}
```

Compile and run this program. Notice how the output looks a bit funny. Fix it so that it becomes readable. Type the following lines of code into the body of method main.

```
System.out.println("high " + 5);
System.out.println("3" + 20 * 2);
```

```
System.out.println(3.4 + 1.6 + " is five");
System.out.println("Is five " + 3.4 + 1.6);
```

Activity 1-5-3 A GUI: JLiveWindow

This GUI can be used over and over again to help debug your programs. Study it carefully.

Question 4. Programming task: Create a project in your IDE using files `JLiveWindow.java` and `MyJLiveWindow.java`. Compile and run the project to check that you have set it up correctly. (If you type in the fields and press the `Ready!` button, nothing happens.)

1. Class `MyJLiveWindow` (in file `MyJLiveWindow.java`) contains method `buttonPressed`. It reads two numbers from **int** fields 0 and 1 and sets **int** field 2 to their sum. But when you run the program, you will also see four **double** fields. Read the comment in method **main** (just after method `buttonPressed`) and change the program so three **int** fields and no **double** fields are created. You need to change only two numbers.

2. Whenever button `Ready` is pressed, the statement

   ```
   int sum= getIntField(0) + getIntField(1);
   ```

   reads the integer in field 0, adds it to the integer read from field 1, and stores the result in variable `sum`. What do each of the following statements do? Type each (one at a time) into method `buttonPressed`, along with a statement to set field 2 to the result. Run the program for each case to check your work.

   (a) **int** `mult= getIntField(0) * getIntField(1);`

   (b) **int** `other= getIntField(0) - getIntField(1);`

   (c) **int** `divResult= getIntField(0) / getIntField(1);`

   What happens if you type 4 in field 0 and 3 in field 1? Where did the decimal point go?

Activity 1-5-4 Exercises on the Java console and GUIs

Be sure to do these exercises!

Activity 1-5-5 Graphics windows

Question 5. Get a piece of graph paper. Draw a square 5 squares across (along the x-axis) and 5 squares down (along the y-axis). Label the upper-left corner (0, 0). The upper-right corner is (0, 5); the lower-right corner is (5, 5); the lower-left corner is (0, 5).

Put a dot at (2, 2), (2.5, 3), and (3, 2). Now draw a circle around each dot with a radius of 1 square. You should have a picture of three overlapping circles.

Using a different color, draw a square around each of the circles. Write on the drawing the coordinates of the top-left corner of each of the squares.

This is the sort of exercise you should do to plan a picture that you want to draw using the Graphics Window.

Activity 1-5-6 Using a graphics window

Question 6. Assuming that a and b are of type **int** and have already been assigned values, what would you expect the following statement to do?

```
int x= Math.max(a, b);
```

Question 7. Programming task: Create a project in your IDE using files Draw1.java and JLiveGraphics.java. Modify method **paint** in class JLiveGraphics1 to draw the diagram you made for activity 1-5-5. Make one square of your graph paper equal to 20 pixels.

Try changing the color of the circles. For a list of some of the available colors, look in the *ProgramLive* index for "Graphics, class" and click on the star beside "Methods and method calls".

Activity 1-5-7 Exercises on graphics windows

Be sure to do these exercises!

Lesson page 1-6. Assertions in programs

Assertions are expressions (about the variables used in a program) that yield one of the values true or false. An assertion can be written in English, Java, math, or any notation that gets its point across. Assertions are important in describing the situation at particular points during program execution.

Activity 1-6-1 Relations about variables and values

Question 1. Define *relation*.

Question 2. What symbol is used in Java to denote the mathematical equality symbol =?

Activity 1-6-2 Simplifying a particular kind of relation

Question 3. *Dogs* can mean *feet* (see the footnote to this activity). □ true □ false

Question 4. Does the following relation express the state of variable wetPeople in all situations? Explain.

If it is raining, wetPeople is true.

Question 5. Rewrite the relation given in the previous question to completely specify wetPeople.

Question 6. Simplify the relation "greater0 is true iff x > 0".

Question 7. Simplify the relation "I'll eat my hat if you're right, but I won't if you're wrong."

Question 8. Simplify (rewrite) the instruction "Set variable rain to true if it is raining and to false if it is not raining."

Activity 1-6-3 Assertions

Question 9. Define "assertion", as it was defined in this activity, and explain why the term "assertion" is used.

Question 10. Define *Hoare triple*.

Question 11. Define *precondition*.

Question 12. Define *postcondition*.

Question 13. Write down what the following means:

```
{(x+y)*y = 82}
x= x+y;
{x*y = 82}
```

Lesson page 1-7. Additional statements and expressions

Lesson page 1-7 is a catchall for a few statements and expressions that come in handy from time to time. You do *not* have to study this page early in your programming course, unless your instructor asks you to do so. Should you see one of these statements in a program, or should you later want to learn about these statements, then turn to this lesson page.

Chapter 2

Methods and method calls

Lesson page 2-1. Methods

The method is a basic building block of all programming. It corresponds to a recipe in a cookbook. In non-object-oriented programming, it has been called a *subroutine*. In this lesson, we show how to write methods and how to use them (or call or invoke them, as we say).

Activity 2-1-1 Methods are recipes

This activity should show you that you already know what a method is; you just have to learn how a method is written in Java.

Question 1. Computers are not intelligent. They follow the instructions they are given precisely, without any extrapolation or imagination. A program that "adds two numbers together" must tell the computer which two numbers and where to store the result. Someone else already told the computer how to add.

Write a sequence of instructions for wrapping a present. Assume the person following the instructions knows what the present is, as well as what paper, scissors, string, tape, pen, and label are. Then try to follow your instructions using real materials; you may find your instructions aren't as detailed as you thought. (Answer this qestion on an extra sheet of paper and clip it to this page.)

Question 2. When you look at a box of cake mix (or a box of pasta, or soup mix, or some other preprocessed food), you find a set of instructions. Write a set of instructions for boiling pasta. Can you make them general enough that you can substitute "potatoes" for "pasta" and have to change only the cooking time? How about for cooking rice? What problems do you run into? (Answer this qestion on an extra sheet of paper and clip it to this page.)

Activity 2-1-2 The blackbox view of a method

The blackbox view of a method is oriented to showing *what* a method does, and not *how* it does it. The blackbox view is what programmers generally use when they want to *use* a method.

Question 3. Define *method*.

Question 4. Define *procedure*.

Question 5. Define *specification*.

Question 6. Write the form of a method header.

Question 7. Define *body*.

Question 8. Define *parameter*.

Question 9. Write the form of a parameter declaration.

Question 10. **int** is a type. ☐ true ☐ false

Question 11. A parameter is a variable. ☐ true ☐ false

Question 12. What does keyword **public** indicate?

Question 13. Write a method header for a method `myFirstHeader` that is **public**, has return type **void**, and has two parameters: a variable `i` and a variable `j`, both of type **int**.

Activity 2-1-3 Check your understanding of terminology

Don't skip this exercise!

Activity 2-1-4 Understanding procedure calls

Your programming will be more effective and easier if you get in the habit of relying on the specification of a method when writing calls on the method. Here, we show you how to do that.

Question 14. What do you need to do in order to figure out what execution of a procedure call does?

Question 15. What does the method call `drawRect(22, 30, 40, 10);` do?

Activity 2-1-5 The general form of a procedure call

Question 16. What are the parts of a procedure call?

1.

2.

3.

Question 17. Define *argument*.

Question 18. Write the rules for the number and types of arguments:

1.

2.

3.

Question 19. This is a valid procedure call:

```
drawLine(0, 10, (3+30)/11, 4);
```

☐ true ☐ false

Lesson page 2-2. Method bodies and method calls

Finally, we get to see what a complete method looks like. After this, you can start writing your own methods!

Activity 2-2-1 The method body

Question 1. Write the steps of execution of a procedure call:

1.

2.

3.

4.

5.

6.

Question 2. Execute the first four steps of this method call: `print3(8*4, (14-6)/2);`

Question 3. Execute the first four steps of the method call `doIt(8*4, (14-6)/2, x);`, where x=12. Here is method `doIt`:

```
// Draw something
public static void doIt(int ) {


}
```

Question 4. Programming task: Write a static method `strangeAdd` that has two **int** parameters and prints the result of adding (two times the first parameter) to (three times the second). Put this method in the following class in the place shown and run it.

```
public class Test {
    public static void main(String args[]) {
        strangeAdd(1, 2);
    }

    // strangeAdd goes here




}
```

Activity 2-2-2 Example of method-call execution

Question 5. Define *frame*.

Question 6. It is so important that you memorize the steps in executing a procedure call that you should now, from memory, try to write those steps:

1.

2.

3.

4.

5.

6.

If you can do it, congratulations! If not, memorize the steps and try again —this is for your understanding of how method calls work.

Activity 2-2-3 Executing inner calls

A method call can occur within another method. There's nothing strange about this; it's like an instruction "Make the white icing on page 54" in the middle of a cake recipe. You will see that there is a frame for each method call that has started but has not yet completed.

Question 7. From memory, write the steps in executing a procedure call:

1.

2.

3.

4.

5.

6.

Question 8. What happened to the frame for method `paint` while method `drawTriangle` was being executed?

Question 9. When method `drawTriangle` finished executing, we restarted execution of `paint` from its beginning. □ `true` □ `false`

Activity 2-2-4 The stack of frames for calls

Question 10. Define the term *stack*. Be sure to mention the two operations on it.

Question 11. What happens to the call stack when (a) a procedure is called, and (b) execution of a procedure call finishes?

Activity 2-2-5 Review of methods

Don't forget to do these exercises!

Activity 2-2-6 Writing procedure calls

Question 12. Define *debugging*.

Question 13. Consider this procedure specification:

```
// Draw a circle that fits in the square with
// top left corner (x,y) and side length w.
public static void drawCircle( int x, int y, int w)
```

Write a method call to draw a circle that fits in the square with top left corner (20,30) and side length 40.

Write a method call to draw a circle with center (40,50) and radius 20.

Lesson page 2-3. Two components of method bodies

The body of a method can use local variables in order to simplify tasks, make the code easier to read, and make it more efficient. Also, the use of a `return` statement can help. This lesson page describes these concepts.

Activity 2-3-1 Local variables

Question 1. Define *local variable.*

Question 2. Write the form of a local variable declaration.

Question 3. Define *initialize.*

Question 4. What do you have to do to a local variable before you use it?

Question 5. Define *scope.*

Question 6. What is the scope of a local variable?

Question 7. Circle the scope of variable aVar in the following method.

```
public void foo() {
    System.out.println();
    int bVar;
    bVar= 3;
    int aVar;
    System.out.println();
    aVar= bVar * 2;
}
```

Activity 2-3-2 Combining declaration and initialization

Question 8. Write the form of an initialized variable declaration.

Question 9. Combine the following declaration and assignment into a single statement:

```
int timeToGetUp;
z= 0530;
```

Question 10. Separate the following statement into a declaration and an assignment that initializes it.

```
boolean youWin= morePoints && gameOver;
```

Question 11. What should you do at the same time that you declare a local variable?

Activity 2-3-3 Check your understanding of local variables

Don't forget to do these exercises!

Activity 2-3-4 The return statement

Question 12. What happens when a `return` statement is executed?

Question 13. A procedure body must have a `return` statement in it. ☐ true ☐ `false`

Question 14. During execution of a procedure body, how many times can `return` statements be executed?

Question 15. Define *overloading*.

Question 16. Look up `println` in the index and turn to the page indicated in Appendix D. You will see something like this:

> **public void println(boolean x)**
> **public void println(char x)**
> . . .
> **public void println(long x)**
>   print x and a line separator

All the functions in the list have the same name, `println`, so the method name is overloaded. But each has a different argument type. The same specification holds for all of them, so the specification is give only once. How many procedures in this list have name `println`?

Lesson page 2-4. Functions

There are two (at this point) forms of method: the procedure, which you have already seen, and the function. In this lesson page we explore the differences between them.

Activity 2-4-1 Form of a function

Question 1. What is the major difference between a procedure and a function?

Question 2. How can you tell whether a method is a procedure or a function?

Question 3. What does the return statement in a function body look like?

Question 4. What is the purpose of the type that replaces keyword `void`?

Question 5. A function body does not need a return statement. ☐ `true` ☐ `false`

Activity 2-4-2 The function call

The major point to remember is that a procedure call is a statement to be executed, while a function call is an expression that evaluates to the value returned by the function.

Question 6. Procedures and functions are _____ mechanisms.

Question 7. A procedure call is a _____.

Question 8. A function call is an _____.

Question 9. Describe the difference between the purposes of a function specification and a function body.

Question 10. Here is a function specification and header and a call on the function. What is the result of the call? (It's not a simple answer.)

```
// = the minimum of x, y, and z
public static int min(int x, int y, int z)


min(a, a+20, a-a)
```

Activity 2-4-3 Evaluating a function call

Question 11. Write the steps for evaluating a function call:

1.

2.

3.

4.

5.

6.

7.

Question 12. How does your answer to the question above differ from the steps in executing a procedure call?

Activity 2-4-4 Check your understanding of functions

Don't skip these exercises!

Lesson page 2-5. Top-down programming

Until now, we have focused mainly on the mechanics of Java programs. This lesson page discusses the process of developing a program.

Activity 2-5-1 Top-down design

Question 1. Define *top-down programming*.

Question 2. Give another name for *top-down programming*.

Question 3. Define *statement-comment*.

Activity 2-5-2 Edgar Allen Poe used top-down design

Question 4. How many lines did Poe decide *The Raven* should be?

Question 5. What was the topic?

Question 6. What was the tone?

Question 7. What would have to be sonorous and susceptible to protracted emphasis?

Activity 2-5-3 Anglicizing integers —functionally

Question 8. In method `tensName`, why is n's range `2 <= n <= 9`? That is, why isn't 1 included?

Activity 2-5-4 Anglicizing integers —using assignments

Question 9. Programming task: Write a function with one parameter, a `String`. The parameter contains a single-digit word: `"zero"`, `"one"`, ..., `"nine"`. The function yields the **int** version of it. For example, a call on your function with argument `"seven"` will evaluate to 7.

Chapter 3
Classes

Lesson page 3-1. Classes

This lesson page begins the important study of *classes*, the basis for object-oriented concepts. The class is used for two different things: as a container for static methods and as a "template" or description of objects (or instances) of the class. The first use of a class is described first.

Activity 3-1-1 The class as a file drawer of methods

Question 1. Write the form of a class definition.

Question 2. If someone asked you how a class is executed, what would you say?

Question 3. In the filing cabinet metaphor, where are static methods kept?

Question 4. Define *public*.

Question 5. What does a Java program consist of?

Question 6. What is the convention for naming the files that contain the classes of a program? What should you name the file that contains class `Foo`?

Activity 3-1-2 Referencing static methods

Question 7. Write the two rules for referring to a static method in a method call:

1.

2.

Activity 3-1-3 Temperature conversion

Question 8. In writing a program, one may have several goals in mind, some of which are listed below. Prioritize them (write "1" next to the most important one, "2" next to the second most important one, etc.).

1. A simple, readable program.

2. Minimize execution time (an efficient program).

3. A correct program.

4. Minimize the programmer's time.

Question 9. What trick did we use to avoid having to work out formulas for the second set of temperature conversion methods?

Activity 3-1-4 Overloading method names

Question 10. Define *overloading*.

Question 11. When a method with an overloaded method name is called, what is used to determine which method is called?

Lesson page 3-2. Class `Math`

Activity 3-2-1 The static methods in class `Math`

Question 1. The following methods in class `Math` are useful in many different situations. Write a short specification of each one:

- `abs(x)`

- `floor(x)`

- `ceil(x)`

- `min(x,y)`

- `max(x,y)`

Question 2. What is the value of the following expression?
`Math.abs(-4 + Math.sqrt(Math.max(2,3) * Math.ceil(2.8)))`

Question 3. Write an expression that yields the absolute value of the sum of `-100` and the minimum of `c` and `d`.

Activity 3-2-2 The constants in class Math

Question 4. Define *static variable.*

Question 5. Define *static field.*

Question 6. Define *class variable.*

Question 7. In Java, a constant is a variable that is declared with modifier
_____.

Question 8. The value pi, or π, is the ratio of the _____
of a circle to its _____.

Question 9. Write a statement that declares variable `area` and initializes
it to the area of a circle with radius 1. (The formula for the area of circle of
radius r is πr^2. Also, `Math.pow(b,c)` is b raised to the power c.)

Question 10. Consider a program that uses the weight of the Earth. The
number 6,000,000,000,000,000,000,000,000 could be used everywhere, but that
would be silly. Instead, a constant will be used. Write a declaration of a
constant `EARTH_WEIGHT` whose value is `6.0E24`.

Activity 3-2-3 Exercises on static methods and variables

Don't forget to do activity 3-2-3!

Question 11. Programming task: Given is class `Stats` (below). Write a
class `Small` whose method `main` prints variable `eW` of class `Stats`.

```
public class Stats {
    public static int eW= -92;




}
```

Activity 3-2-4 Trigonometric functions

This activity is included as a reference for those who may need to brush up on trigonometry. We provide no questions on it.

Lesson page 3-3. Classes and objects

This lesson page begins the explanation of the second, more important, use of the class, as a description of objects (or instances) of the class. Activity 3-3-1 introduces the concept of an object, and activity 3-3-2 describes how to reference the "fields" of an object.

Activity 3-3-1 Using an object to aggregate information

Question 1. At this point, how do we define an object? How is an object drawn —what does it look like? Where is the name of the object placed? (This information appears to the right of the activity icon after the activity has completed.)

Question 2. Define *aggregate*.

Question 3. Define *field*.

Activity 3-3-2 Referencing an object and its fields

Question 4. Suppose variable obj contains the name of an object. What expression would you write to refer to field x of that object?

Question 5. Assume that variable r contains the name of an object and that variable s is of the same type as r. Write a statement that makes s refer to the same object as r.

Activity 3-3-3 Definition of a class

Here we get to the important point: a class is just a description of (or a template for) objects.

Question 6. Write down the format of a class definition.

Question 7. What does the declaration of a field of an object look like?

Question 8. In a class definition, one variable declaration can declare a field that belongs to all objects of that class, and another declaration can declare a variable that belongs to the class itself (and goes in its file-cabinet drawer). How are these two kinds of declarations distinguished?

Question 9. In the file-cabinet metaphor, where are objects placed?

Question 10. In the file-cabinet metaphor, nonstatic variables belong in the drawer for the class in which they are defined. ☐ true ☐ false

Question 11. Write a definition of a class `Animal` with fields `weight`, `numberOfLegs`, and `color` .

Activity 3-3-4 A class as a type

Question 12. Define *type*.

Question 13. Define *primitive type*.

Question 14. Define *class type*.

Question 15. What is the value **null** used for?

Question 16. Below is a class named `Person`. Write a declaration of a variable Sam of type `Person`. Draw an object of class `Person` (draw it as a manila folder).

```
public class Person {
    public String name;
    public Person father;
    public Person mother;
}
```

Lesson page 3-4. Creating and initializing objects

Activity 3-4-1 Creating objects

Question 1. Write the form of a `new` expression.

Question 2. Describe evaluation of a `new` expression.

Question 3. What is a synonym for "an instance of class C"?

Question 4. Below is an assignment statement, where class `Person` is defined in this *Companion* in the previous activity 3-3-4. Execute this assignment, drawing the box for variable `p1`, creating the object (drawn as a manila folder), etc.

```
Person p1= new Person();
```

Activity 3-4-2 Creating String objects

Question 5. Below is a sequence of four assignments. Execute each assignment, drawing all the variables and objects that are created.

```
String s1= new String();
String s2= new String("");
String s3= "";
String s4= "Yes!";
```

Question 6. There are three ways to create a `String` object and assign its name to a variable. Only two of them allow you to state the contents of the `String`. Complete the two statements below to create a `String` that contains "Elaine" in two different ways.

```
String s=

String s=
```

Question 7. What happens when no variable refers to an object? (Hint: read the footnote following the activity.)

Activity 3-4-3 Using field declarations to initialize fields

Question 8. Write the default values for fields of the following types:

- **byte**, **short**, **int**, **long**.

- **float**, **double**.

- **boolean**.

- **char**.

- Class-type.

Question 9. Consider this class:

```
// Container for Pez, a type of candy
public class PezDispenser {
    String flavor;   // Flavor of this Pez container
    int numberOfPez; // No. candies in this Pez container
}
```

Draw the picture that represents the result of the following program segment:

```
PezDispenser p;
p= new PezDispenser();
```

Question 10.   Most Pez dispensers contain 20 Pez when you buy them. Change the class (write on the class given above) to reflect this —that is, include an initialization for one of the two instance variables.

Question 11.   Suppose `Animal` is a class. What value is initially in variable `sq1` (declared below), and what does that mean? Also, what values can be placed in variable `sq1`?

```
Animal sq1;
```

Question 12.   Programming task: The pet store needs to keep track of information about each animal in the store. Write (on another piece of paper) a class `Animal` that includes information about the animal name (a `String`), species (a `String`), age (an **int**), and whether they have had their shots (a **boolean**).

Here is a main program that uses your class. Note that it creates and initializes two `Animals` and then prints their information. Read this code carefully; it has clues about what you should name your variables. Be sure to compile and run your program to make sure that it does what you expect.

```
public class SPCA {
    public static void main(String[] args) {
        // Create and initialize the first Animal
            Animal a1= new Animal();
            a1.name= "Teabag";
            a1.species= "cat";
            a1.age= 14;
            a1.hasShots= true;

        // Create and initialize the second Animal
            Animal a2= new Animal();
            a2.name= "Beanbag";
            a2.species= "cat";
            a2.age= 3;
            a2.hasShots= false;
```

```
        // Print the information for the first Animal
        System.out.print(a1.name + ", " + a1.species
            + ", age " + a1.age + ", ");
        if (a1.hasShots) {
            System.out.println("is vaccinated.");
        } else {
            System.out.println("is not vaccinated.");
        }

        // Print the information for the second Animal
        System.out.print(a2.name + ", " + a2.species
            + ", age " + a2.age + ", ");
        if (a2.hasShots) {
            System.out.println("is vaccinated.");
        } else {
            System.out.println("is not vaccinated.");
        }
    }
}
```

Here is the expected output:

```
Teabag, cat, age 14, is vaccinated.
Beanbag, cat, age 3, is not vaccinated.
```

Lesson page 3-5. Scope boxes and constructors

Activity 3-5-1 The scope box of a frame

Question 1. What two things might the scope box of a frame contain?

1.

2.

Question 2. What is the purpose of the scope box?

Activity 3-5-2 The constructor

Question 3. How do constructors differ from procedures and functions?

Question 4. What are the steps in evaluating a **new** expression?

1.

2.

3.

Question 5. If a class does not contain a constructor, what default constructor is used?

Question 6. Below is a class `Person`. It contains a constructor. Execute the assignment statement `Person sam= Person("Sam Hall");`, drawing all the boxes and following the steps of the call of the constructor.

```
public class Person {
    public String name;    // The person's name
    public Person father;
    public Person mother;

    // Constructor: a person named s with no mother or father
    public Person(String s)
        {name= s;}
}
```

Activity 3-5-3 Calling a constructor from a constructor

Question 7. What is the form of a call of a constructor from within another constructor?

Question 8. Programming task: Rewrite the Pez example (on a separate piece of paper) to provide two constructors:

- A constructor with two parameters: the flavor and the number of initial Pez, and

- A constructor with only one parameter: the flavor. It should call the other constructor with a value 20 for the number of Pez.

Test both constructors using suitable code in a method `main`:

```
Pez p1;
p1= new Pez("strawberry", 12);
Pez p2;
p2= new Pez("grape");

System.out.println("Pez 1 information: " +
        p1.flavor + " " + p1.numberOfPez);
System.out.println("Pez 2 information: " +
        p2.flavor + " " + p2.numberOfPez);
```

Lesson page 3-6. Nonstatic methods

Activity 3-6-1 Nonstatic methods

Question 1. Define *nonstatic method*.

Question 2. Define *instance method*.

Question 3. Consider the following class.

```
public class TaxiRide {
    public double distance; // Miles traveled so far
    public String driver; // Cab driver's name

    // Constructor: an instance with driver d
    public TaxiRide(String d)
        { driver= d; }

    // = the per-mile fare for every taxi, in dollars
    public static double getStandardRate()
        { return 1.25; }

    // = the amount owed for this ride
    public double getFare()
        { return distance * getStandardRate(); }
}
```

Assuming that the box below represents the object that is created by evaluation of the expression **new** TaxiRide(), fill in the four members of the
object.

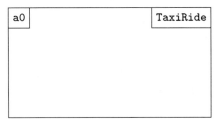

Question 4. In the previous question, distance was not explicitly initialized.
Why not?

Question 5. Assume that TaxiRide variable t refers to an instance of class
TaxiRide. Write a statement to declare double variable cost and set cost
to the fare owed for the ride t.

Question 6. Execute the following sequence of statements. You need not
execute the constructor call explicitly; just execute it according to its specification. But do draw the frames for the other method calls.

```
Taxi t= new Taxi("Sage");
t.distance= 3;
double perMileFare= TaxiRide.getStandardRate();
double cost= t.();
```

Question 7. Write a specification for a new instance method increment-Distance that will add 1 to the miles traveled. Be sure to use the "this" convention in writing its specification.

Activity 3-6-2 Creating an instance of Circle

No questions are provided for this activity.

Activity 3-6-3 Using instance methods of class Circle

No questions are provided for this activity.

Activity 3-6-4 Hiding instance variables

Now that we have all the necessary technical details defined, we get to a very important topic, hiding instance variables. In general, in almost every class, its instance variables should be hidden by making them **private**.

Question 8. Define *private*.

Question 9. Define *getter method*.

Question 10. Define *setter method*.

Question 11. Rewrite class TaxiRide to hide its two instance variables; write getter methods for the two instance variables.

Question 12.   There is currently no way to set variable `distance` of an instance of class `TaxiRide`. Write a setter method for it. Ensure that the distance is always at least zero.

Activity 3-6-5 Reasons for using modifier `private`

Question 13.   Write two reasons for making instance variables of a class private:

1.

2.

Activity 3-6-6 Check your understanding of nonstatic methods

Be sure to do these exercises!

Lesson page 3-7.   Consequences of using objects

Activity 3-7-1 The scope box for a call of an instance method

Question 1. What is a scope box used for?

Question 2. What is inside the scope box for an instance method?

Question 3. What is inside the scope box for a static method?

Question 4. Draw a diagram of the frame for a method call, showing all its components. The footnote for this activity may help.

Question 5. Write the steps for executing a function call:

1.

2.

3.

4.

5.

6.

7.

Question 6. Read the footnote to this activity, then complete this chart:

For one of these	The scope box contains
Constructor	Name of the newly created object
	Name of the class
	Name of the object in which the method resides

Question 7. This exercise concerns testing for equality of two objects. Write an instance method `equals` for class `TaxiRide` (see page 87) with the following heading:

```
// = ''this instance and t are equal (have the
//      same driver and went the same distance)''
public boolean equals(TaxiRide t)
```

Question 8. Define *aliasing*.

Activity 3-7-2 Method `toString`

Question 9. What is method `toString` used for?

Question 10. Which of the following statements (circle them) have an implicit call on method `toString` in the object to which `e` refers?

```
Employee e= new Employee();
System.out.println(e);
Employee f= e;
String s= "" + e;
System.out.println("" + e);
String t= e + "";
```

Activity 3-7-3 Evaluating a call on method `toString`

Question 11. What is the output of the following program segment?

```
Employee e= new Employee();
Employee f= new Employee();
e.name= "Paul";
e.start= 1997;
e.salary= 100000;
f.name= "Petra";
f.start= 2000;
f.salary= 200000;
System.out.println(f);
System.out.println(e);
```

Activity 3-7-4 Further examples of method `toString`

Question 12. **Programming task:** Write a method `toString` for class TaxiRide that returns a String containing the name of the driver, the distance traveled, and the fare for the trip. Determine the fare by calling method getFare. Be sure to test your code to verify that it works.

```
public class TaxiRide {
    private double distance= 0; // Miles traveled
    private String driver; // Cab driver's name

    // Constructor: instance with driver d, distance 0
    public Taxi(String d)
        { driver= d; }

    // = the per-mile fare for every taxi, in dollars
    public static float getStandardRate()
        { return 1.25; }

    // Add 1 to the distance of this tax ride
    public void increment()
        { distance= distance+1; }

    // = the amount owed for this ride
    public float getFare()
        { return distance * getStandardRate(); }
}
```

Activity 3-7-5 Exercises on objects

Don't forget to do this exercise!

Lesson page 3-8. Object-oriented design

The design of a large object-oriented program is a difficult task, and it's even more difficult to explain how to do it. Lesson page 3-8 makes an attempt at this explanation, but it is only a beginning.

Activity 3-8-1 Designing the classes of a program

Question 1. Define *problem domain*.

Question 2. What does the specification of a class consist of?

Question 3. Write the basic steps in object-oriented design:

1.

2.

3.

4.

Activity 3-8-2 Problem statement: reading a clock

Question 4. What information is requested in the first two windows shown to the player?

Question 5. Describe the four levels of play:

1.

2.

3.

4.

Question 6. When is the level incremented?

Activity 3-8-3 Identifying the classes

Question 7. After listening to activity 3-8-3, get a fresh sheet of paper and, based on your knowledge of the game, write down as many objects as you can think of that this game uses. Your list does not have to be the same as that of this activity. When you are finished, compare your list to the list produced in this activity.

Activity 3-8-4 Designing classes `Clock` and `Time`

Question 8. Write down the specifications of class `Clock` and `Time` (or print the Exposition text). Study the specifications; ask yourself which of these specifications you would have also written.

Activity 3-8-5 Implementing `ClockWindow`, `Clock`, and `Time`

There are no questions for this activity.

Activity 3-8-6 Designing the player and the game

Question 9. Write down the specifications of class `Player` and `ClockGame` (or print the Exposition text). Study the specifications; ask yourself which of these specifications you would have also written.

Activity 3-8-7 Implementing the player and the game

There are no questions for this activity.

Activity 3-8-8 Putting it all together

Question 10. Programming task: Obtain the .java files for the clock game (see the introduction to activity 3-8-2), construct a project from these files, and play the game. Spend some time studying the implementations of the various classes.

Chapter 4

Subclasses and inheritance

Lesson page 4-1. Subclasses

This lesson discusses the notion of a subclass of a class and related notions and mechanisms. It is the subclass and inheritance that makes object-oriented programming different and exciting. These mechanisms provide suitable facilities for structuring and maintaining larger programs.

Activity 4-1-1 The need for better structuring mechanisms

There are no questions about this activity, for it just illustrates problems that could arise in extending a program with the tools currently available.

Activity 4-1-2 The subclass

Question 1. Define *subclass*.

Question 2. Define *superclass*.

Question 3. Define *inheritance*.

Question 4. If class A is defined as "**public class A extends** B {...}", then _____ is a superclass of _____. Also, every instance method of _____ is an instance method of _____.

Question 5. Draw an instance of class Exec of this activity.

Activity 4-1-3 The subclass (continued)

Question 6. Each subclass of a class C inherits all the fields and methods of C, and each can also have other fields and methods. ☐ true   ☐ false

Question 7. Below are two classes and an assignment to a variable b of class-type Book. Below that, we show variable b and the instance created by the assignment. Fill in the fields and methods in the object.

```
public class LibraryItem {
    private String deweyDecimalNumber;

    // = the Dewey Decimal Number of this instance.
    public getDeweyDecimalNumber()
        {return deweyDecimalNumber;}
}
public class Book extends LibraryItem {
    private String title;
    private String author;

    // Constructor: a Book with title t and author n
    public Book(String t, String n) {
        title= t; author= n;
}

    // = the title of this Book
    public String getTitle()
        { return title; }

    // = the author of this Book
    public String getName()
        { return author; }
}
    . . .
```

Book b= **new** Book("Companion", "Gries, Hall, Gries");

```
                           ┌──────────────────────────────┐
                           │ a0              │ LibraryItem │
                           │                 └─────────────┤
                           │                              │
                           │                              │
                           │                              │
                           ├──────────────────┌───────────┤
                           │                  │    Book   │
Book b  ┌──────┐           │                  └───────────┤
        │      │           │                              │
        └──────┘           │                              │
                           │                              │
                           └──────────────────────────────┘
```

Lesson page 4-2. Constructors and inherited methods

Activity 4-2-1 Writing a constructor for a subclass

Question 1. It is best to initialize inherited fields using (0) a call on a constructor in the superclass or (1) using some assignment statements in the subclass constructor (circle one).

Question 2. Write the form for a call of a constructor in the superclass and indicate where such a call may used.

Activity 4-2-2 Overriding an inherited method

Question 3. Define *override*.

Question 4. State an advantage of the ability to override (see the discussion of the activity).

Activity 4-2-3 Calling an overridden method of the superclass

Question 5. To reference a method of the superclass, precede its name by _____.

Activity 4-2-4 Use of keywords this and super

Question 6. What are the two uses of keyword **super**?

    1.

    2.

Question 7. What are the two uses of keyword **this**?

1.

2.

Activity 4-2-5 Exercises on subclasses

Be sure to do these exercises!

Activity 4-2-6 Access modifier protected

Question 8. In the programs you generally write, as a beginner, there is no difference between protected and public. ☐ true ☐ false

Question 9. Where can a protected instance variable or method be referenced?

Question 10. From where are fields with no access modifier accessible?

Activity 4-2-7 The class hierarchy

Question 11. Which class is at the top of the class hierarchy —in other words, which class is automatically the superclass of classes that are not explicitly defined to be subclasses?

Question 12. What are the two most useful methods that are defined in class Object?

Question 13. **Programming task:** Do the following:

1. Write a constructor for class Hourly that initializes Hourly's instance variables. Make use of class Employee's constructor!

2. Test your new code.

Question 14. If a class `Temp` extended `Hourly` where would it appear in the class hierarchy?

Lesson page 4-3. Casting and a new model of execution of method calls

We now investigate two things. First, just as we have widening and narrowing casts for primitive types, we have widening and narrowing casts for class-types. Second, we extend the model of execution to include subclasses.

Activity 4-3-1 Widening

Question 1. Define *wider class-type*.

Question 2. Widening of a class-type has to be done explicitly; Java won't do it implicitly when it is necessary. ☐ `true` ☐ `false`

Question 3. If an instance of class `SC` is widened to a superclass `C`, then the only instance names (of variables and methods) that are accessible are those accessible in class `C`. ☐ `true` ☐ `false`

Question 4. Assume that class `B` extends class `A`. Circle the legal statement and cross out the illegal one:

- `B b= new A();`

- `A a= new B();`

If you aren't sure which is legal, declare two such classes (they can even be empty classes), write the two statements in a `main` method, and try compiling.

Question 5. Consider a class `Animal` and a subclass `Cat` of `Animal`, both of which define an instance function `noise()`, which returns the noise that an instance makes. Consider the following two statements:

```
Animal s= new Cat();
System.out.println(s.noise());
```

What is the apparent class of `s`? The real class?

Question 6. In the previous question, which function `noise` will be called when the `println` statement is executed, the one defined in `Animal` or the one defined in `Cat`? Understanding this is important for the proper use of subclasses.

Activity 4-3-2 Narrowing

Question 7. Define *narrower class-type*.

Question 8. Suppose class B extends class A. Each of the two assignments given below has an explicit type cast. Which cast does not have to be explicit?

- A a= (A) new B();

- B b= (B) a;

Question 9. Suppose class B extends class A. The following statement creates an instance of B, widens it to A, and then narrows it back to B before assigning it to variable x. Because of the widening cast, information is lost, and the resulting instance doesn't have all the fields and values that it had upon creation. ☐ true ☐ false

        B x= (B) ((A) (new B()));

Question 10. Write down the meaning of the expression x **instanceof** C. That is, write down what the result is.

Question 11. Write a boolean expression that evaluates to **true** iff variable a contains the name of an instance of class C.

Activity 4-3-3 Execution of a method call

This activity and the next discuss the final model of execution of method calls, taking into account subclasses, and the algorithm for determining what a name (e.g. the name of a method) refers to. We won't extend the execution model any further.

Question 12. What is the difference between a function call and a procedure call?

Question 13. Using class C as shown in the activity window, execute a call on method main of class D below. (Assume that the constructor call C(5) sets C's field d to 25.) Below the code, we show the frame for the call on main at the point where the new expression is to be evaluated, so evaluate the new expression and complete the assignment statement.

```
public class D {
    public static void main(String[] args) {
        C c= new C(5);
    }
}
```

Activity 4-3-4 Referencing an item within a method body

Question 14. Study the algorithm for determining what a name refers to. Most of it you know already; this is just a summary. The crucial point for object-oriented programming is the following: Consider a class Animal and a subclass Cat of Animal, both of which define an instance function noise(), which returns the noise that an instance makes. Consider the following two statements:

```
Animal s= new Cat();
System.out.println(s.noise());
```

Which function noise will be called when the println statement is executed, the one defined in Animal or the one defined in Cat? Indicate the part of the algorithm for determining to what a name refers in order to explain your answer.

Question 15. Do lab 3 of this lesson (use the Labs icon to get to it).

Activity 4-3-5 A final look at class Employee

Question 16. Programming task: First, finish class Hourly. Second, write a class Temp that extends Hourly. Include a constructor for Temp that makes use of Hourly's constructor and also sets Temp's end date. Test your code.

Lesson page 4-4. Object-oriented design

Question 1. Define *problem domain*.

Activity 4-4-1 Object-oriented design with subclasses

Question 2. Did we use noun phrases or verb phrases to identify the objects?

Question 3. If class B extends class A, then every A is a B. □ true □ false

Question 4. Copy the three guidelines for object-oriented design:

-

-

-

Activity 4-4-2 Classes Shape and `Parallelogram`

This activity and the following two are a case study in object-oriented design with subclasses. There are no questions associated with the activities, but be sure to study them carefully.

Activity 4-4-3 Sublasses `Rhombus` and `Square`

Activity 4-4-4 Using the shape classes

Lesson page 4-5. Abstract classes

Activity 4-5-1 Abstract classes

Question 1. What is the reason for placing method `drawShape` in class `Shape`? (See the second paragraph of the Exposition Text for the answer.)

Question 2. What is the reason for making a class abstract?

Question 3. What is the reason for making a method abstract?

Chapter 5

Some useful classes

Lesson page 5-1. Numerical wrapper classes

The activity on this lesson page discusses only wrapper class `Integer`, because the other numerical wrapper classes are similar. Look in the footnotes on this lesson page for information about wrapper classes `Byte`, `Short`, `Long`, `Float`, and `Double`.

Activity 5-1-1 Wrapper-class `Integer`

Question 1. The value that is wrapped by an instance of class `Integer` can be changed. ☐ `true` ☐ `false`

Question 2. Write a statement that subtracts 5 from the value referenced by `Integer` variable d. The last sentence is a bit misleading; you will have to create a new `Integer` (that will contain the value) and store its name in d.

Activity 5-1-2 Instance methods of class `Integer`

Question 3. How can you get the `String` representation of an `Integer` object?

Activity 5-1-3 Static constants and methods of class `Integer`

Question 4. Write a Java statement that prints the smallest possible `int` value.

Question 5. Write a Java expression whose value is the `String` representation of the `int` literal 270.

Question 6. Write a Java expression that whose value is the **int** representation of the String literal "456".

Lesson page 5-2. Wrapper classes Boolean and Character

No questions are placed here because the wrapper classes Boolean and Character are so similar to wrapper class Integer. Use the lesson page as a reference when you are looking for methods or constants that deal with boolean values and characters.

Lesson page 5-3. Strings

Question 1. Define *literal*.

Question 2. Write down the escape sequences that can be used within a String for the single-quote character, the double-quote character, the backslash, and the newline character.

Question 3. What is the value of the following Java expression? Type it in a program and verify your answer.

```
"What !\\$\"".length()
```

Question 4. What is the length of the String "abdcefg"? Write an expression whose value is the length of this String.

Activity 5-3-1 String literals

Question 5. Write beside each line the String that produced the output. The first one is done for you.

Output	Java String
What?!?	"What?!?"
Who's this?	
When are they arriving?	
Sage said "Ah!" and ate.	

Activity 5-3-2 Variables of type `String`

Question 6. In the space below, declare a variable of type `String` and assign it your name.

Question 7. Write a `String` that, when printed, produces the output:

"Isn't there more?" they chorused.

Activity 5-3-3 Operation catenation

Question 8. Assume `String` variables, `name` and `job` have already been declared and assigned values. Write a print statement that would produce the line below if `name` contained `"Sam"` and `job` contained `"sorting socks"`.

Sam's job is sorting socks.

Activity 5-3-4 Operation catenation (continued)

Question 9. In what contexts is method `toString` automatically called?

Question 10. What is the output of the following program? Place your answer here:

```
// Used to test class River.
public class RiverTest {
    public static void main(String args[]) {
        River redRiver= new River();
        River slowRiver= new River();
        slowRiver.avgSpeed= 0.2;
        redRiver.avgDepth= 16;
        System.out.println(slowRiver);
    }
}

// Keeps track of the average depth of a
// river in meters and the average speed in knots.
public class River {
    public double avgDepth= 4.5; // in meters
    public double avgSpeed= 3.2; // in knots

    public String toString() {
        return "Average: " + 1 + " depth - " +
                avgDepth + 2 + " speed - " + avgSpeed;
    }
}
```

Activity 5-3-5 Referencing the characters of a String

Question 11. What is the result of evaluating `"ABCD".charAt(2)`?

Question 12. The lines are out of order in the following program. Rearrange them so that the output is `"My name is Leonardo da Vinci."` (You can just number the lines in the correct order.)

```
public class StringMess {
    public static void main(String args[]) {
        System.out.print(s77);
        String s25= "n" + s77.charAt(1) + "me ";
        String s18= "r" + s77.substring(0,1) + s5.charAt(2);
        System.out.print(s23);
        System.out.print(s25);
        System.out.print("My ");
        String s5= "Leo" + s25.substring(0,2);
        System.out.print(s2);
        String s23= "Vinc" + s2.charAt(0);
        System.out.print(s5);
        String s2= "is ";
        String s77= "da ";
        System.out.println(".");
        System.out.print(s18 + s2.charAt(2));
```

```
        }
    }
```

Activity 5-3-6 Equality of Strings

Question 13. Will the following code print `true` or `false`? Why?

```
String s= "Sam";
String t= "Sam";
System.out.println(s==t);
```

Question 14. Does the following code print **true** or **false**?. If the latter, change the argument of `println` so that the comparison of s and t prints **true**.

```
String s= "Sam";
String t= "Sa" + "m";
System.out.println(s==t);
```

Question 15. Programming task: It is usually wrong to use operator `==` when comparing `Strings` because operator `==` compares what is stored in the variable. A variable of a class type contains the name of an object, and not the object itself.

Given class `Fraction` below, fill in the body of method `equals`. (Remember that members of a class can access the private variables of the class.)

```
// An instance is a fraction in the form of a numerator
// and a denominator. This is a naive, poor version, in
// which 2/2 and 3/3 are considered to be different.
public class Fraction {
    private int numerator= 1;   // Default value of
    private int denominator= 1; // fraction is 1

    public Fraction(int num, int denom) {
        numerator= num;
        denominator= denom;
    }

    public boolean equals(Fraction f) {



    }
```

Question 16. Programming task: Write method `equals` for class `Book`:

```
// A Book has a title, a number of pages and a price
public class Book {
    private String title= ""; // no title
    private int numPages= 0; // empty book
    private double price= 0; // price per book

    public Book(String t, int p, double pr) {
        title= t;
        numPages= p;
        price= pr;
    }
}
```

Question 17. Programming task: Write a program that swaps the first and last vowels in a word and then prints the original word followed by the altered version. For example, if your program processed the word `"value"`, output would be: `value velua`. If you know how to get input from the user, do so. Otherwise, use a `String` literal.

Lesson page 5-4. Class `StringBuffer`

Question 1. Define *mutable*.

Question 2. Define *immutable*.

Question 3. Programming task: Write a method `main` that does the following. Input a word from the user (use an input method of your own choosing) and store it in a `StringBuffer`. Then, if the word is longer than 5 letters, reverse the letters and prepend the letter `"i"`. Finally, print the mangled word.

For example, if the word was `"bate"`, the output would be `"bate"`. If the word was `"envelope"` the output would be `"iepolevne"`.

Lesson page 5-5. Class Vector

Question 1. What is the *capacity* of a Vector?

Activity 5-5-1 Adding objects to a Vector

Question 2. The number of elements in a Vector cannot get larger than an amount that is known when the Vector is created. □ true □ false

Question 3. All elements in a Vector are viewed as being of class Object. □ true □ false

Question 4. Are there bugs in the following program? If so, where are they and why do they cause problems?

```
import java.util.*;
public class Test {
    public static void main(String args[]) {
        Vector v= new Vector(45);
        v.addElement(3);      }
}
```

Question 5. Are there bugs in the following program? If so, where are they and why do they cause problems?

```
public class Test {
    public static void main(String args[]) {
        Vector v= new Vector(45);
        v.addElement("3");
    }
}
```

Question 6. Are there bugs in the following program? If so, where are they and why do they cause problems? (Class Byte is a wrapper class.)

```
public class Test {
    public static void main(String args[]) {
    Vector v= new Vector(45);
    v.addElement(new Byte((byte)3));
    }
}
```

Activity 5-5-2 Referencing and changing objects in a `Vector`

Question 7. Consider a `Vector v`, whose elements are really of class `Integer`. Write a statement to store in `Integer` variable `x` the fifth element of `v`.

Question 8. If `Vector v` contains at least one object of any class type, the following code will always work. It is not necessary to cast the element. Why not?

```
System.out.println(v.elementAt(0));
```

Question 9. Assuming `Vector v` has at least three `Integer`s stored in it, write the code to get the `Integer` at position 0, add it to the `Integer` stored at position 1, and then set the element at position 2 to the result.

Activity 5-5-3 Other `Vector` methods

Question 10. A `Vector v` with size 3 and capacity 3 will have size 4 and capacity 8 after the call `v.insertElementAt(...)`. □ true □ false

Question 11. Programming task: Write a method that has a `Vector` as a parameter and does the following:

1. If the `Vector` is empty, print `"The Vector is empty."`.

2. If the `Vector` contains an even, positive number of elements, print `"The Vector is even."`, remove the last element, and insert it at the front of the `Vector`.

3. If the `Vector` contains an odd number of elements, print `"This was an odd Vector."` and then remove the middle element.

4. Finally, get a `String` representation of the entire `Vector`, remove all the elements, and return the `String` representation.

Lesson page 5-6. Class `Date`

Question 1. The method of estimating how long it takes to execute a method as shown on the lesson page isn't very accurate because the measured amount of time may include other instructions the computer was trying to execute. ☐ true ☐ false

Question 2. Programming task: Create an object of type `Date` and use the object to print the current date and time.

Lesson page 5-7. Reading from the keyboard and files

Question 1. Define *stream*.

Question 2. Define *input stream*.

Question 3. Define *output stream*.

Activity 5-7-1 Linking to the keyboard

Question 4. What is the standard input, usually?

Question 5. Which variable represents the standard input?

Question 6. Write a statement that creates an `InputStreamReader` that is hooked up to the standard input.

Question 7. Write a statement that creates a `BufferedReader` that is hooked up to the standard input.

Activity 5-7-2 Reading a line at a time from the keyboard

Question 8. Write a statement that reads a line of text from the keyboard. Use the `BufferedReader` variable that was created in the previous question.

Activity 5-7-3 Handling an IO exception

Question 9. When doing input, what `import` statement is necessary?

Question 10. If a method does input, what must appear at the end of the method header?

Question 11. How many different `BufferedReader` objects can read from the standard input at one time?

Activity 5-7-4 Reading numbers

Question 12. What is wrong with this expression?

```
Integer.parseInt(" 77 ")
```

Question 13. Write a program that reads two **int**s (one per line of input) and prints their sum.

Activity 5-7-5 Reading from a file

Question 14. In this Activity, two `BufferedReader`s were created. What were they linked to?

Question 15. How did the program get the name of the file to read?

Question 16. What does method `readLine` return when there are no more lines in a file?

Activity 5-7-6 Using a dialog box

Question 17. Write Java expressions that correspond to these statements:

- Create a `JFileChooser` object.

- Set the title of the file chooser window.

- Show the dialog.

- Get the file name that the user selected.

Question 18. **Programming task:** To get a second file name from the user, you can simply show the dialog again. Write a program to read the first lines of two files, whose names are obtained from the user, and print `"same"` if the first lines are the same and `"different"` if they are different.

Lesson page 5-8. Writing to the Java console and files

Activity 5-8-1 Writing a file

Question 1. Write a statement that creates a `PrintStream` that is hooked up to a file called `"f.txt"`.

Question 2. **Programming task:** Write a program that (a) reads a line from a file that the user chooses and (b) writes that line to another file that the user chooses.

Question 3. **Programming task:** Write a program that (a) reads a line from a file that the user chooses and (b) appends (not overwrites!) that line to another file that the user chooses.

Question 4. **Programming task:** Write a program that reads a line from a file that the user chooses, asks the user whether to append or to overwrite, and then appends or overwrites the line to another file that the user chooses.

Chapter 6
Primitive types

Lesson page 6-1. Primitive types

A *type* describes a set of values and some operations on them. In mathematics, type *integer* describes the set of integers $\{\ldots, -2, -1, 0, 1, 2, 3, \ldots\}$ and the operations negation $(-)$, addition $(+)$, multiplication $(*)$, and so forth. In Java, each variable has a type, which defines the set of values that can be associated with the variable. In fact, each expression has a type, which defines the set of values that might be the result of its evaluation.

Java has two kinds of types: *primitive types* and *class types*. This lesson discusses Java's seven primitive types, which can be further classified as the *integral types* (called that because their values are integers), the *floating-point types*, and type `bool`.

Question 1. Why doesn't Java include the mathematical type *integer* as a primitive type?

Question 2. List the five integral types in Java:

1.

2.

3.

4.

5.

Question 3. List the two floating-point types in Java:

1.

2.

Question 4. Which integral type has the largest range?

Question 5. Which floating-point type has the largest range?

Question 6. Which primitive type has only two values?

Question 7. Fill in the following table with the smallest and highest value of each type.

type	smallest value	largest value
boolean		
long		
int		
short		
byte		

Lesson page 6-2. The integral types

Activity 6-2-1: Integral constants (literals)

Question 1. Define *literal*.

Activity 6-2-2: Operations on type int

Question 2. Fill in the following table (we did one row for you) for the two unary and five binary operations in type int.

	Symbol	Name of operation	Example
unary operator:			
unary operator:			
binary operator:	+	addition	4 + 6 = 10
binary operator:			
binary operator:			
binary operator:			
binary operator			

Question 3. Java stops running your program and gives an error message if integers get too large. □ true □ false

Question 4. In Java, what does -2147483648-1 evaluate to?

Question 5. What does 5-(6/7) evaluate to?

Question 6. What is different about a division like 6/7 in Java as opposed to mathematics?

Question 7. How many operations are there on type **byte**? Type **short**?

Activity 6-2-3: Promoting integer values to a wider type

Question 8. All values in one of these integral types are contained in a wider integral type. □ true □ false

Question 9. When assigning a **byte** to an **int**, Java will automatically promote a **byte** to an **int**. □ true □ false

Question 10. List the four integral types mentioned in this activity, from narrowest to widest:

Activity 6-2-4: Casting integer values

Question 11. Define *cast*.

Question 12. Write an expression that will cast the value of the expression 32768 - 32765 to type **byte**.

Question 13. Circle the error(s) in the following sequence of statements:

```
byte b= 3.5;
short s= b;

short j= 4;
long l= (long)j;

byte k= 440;
int i= k;
```

Activity 6-2-5: Review of integer types

Participate in this activity for futher confirmation of your understanding.

Lesson page 6-3. A minimalist view of floating-point

Activity 6-3-1: Literals of type double

Question 1. Below, circle the literals that represent the number 4500.0 in Java as a **double**. (If you are unsure, put them into print statements and run the code —all of these **double** values will be printed in the format 4500.0.)

```
4500.    45e2        45e2D
4500d    45000e-1    4500e0
.45e4    4500.0      4500
```

Activity 6-3-2: Values of type double and operations on them

Question 2. How do you write 108.225×10^5 in Java?

Question 3. See the bottom of lesson page 6-3 for the information necessary to fill in the blanks below.

1. If at least one operand is a _____, the result is a _____; otherwise

2. If at least one operand is a _____, the result is a _____; otherwise

3. If at least one operand is a _____, the result is a _____; otherwise

4. All operands are of type _____, _____, _____, or _____, and the result is an _____.

Question 4. Fill in the blanks for the widening conversion rules (see the bottom of lesson page 6-3).

1. _____ → _____ → _____ → _____ → _____ → _____

2. _____ → _____ → _____ → _____ → _____

Lesson page 6-4. Remarks about floating point

Question 1. What does this statement print?

```
System.out.println( 100100100100100100.0 );
```

Lesson page 6-5. Type char

Activity 6-5-1: Literals of type char

Question 1. A **char** literal begins and ends with a single quotemark. ☐ true ☐ **false**

Question 2. A String literal begins and ends with a double quotemark. ☐ true ☐ false

Question 3. What is an "escape sequence"? What do the Java escape sequences begin with?

Question 4. Write the **char** literals for the following symbols:

Java literal	symbol it represents
	backslash
	single quote
	double quote
	line feed, or newline
	carriage return
	tab
	form feed
	backspace

Question 5. What does ASCII stand for? How many bytes does an ASCII character take?

Question 6. Java uses ASCII, not Unicode, to represent characters. □ true
□ false

Activity 6-5-2: char as an integral type

Question 7. Assume that **int** variable i contains a single-digit number.
Complete the following assignment statement so that c will contain the **char**
representation of i. For example, if i contains 3, c should be set to '3'.

```
char c=                    ;
```

Question 8. Assume that **char** variable c contains a character. Complete the
following assignment statement so that i will contain the **int** representation
of c. For example, if c contains 'A', i should be set to 65.

```
int i=                  ;
```

Activity 6-5-3: A loop to sequence through characters

Don't participate in this activity if you have not yet learned about loops.

Question 9. Which is larger, 'a' or 'A'?

Question 10. Write a Java expression to produce the uppercase version of
lowercase **char** c.

Activity 6-5-4: Execution of the loop

Question 11. What Java statement will increment **char** variable c?

Question 12. Programming task: Write a Java **boolean** expression that
evaluates to the value of "**char** c is an uppercase letter". Write a short program and run it to test your answer on a few examples.

Lesson page 6-6. Type `boolean`

Activity 6-6-1: The literals and operations of type `boolean`

Question 1. What are the two literals of type **boolean**?

Question 2. What are the three names for operator ! ?

Question 3. Complete the following truth table. Rather than just copying it, try to reason it through —every computer scientist needs to have a thorough understanding of these rules.

b	c	b&&c	b‖c	!b	b==c	b!=c
true	true					
true	false					
false	true					
false	false					

Question 4. List the precedences of the mathematical and boolean operators from highest to lowest:

1.

2.

3.

4.

5.

6.

7.

Question 5. Write down the value of this expression: (**true** || **false**) || 5 < 3 + 2.

Question 6. Define *equivalence*.

Question 7. Define *inequivalence*.

Activity 6-6-2: Short-circuit evaluation

Question 8. Define *short-circuit evaluation*.

Question 9. For operator &&, when is the second operand not evaluated?

Question 10. For operator ||, when is the second operand not evaluated?

Question 11. Suppose x contains 0. Indicate whether or not the following expression can be evaluated and, if so, what its value is: x==0 || 50/x>2.

Question 12. Suppose x contains 0. Indicate whether or not the following expression can be evaluated and, if so, what its value is: x==0 && 50/x>2.

Activity 6-6-3: Properties of `boolean` operators

Question 13. Write the formula that indicates that && is symmetric.

Question 14. Write the formula that indicates that ‖ is associative.

Question 15. Write the formula that indicates that && is idempotent.

Question 16. Write the formulas Excluded middle and Contradiction.

Question 17. Write De Morgan's laws.

Question 18. According to the boolean properties listed in the footnote of this activity, is the following expression true or false? Here, b is a **boolean** and i and j are **int**s. (Hint: use De Morgan and double negation.)

```
!(!b ‖ i >= j) == (a && i > j)
```

Activity 6-6-4: Exercises on type `boolean`

Participate in this activity for further confirmation of your understanding.

Activity 6-6-5: The mark of a boolean tyro

Question 19. Define *tyro*.

Question 20. Write down three marks of the boolean tyro.

   1.

   2.

   3.

Question 21. Simplify the following boolean expression. Hint: Remove the marks of a tyro and use De Morgan, the definition of `!=`, and the law of the Excluded Middle. Another hint: the answer is really simple.

```
!((a != true) && (a == true)) == true
```

Chapter 7
Iteration

We study loops, which provide for the repeated execution of a statement (called the repetend, or loop body). The loop is more complicated than other statements we have seen —like the assignment and the if-statement. So it will take more time and effort to learn to use it well. But the time will be well spent, for the loop is a very useful tool.

Lesson page 7-1. Iteration

Activity 7-1-1 Introduction to the `while` loop

Question 1. Write the form of a `while` loop.

Question 2. Draw the flaw chart for a `while` loop.

Question 3. Define *iteration*.

Question 4. Define *repetend*.

Question 5. Define *loop body*.

Question 6. Define *loop condition*.

Question 7. The first iteration of a loop execution is called iteration 0.
☐ true ☐ false

Activity 7-1-2 The invariant of a while loop

Question 8. Define *invariant*.

Question 9. Consider this annotated sequence of five statements:

```
s= '''';
// { s is the catenation of the first 0 capital letters}
s= s + ''A'';
// { s is the catenation of the first 1 capital letters}
s= s + ''B'';
// { s is the catenation of the first 2 capital letters}
s= s + ''C'';
// { s is the catenation of the first 3 capital letters}
s= s + ''D'';
// { s is the catenation of the first 4 capital letters}
s= s + ''E'';
```

Below is a corresponding loop, without the loop invariant. Write down the invariant, which is found by generalizing each of the preconditions of the sequence above, replacing a constant by k.

```
int k= 0;
s= '''';
// inv:


while (k != 5) {
    s= s +''ABCDE''.charAt(k);
    k= k+1;
}
```

Activity 7-1-3 Understanding the loop in terms of its invariant

Question 10. Define *falsify*.

Question 11. Define *truthify*.

Question 12. Define *Hoare triple*.

Question 13. Write the four steps in understanding a loop in terms of its invariant:

  1. _____ must truthify the invariant.

  2. _____ must maintain the invariant (keep it true).

  3. _____ must make progress toward termination.

  4. The falsity of the loop condition together with _____ must imply that the desired result it true.

Activity 7-1-4 Summing the first n-1 positive numbers

Question 14. Define *fresh variable*.

Question 15. How do you complement a relation?

Question 16. Write the five steps in developing a loop (look in the footnote for this activity).

  1. Find the _____.

  2. Develop _____ to truthify the invariant.

3. Find _____ by finding a relation that describes when the loop can terminate and complementing that relation.

4. Begin writing the repetend to _____ toward termination.

5. Change the repetend (if necessary), to _____.

Question 17. What does 3+...+4 equal?

Question 18. What does 3+...+3 equal?

Question 19. What does 3+...+2 equal?

Question 20. We used a trick to develop the invariant from the postcondition. What was it?

Activity 7-1-5 Executing the summing loop

Question 21. What value should variable x have when k = 3 for the following relation to be true? x = 1+...+(k-1).

Activity 7-1-6 Understanding a loop in terms of its invariant

This activity deals with the following loop:

```
// Store 1+2+...+(n-1) in x (given n > 1)
    x= 0;    int k=1;
    // {invariant: x = 1+...+(k-1) and 1 <= k <= n}
    while (k != n) {
        x= x+k;
        k= k+1;
    }
    // {x = 1+...+ (n-1)}
```

Question 22. For a given value of n, how many iterations are performed during one execution of the loop?

Question 23. How many iterations are left to perform when k = n-1?

Question 24. How many iterations are left to perform when k = n?

Question 25. Write an integer expression involving k and n that expresses how many iterations are left to perform. For example, when k = 1, your expression should evaluate to the total number of iterations, and when the loop condition is false, your expression should evaluate to zero.

Activity 7-1-7 Summing the first n positive numbers

Here is the loop that was developed in this activity:

```
// Store 1+2+...+n in x
   x= 0;
   int k= 0;
   // {invariant: x = 1+...+k}
   while (k != n) {
       x= x+(k+1);
       k= k+1;
   }
```

The two invariants for the two summing loops discussed in this lesson page look alike (see the previous activity). But they differ on the details, which make sense because one adds n numbers and the other adds n-1. The following questions ask you about the differences and similarities.

Question 26. In both loops, what value does k have when the loop terminates?

Question 27. Why do they have a different sum if k ends up with the same value?

Question 28. In the two loops, which parts (the initializations, the repetends, or the conditions) cause these two loops to do different things?

Question 29. The ranges on k are different. What is the size (number of values) of the range for k in the first loop? In the second loop?

Question 30. In both cases, the range includes one more number than is summed. Why?

Activity 7-1-8 Exercises on loops

Participate in this activity to check your understanding of terminology.

Lesson page 7-2. Several examples of loops

Activity 7-2-1 Developing invariants

Question 1. Often, a good choice for a loop invariant is the _____ with one of its expressions replaced by a _____.

Question 2. When does this technique work especially well?

Question 3. The footnote that appears upon completion of this activity contains an annotated loop. Copy it here:

Question 4. Define *weaker*.

Question 5. Define *stronger*.

Question 6. Define *conjunction*.

Question 7. Define *conjunct*.

Activity 7-2-2 The roach explosion

Question 8. Simplify `!(a <= b)`.

Question 9. If x is of type `int`, 5x/4 and `1.25x` are equal. ☐ true ☐ false

Activity 7-2-3 Exponentiation

Question 10. $b^{2 \times i} = (2 \times b)^i$ ☐ true ☐ false

Question 11. $b^{2 \times i} = (b^2)^i$ ☐ true ☐ false

Question 12. If $z \times x^y = b^c$, what are x and y when $z = 1$?

Question 13. Below is method `exp`, with some parts removed. Using the invariant (which is given), develop the missing parts. This exercise should show you that if you know the invariant, you can develop the loop.

```
// return b^c, given c >= 0
public static int exp(int b, int c) {
    int x=              ;

    int y=              ;

    int z=              ;

    // {invariant: z*x^y = b^c and 0 <= y <= c}
    while (                        ) {
```

```
    }// {z = b^c}
    return z;
}
```

Activity 7-2-4 The spiral

Question 14. Open the program in your favorite IDE and test it with various values for the angles. You'll need files JLiveWindow.java, MJLiveWindow.java, and Spiral.java. MyJLiveWindow.java contains method main. Just type the angle in the integer field and click button Ready!

Lesson page 7-3. Loop schemata

Activity 7-3-1 A counting-loop schema

Question 1. Define *schema.*

Question 2. Define *loop schema.*

Question 3. Define *natural number.*

For later use, here is the loop schema.

```
// Process natural numbers 0..(n-1) --for n >= 0
    int k= 0;
    // {invariant: 0..k-1 have been processed}
    while (k != n) {
        Process k;
```

```
         k= k+1;
      }
// {0..(n-1) have been processed}
```

Activity 7-3-2 Counting the w's

Question 4. The schema (see above) uses variable n for the upper end of the range. What was it replaced by for this particular problem?

Question 5. What did it mean to process k in this problem?

Question 6. What is the only difference between the invariant and the postcondition?

Activity 7-3-3 Testing primality

Question 7. Define *prime*.

Question 8. What did we do to modify the schema (see above) to handle a range other than 0..(n-1)?

Question 9. How can you check whether i divides j (i.e. with a remainder of 0)?

Activity 7-3-4 Loop schema for reading/processing nonzero integers

Here is the loop schema:

```
// Read and process a list of nonzero values
// that is followed by a 0
    int v= JLiveReadreadInt();
    // {inv: v contains the last value read and
    //       input values before v were processed}
    while (v != 0) {
        Process v;
        v= JLiveRead.readInt();
    }
    // {all nonzero input was read and processed,
    //  and the final 0 was read}
```

Question 10. If the first input value is 0, how many iterations are performed?

Activity 7-3-5 Summing the nonzero input

Question 11.   Programming task: Using the loop schema given above, write a loop that reads nonzero integers and prints every integer that is divisible by 5. For example, with input 3 115 7 5 8 0, your loop should print 115 and 5.

Question 12.   Programming task: Here's a tough one. Using the loop schema given above, write a loop that reads nonzero integers and prints every integer that is divisible by the previously–read integer. For example, with input 3 9 7 2 8 0, your loop should print 9 and 8.

Lesson page 7-4. The for loop

Activity 7-4-1 The for loop

Question 1. A *loop counter* is a variable that is _____ just before a while loop and is _____ or _____ at the _____ of the repetend of the while loop.

Question 2. When is a `for` loop particularly suitable?

Activity 7-4-2 Syntax and semantics of the `for` loop

Question 3. Write the syntax of a `for` loop.

Question 4. Rewrite this loop as a `while` loop:

```
b= p>1;
for (int k= 2; k != p; k++) {
    b= b && (p%k == 0);
    k= k+1;
}
```

Activity 7-4-3 Developing a `for` loop

Question 5. Below is the loop that was developed in this activity, with parts removed. Begin by writing the invariant. Then fill in the other parts, using the checklist for developing a loop.

```
// Print 9, 8, down to 2
    // {inv: 9, 8, down to                              }

    for (int k=        ;                  ;             ) {



    }

// {R: 9, 8, down to 2 have been printed}
```

Question 6. Fill in the schema for processing natural numbers, including the missing parts of comments:

```
// Process natural numbers 0..(n-1), where n >= 0

// {invariant: 0..              have been processed}
```

```
for (int k=        ; k !=          ;                  ) {




}
// {postcondition: 0..    have been processed}
```

Activity 7-4-4 Exercises on `for` loops

Participate in these activities to confirm your understanding.

Lesson page 7-5. Making progress and stopping

Activity 7-5-1 The bound function

Question 1. A bound function is an integer expression F that is an _____ _____ bound on the number of _____. It has two properties:

1. Each iteration _____ F.

2. As long as there is another iteration to perform, _____.
   We state this property as: the invariant together with the _____ _____ imply _____.

Activity 7-5-2 The stopping condition `k!=n`

Question 2. If both k < n and k != n can be used as a loop condition, which is the better one to use, and why?

One implication of this activity is that the earlier errors are detected, the better off you (and the company you work for and own stock options in) are.

Activity 7-5-3 Using the condition `k<n`

Question 3. Define *conjunction*.

Question 4. The condition in this activity actually *could* have been written using != *twice*. That is, the condition could have been written using a conjunction, one conjunct being k!=n. What is the other conjunct?

Activity 7-5-4 Off-by-one errors

Question 5. Define *relation*.

Question 6. Define *off-by-one error*.

Question 7. To prevent off-by-one errors, find a loop condition in this way: First, find a _____ r such that r together with the loop invariant imply the _____ of the loop. Then use the _____ of r as the loop condition.

Question 8. Here are a loop invariant and postcondition. Variable s is a String and b is **boolean**. Write a suitable loop condition.

```
inv:  b = ''All chars in s[0..k] are lowercase''
post: b = ''All chars in s[0..s.length()-1] are lowercase''
```

Question 9. Here are a loop invariant and postcondition. Write a suitable loop condition.

```
inv:  All numbers in a..b have been processed
post: All numbers in 0..b have been processed
```

Question 10. Here are a loop invariant and postcondition. Write a suitable loop condition.

```
inv:  All numbers in a..b have been processed
post: All numbers in a..50 have been processed
```

Lesson page 7-6. Miscellaneous points about loops

Question 1. Define *empty statement.*

Question 2. How many iterations will the following loop perform? Be careful.

```
i= 0;
while (i != 100) ; {
    System.out.println(i);
    i= i+1;
}
```

Activity 7-6-1 Counting primes

Question 3. Read the glossary entry for *top-down programming.*

Question 4. Programming task: We used a loop from a previous activity to test whether a particular variable was prime. This is an example of *code reuse*, which saves a great deal of time. However, we simply copied and pasted the code where we needed it. A better technique would be to write a boolean function isPrime(**int**) that contained that loop and then to call isPrime(p) from within the outer loop. Do it!

Activity 7-6-2 About nested loops

Question 5. Define *statement-comment.*

Question 6. Rate the singers on a scale of 1 to 10, with 10 being the best.

Activity 7-6-3 How not to design loops

Question 7. Concisely describe the student's programming strategy.

Question 8. Summarize the strategies espoused in this livetext. If you have to, study lesson 5, and especially lesson page 5-4.

Chapter 8
Arrays

Lesson page 8-1. Introduction to arrays

Activity 8-1-1 Introduction to arrays

An array consists of a list of *elements*, all of the same type. The number of elements is given when the array is created.

Question 1. Define *base type of an array*.

Question 2. Suppose T is a type. What is T[]?

Question 3. What is the result of evaluation of the expression **new long**[30]?

Question 4. Write a declaration of a variable b that can contain an array of Strings; then write an assignment that assigns to b an array of length 40.

Question 5. Write a single statement that declares a variable to be (the name of) a String array and assigns to it a 5-element array.

Question 6. Can a single array contain one element of type **int** and another of type **long** at the same time? Why or why not?

Activity 8-1-2 The length of an array

Question 7. Suppose `temps` is an array variable. Write an expression that yields the length of array `temps`.

Activity 8-1-3 Referencing array elements

Question 8. Write the form of a subscripted variable:

Question 9. Define *index*. What are the two alternatives for its plural?

Question 10. Why is the last element of array `g` numbered `g.length-1`, rather than `g.length`?

Question 11. Complete the following program segment:

```
// Print the elements of array arr, one to a line
    for (int i=        ;                    ; i= i+1) {
        System.out.println(arr[i]);
    }
```

Question 12. Using array `arr`, which is initialized in the following program segment, write a single statement that prints `My cat eats socks.`; the statement should not use any `String` literals. What is the output?

```
String[] arr= new String[4];
arr[0]= "socks.";
arr[1]= "My ";
arr[2]= "eats ";
arr[3]= "cat ";
```

Question 13. Add two appropriate statement-comments in the code below, just before the two loops:

```
public class Test {
    public static void main(String args[]) {
        // The first 5 letters of the alphabet
        String[] arr= new String[5];
        //
            for (int i= 0; i != arr.length; i= i+1) {
                arr[i]= "" + (char)('a'+i);
            }
        //
            for (int k= 0; k < arr.length; k= k+2) {
                System.out.print(arr[k]);
            }
    }
}
```

Activity 8-1-4 Array initializers

Question 14. The following array initalizations won't work. Explain why each one is syntactically incorrect.

```
String[] arr= {"Eat", 'a', "tomato."};
int[] nums= {3, 4, 5, 6. 7, 8};
String[] arv=
    (new String(), new String("bye"), new Object());
```

Question 15. Execute the following sequence of statements, drawing variables pop, etc. and the created arrays as done in this and previous activities.

```
int[] pop= {2, 44, 2};
int[] bees;
int x= pop[0];
bees= new int[x];
bees[0]= pop[2];
pop[2]= 93;
bees[1]= 0;
bees[1]= bees[0] + pop[1];
```

Activity 8-1-5 Where can array initializers be used?

Question 16. The following code is illegal. Explain why.

```
Object[] ob= new Object[2];
ob= {new Object(), new Object()};
```

Lesson page 8-2. Talking about array segments

Activity 8-2-1 The notation b[i..j]

Question 1. What elements are in b[1..4] for the array below?

```
int[] b= {2, 44, 2, 45, 2, 46};
```

Question 2. How many elements are in the subsection b[1..5]?

Question 3. Give a formula for the number of elements in the segment b[i..j-1].

Question 4. How would you refer to the segment of array b from position 3 through the penultimate (next to last) element of the array?

Activity 8-2-2 Picturing array elements

The questions for this activity refer to this picture of array x:

Question 5. The first segment can be denoted by x[b..c-1] and by x[b..3]. Write two such descriptions of the second segment.

Question 6. Remembering that the picture describes the whole array, write the value of each variable: a = -1, b = _____ , c = _____ , e = _____ , and d = _____ .

Question 7. It's important to know the formula for the number of values in a segment. It's best to memorize the formula for the number of values in a segment whose denotation has the form

    x[c..e-1]

because you can then easily figure out the number of values in x[3..e-1], x[c..d], and x[3+1..d]. Answer the following questions (the first one is done for you).

1. The segment x[c..e-1] has e-c values.

2. The segment x[c..d] has _____ values.

3. The segment x[3..e-1] has _____ values.

4. The segment x[3..e] has _____ values.

5. Write the formula that restricts x[c..e-1] to be empty: _____.

6. Write the formula that restricts x[c..d] to be empty: _____.

Activity 8-2-3 Using pictures to present relations about arrays

The questions below refer to the following array:

Question 8. The first segment has length 2. ☐ true ☐ false

Question 9. The second segment is b[2..m]. ☐ true ☐ false

Question 10. The last segment is b[n..length-1]. ☐ true ☐ false

Question 11. You can tell which is the smallest segment. ☐ true ☐ false

Question 12. If the base type of array b was **int** and you wanted to indicate that all the elements in b[0..2] were at most 3, what would you write in that segment in the picture?

Question 13. If the base type of array b was **int** and you wanted to indicate that all the elements in b[0..2] were greater than the elements in the rest of the array, what would you write in that segement of the picture?

Lesson page 8-3. Some programs that use arrays

Activity 8-3-1 A schema for processing array segments

Here are two schema for processing elements of an array segment.

```
// Process elements of c[h..k-1]
    // invariant: h <= i <= k and
    //               c[h..i-1] has been processed
    for (int i= h; i != k; i= i+1) {
        Process c[i]
    }

// Process c[h..k]
    // invariant P: h <= i <= k+1 and
    //               c[h..i-1] has been processed
    for (int i= h; i <= k; i= i+1) {
        Process c[i]
    }
```

Question 1. Consider a program that uses an array **z** of **int**s. The program prompts the user in some fashion for two values that give the beginning and end indices of an array segment and stores them in variables `start` and `end`, so the segment is `z[start..end]`.

1. If `end = start-1` what is the size of the array segment?

2. Use one of the schemata given above to write a program segment that prints each element of `z[start..end]`. You may assume that `0 <= start <= end+1 <= z.length()`.

Activity 8-3-2 Processing array segments in reverse order

Question 2. Write the two schemata for processing segments `c[h..k-1]` and `c[h..k]` in reverse order.

Read the following program segment and then answer the questions below.

```
// Print the elements of z with even indices.
    // {inv: elements in z[0..i-1] with even indices have
    //        been printed.}
    for (int i= 0; i<z.length; i=i+2) {
        System.out.println(z[i]);
}
```

Question 3. State the invariant:

Question 4. Which is the first element to be printed?

Question 5. Which is the last element to be printed?

Question 6. Rewrite the loop (show it below) so that every element of the first half of the array is printed.

Question 7. Rewrite the loop (show it below) so that every element of the last half of the array is printed, in reverse order (starting at the last element).

Activity 8-3-3 Printing input values in reverse order

Question 8. Programming task: This activity discusses a program that reads a fixed number of integers from the keyboard and prints them in reverse order. This program uses class JLiveRead to read from the keyboard. Without copying the program in the activity, write a program that reads 5 integers and prints their squares in reverse order.

Instead of using class JLiveRead, try using a BufferedReader as shown on *ProgramLive* lesson page 5-7. Remember: only one BufferedReader should be linked to the keyboard per program, so create one in your main method and pass it as a parameter to any methods that will read input directly from the keyboard.

Activity 8-3-4 Finding the number of smaller elements

Question 9. After listening to this activity, try to develop the method yourself. When finished, compare your answer to the algorithm developed in the activity and fix any mistakes you made:

```
// = number of elements of b that are less than v
public static int numberLess(int[] b, int v) {




    }
```

Question 10. Think of a situation (and write it down) where you might want to find smaller values in an array of **doubles**.

Activity 8-3-5 Testing function `numberLess`

Question 11. Programming task: The following method pp has some problems with it. Change it to meet its specification, and debug it on the computer. We have included a class and method **main** that can be used to test it.

```
// Test of method pp
public class Test {
    public static void main(String args[]) {
        String[] lines= "Jack", "Sage", "Theo";
        pp(lines);
    }

    // On the first line, print the first char of each element of b
    // On the second line, print the second char of each element of b
    // On the third line, print the third char of each element of b
    // On the fourth line, print the fourth char of each element of b
    public static void pp(String[] b) {
```

```
    // output the first line
        for (int i=0, i<=b.length, i= i+1) {
            System.out.print(b[i].charAt(0));
            i= i+1;
        }
        System.out.println();

    // output the second line
        while (i<b.length) {
            System.out.print(b[i].charAt(1));
            i= i+1;
        }
        System.out.println();

    // output the third line
        while (i<b.length) {
            System.out.print(b[i].charAt(1));
            i= i+1;               }
        System.out.println();

    // output the fourth line
        while (i<b.length) {
            i= i+1;
            System.out.print(b[i].charAt(2));
        }
    }
}
```

Question 12. Will the following call on method pp of the previous question work? Try it. What is wrong? Change the specification of method pp (and also change the body to fit the specification, if necessary) to handle such cases —you get to decide what should happen in such cases.

```
String[] bb= {"Mel", "Mary", "Jo"};
pp(bb);
```

Activity 8-3-6 Checking for equality of arrays

Question 13. Programming task: Complete the body of the following method. The method developed in the activity worked only for **int** arrays; this one should work for all arrays whose base type is a class-type. Hint: remember method equals.

```
// = "arrays b and c are equal"
public static boolean equals(Object[] a, Object[]b)
```

Activity 8-3-7 Returning an array

Question 14. This question is designed to let you see the different effects between arguments that are objects (i.e. names of objects) and arguments that are values of a primitive type. The program given below produces the following output:

```
2, 3, 4, 5
m: 101
```

Compare the program and its output, with an eye to understanding that a, b, and m were changed but n was not. If necessary, execute the program yourself, by hand, drawing all frames and objects that are produced.

```
public class Test {
    private static int[] a= {1,2,3,4};
    private static int m= 100;

    public static void main(String args[]) {
        addOneToArray(a);
        addOne(m);

        Test.printArray(a);
        System.out.println("m: " + m);
    }

    // Add 1 to each element of x
    public static void addOneToArray(int[] x) {
        for (int i= 0; i!=x.length; i= i+1)
            {x[i]= x[i]+1;}
    }
```

```
    // add 1 to x
public static void addOne(int x)
    {x= x+1;}

    // print x's elements on a line, separated by ", "
public static void printArray(int[] x) {
    for (int i= 0; i!=x.length; i= i+1) {
        System.out.print(x[i]);
        if (i < x.length-1)
            {System.out.print(", ");}
    }
    System.out.println();
    }
}
```

Lesson page 8-4. Arrays and classes

Activity 8-4-1 Class Student

Question 1. To access method getGrade in class Student, a new Student would have to be created. □ true □ false

Question 2. What is the name of a Student when it is first created?

Question 3. Programming task: Comment out the constructor for class Student and write a new constructor that automatically requests a name and a grade. (Use methods already in class Student.)

Activity 8-4-2 Class StudentReport

Question 4. What would have to be changed in method main if it was moved to a new class ReportTester?

Activity 8-4-3 Class StudentReport (continued)

Question 5. Programming task: Add a private variable title to class Student Report. Write a method getTitle and call this method before the data on the students is collected. Change printReport so that a blank line and then the title is print before the report.

Activity 8-4-4 Private leaks

Question 6. After execution of the last statement of method `main` in the program below, what does array y contain? What does the array in object x contain?

```
public class Test {
    private int[] a= {1,2,3,4};

    public static void main(String args[]) {
        Test x= new Test();
        int[] y= {11,12,13,14};
        y[2]= 99;
        y= x.doThis();
        x.doThat();
    }

    // = array a
    public int[] doThis() {return a;}

    // swap the first and last elements of a
    public void doThat() {
        int x= a[0];
        a[0]= a[a.length-1];
        a[a.length-1]= x;
    }
}
```

Activity 8-4-5 Using class `DynamicArray`

Question 7. Rewrite the following program segment to use class Dynamic-Array instead of an int array.

```
int[] x= new int[20];
// Print the squares of the elements of x, with comma after each
    // {inv: the squares of x[0..i-1] have been printed}
    for (int i= 0; i < x.length; i++) {
        x[i]= i*i;
        System.out.print(x[i] + ", ");
    }
```

Activity 8-4-6 Explaining class DynamicArray

Question 8. Below are the headers of the methods in class DynamicArray. Fill in the method specifications.

```
//
public DynamicArray()

//
public DynamicArray(int e)

//
public int length()

//
public int allocatedLength()

//
public int get(int i)

//
public void set(int i)
```

Question 9. The question in the previous activity asked you to rewrite a program segment to use a DynamicArray. Rewrite that program segment once again, this time so that when the DynamicArray is created, it has exactly 20 elements. Also, in the loop condition, use a function call that yields the number of array elements allocated.

Question 10. Instead of an array of size 15 that contains one class of Students, it would be useful to use a DynamicArray. Explain why.

Lesson page 8-5.   Some basic array algorithms

Activity 8-5-1 Finding the first value

> **Question 1. Programming task:** Type in method `linearSearch`. Change it so that the first parameter has type `Object[]` instead of **int**`[]` and the third parameter has type `Object` instead of **int**. Test it using an array of base type `String`.

Activity 8-5-2 Another version of linear search

> **Question 2.   Programming task:** Write a function `lastLinearSearch` that returns the index of the last occurrence of x in an array b, or -1 if x is not in b.

> **Question 3.   Programming task:** Fill in the body of the method shown below by modifying method `linearSearch` of this activity.

```
// Print the index of each occurrence of x in b and return
// the index of the first occurrence of x (-1 if none)
public static int linearPrint(Object[] b, Object x) {
```

Activity 8-5-3 Finding the minimum value

> **Question 4.** Write a function that returns the maximum value in a nonempty **int** array.

Activity 8-5-4 Inserting into a sorted array segment

Question 5. Programming task: Class `String` has an instance method `compareTo(String s)`, which returns a positive integer, 0, or a negative integer depending on whether this `String` is greater (in the dictionary sense) than s, equal to s, or less than s. Rewrite the following method (from the activity) so that b is an array of `Strings`.

```
// b[h..k-1] is sorted. Sort b[h..k]
public static void insertValue (int[] b, int h, int k) {
    int v= b[k];
    int i= k;
    // inv: (1) Placing v in b[i] makes b[h..k] a
    //             permutation of its initial value
    //          (2) b[h..k] with b[i] removed is initial b[h..k-1]
    //          (3) v < b[i+1..k]
    while (i!=h && v<b[i-1])
        {b[i]= b[i-1];   i= i-1;}
    b[i]= v;
}
```

Activity 8-5-5 Partitioning an array segment

Question 6. Suppose integer i is supposed to contain the index of the largest element of array d that is at most 5. What are the possible values of i?

```
int[] d= {3, 4, 5, 5, 6, 9, 4435};
```

Question 7. The heart of algorithm `partition` is a loop that starts with Q true and terminates with R1 true:

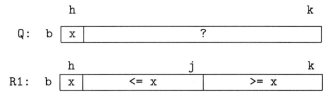

Invariant P of the loop has four segments, corresponding to the four different segments that are in Q and R1. If you can draw P, based on Q and R1, you are well on your way to mastering algorithm `partition`. Draw P below. Then compare it against the invariant in the activity to make sure P is right.

Now develop the loop and its initialization:

```
// Given Q true, truthify R1
    i=                ;
    j=                ;
    // {inv: P (shown above)}
    while (                          ) {




    }
```

Activity 8-5-6 Median of three

> **Question 8. Programming task:** Fill in the bodies of the following methods. Method `swap` is to be used in method `sort3`.

```
// Swap b[i] and b[j]
public static void swap(int[] b, int i, int j)




// Swap b[h], b[(h+k)/2], and b[k] (if necessary)
// so that b[h] <= b[(h+k)/2] <= b[k].
// Precondition: b[h..k] has at least three elements
public static void sort3(int[] b, int h, int k)
```

Activity 8-5-7 Merging two sorted array segments

> **Question 9. Programming task:** Fill in the missing code in the following method:

```
// = a sorted array containing the elements of x and y.
// Precondition: x and y are in ascending order.
public static int[] arrayMerge(int[] x, int[] y) {
    int[] merge= new int[                        ];
    int m= 0;
    int i= 0;
    int j= 0;

    // {inv P: merge[0..m-1] contains x[0..i-1] and y[0..j-1]
    //         and merge[0..m-1] is in ascending order}
    while (i != x.length && j != y.length) {




    }

    // copy into merge the end of whichever array
    // has yet to be completely copied
        while (i != x.length) {


        }
        while (j != y.length) {


        }
    return merge;
```

Activity 8-5-8 Binary search

> **Question 10.** You know algorithm binary search if you can (0) develop invariant P from the postcondition and (1) write the loop and its initialization, given P. Below is a skeleton of the method. Fill in the invariant and then compare it to the invariant given in the activity. After that, fill in the rest of the method and then compare it to the method given in the activity.

```
// Assume virtual elements b[-1] = −∞ and b[b.length] = +∞
// Return an index i that satisfies: R: b[i] <= x < b[i+1]
public static int binarySearch(int[] b, int x) {

    int i=

    int j=


    // {inv P:                                           }
    while (                        ) {

        int e=

        // {-1 <= i < e < j <= b.length}
        if (                      ) {i=              ;}

        else {j=            ;}
    }
    return            ;
}
```

Question 11. Below is a method **main**. Trace execution of the **while** loop in each call of **binarySearch**. The first one has been done for you.

```
public static void main(String args[]) {
    int[] x= {3, 5, 6, 9, 20};
    System.out.println(binarySearch(x, 33));
    System.out.println(binarySearch(x, 5));
    System.out.println(binarySearch(x, 8));
}
```

i	j	e		i	j	e		i	j	e
-1	5	2								
2		3								
3		4								
4										

Lesson page 8-6. Selection sort and insertion sort

Question 1. An array is sorted when it is in descending order (meaning the largest element is first, then the second largest, etc). ☐ true ☐ false

Question 2. An array is sorted when it is in ascending order (meaning the smallest element is first, then the second smallest, etc). ☐ true ☐ false

Question 3. The array shown below is not in ascending order or descending order, but its values ARE in a certain order. Can you see what this order is?

```
String[] s= {"c", "abc", "Giggle", "broadloom"};
```

Activity 8-6-1 Selection sort

Question 4. You know algorithm `selectionSort` if you can (0) draw the precondition `Q` and postcondition `R` as pictures, (1) draw invariant `P`, and then write the loop and its initialization based on `P`, `Q`, and `R`. Below, we have started drawing the three pictures and the body of method. Fill everything in. Compare your work to the method in the activity.

```
               0                                    length
       Q: b  |                 ?                        |

               0                                    length
       R: b  |               sorted                     |

               0                      j              length
       P: b  |                   |                      |

int  j=                          ;
// {inv: P (see above)}
while (                          ) {



       }
```

Activity 8-6-2 Selection sort revisited

Question 5. Why would you use a statement-comment?

Question 6. Finish the following program segment.

```
// Store in p the index of the minimum of b[j..]
    int p= j;
    // {inv: b[p] is the minimum of b[j..i-1]}
    for (                ;                 ;                ) {


    }
```

Activity 8-6-3 Insertion sort

Question 7. **Programming task:** Change `insertionSort`, given below, so that it sorts b into descending order. You will have to change `insertValue` as well —this method is discussed in activity 8-5-4 on page 157.

```
// Sort b --put its elements in ascending order.
public static void insertionSort(int[] b) {
    // {inv P: b[0..j-1] is in ascending order}
    for (int j= 1; j != b.length; j= j+1) {
        insertValue(b, 0, j);
    } }


// b[h..k-1] is sorted. Sort b[h..k]
public static void insertValue (int[] b, int h, int k) {
    int v= b[k];
    int i= k;
    // inv: (1) Placing v in b[i] makes b[h..k] a
    //          permutation of its initial value
    //      (2) b[h..k] with b[i] removed is initial b[h..k-1]
    //      (3) v < b[i+1..k]
    while (i!=h && v<b[i-1])
        {b[i]= b[i-1];   i= i-1;}
    b[i]= v;
}
```

Chapter 9

Multidimensional arrays

Lesson page 9-1. Multidimensional arrays

Activity 9-1-1 Declaring and creating two-dimensional arrays

Question 1. How many rows does array `fred` have?

```
int x= 44
int[][] fred= new int[x+2][3];
```

Question 2. Declare a two-dimensional array with 2 rows and 3 columns that can hold (at least) `String` and `Integer` objects.

Activity 9-1-2 Referencing an array element

Question 3. Subscripted variable `b[r][c]` refers to an element of two-dimensional array `b`. What types can `r` and `c` be, and what is the possible range of their values?

Activity 9-1-3 Referencing the number of rows and columns

Question 4. To reference the number of rows of rectangular array `b`, use

_____.

To reference the number of columns, use _____.

Question 5. Finish the following program segment:

```
// Add one to each element of rectangular
// int array b
    for (int i= 0;                     ; i= i+1) {
        for (int j= 0;                     ; j= j+1) {
            b                     ;
```

Activity 9-1-4 Exercises on two-dimensional arrays

Don't forget to do these exercises!

Activity 9-1-5 A non-Java notation for a subarray

The following questions refer to this array (**int** [] [] b):

1	3	3	
2	4	4	

Question 6. Using non-Java notation, how would you refer to the initalized section of b?

Question 7. Below are some assertions concerning array b, with some missing information. Fill in the information so that the assertions describe the largest set of array elements for which the assertion is true.

1. b[   ] [   ] = 3

2. b[   ] [   ] < b[0..1] [1..2]

3. b[   ] [   ] are even

4. 0 < i < 1 && 0 < j <   &&

   b[i-1] [j-1] $\leq$ b[   ] [   ]

Activity 9-1-6 Two-dimensional array initializers

Question 8. What are the dimensions of the following arrays? (The first question is answered for you.)

1. **int** [] [] yet= {{1},{2}};   **2x1 (2 rows, 1 column)**

2. **int** [] [] yap= {{1,1,1}, {2,2,2}, {3,3,3}};

3. **int** [] [] yak= {{2, 2, 2, 2}, {3, 3, 3, 3}};

4. **int** [] [] [] yo= {{{1},{2}},{{3},{4}},{{5},{6}}};

Question 9. Write the initalizer that creates the array oz represented by the picture below.

1	3	5
3	5	7
5	7	11
7	11	13

Lesson page 9-2. Some programs that use two-dimensional arrays

Activity 9-2-1 Printing a table of values

Question 1. Below is the body of method `printTable`, revised to print `Integer` array b. Study it. Then write down the output of the program segment and explain why you wrote what you did. This is in some sense a trick question, so think carefully.

```
// Integer[][] b= new Integer[3][2];
// Print array b, one row per line
// Precede each row with the integer 1+(row number)
    // inv: rows 0, ..., r-1 have been printed
  for (int r= 0; r!=b.length; r++) {
      // Print row b[r] (on the next line)
        System.out.print((1+r) + " ");
        // inv: elements b[r,0..c-1] have been printed
        for (int c= 0; r!= c[r].length; c++) {
            System.out.print("   " + d[r][c]);
        }
  }
```

Activity 9-2-2 A schema for processing a two-dimensional array

Question 2. Define *row-major order*.

Question 3. Define *column-major order*.

Question 4. Write the schema for processing a two-dimensional array d in row-major order:

Question 5. Rewrite the schema of the previous question so that it processes d in column-major order. Assume it is a square array, so that d.length == d[r].length.

Activity 9-2-3 An interest(ing) table

Question 6.   Programming task: Use the schema for processing a two-dimensional array of nonnegative integers to print, for each element, the sum from 1 to that element. For example, if b[2][3] = 5, then for b[2][3] the value of 1+2+3+4+5 would be printed. Print the result in a nice, clear table.

Hint: the formula for the sum from 1 to n is:

$$\sum_{i=1}^{n} i = n(n+1)/2$$

Activity 9-2-4 Class Coordinates

Question 7. Are fields r and c of class Coordinates private or public?

Activity 9-2-5 Row-major search

Question 8. What is the position of the first (in row-major order) occurrence of "Susie" in this array? In column-major order?

```
String[][] s= {{"Phred", "Susie", "Max"},
               {"Susie", "Barbara", "Olga"}};
```

Question 9. Row-major search is an important algorithm, and you should be able to write it fairly easily. Practice, by writing it here:

```
// = index (r,c) of the first (in row-major order) element
// x in d (or the pair (d.length,0), if x is not in d)
public static Coordinates search(int[][] d, int x) }
```

```
}
```

Activity 9-2-6 Saddleback search

Question 10. Which of the following two arrays are arranged as required by saddleback search?

1	3	5
3	5	7
5	7	11
7	11	13

1	3	5
3	5	7
5	7	7
7	7	7

1	3	5
3	5	7
5	7	6
7	7	6

Question 11. Using pencil and paper, execute the following program, keeping track of all the variables by hand.

```
public class Test {
    public static void main(String args[]) {
        int[][] d= {{1,2,3},{2,3,4},{3,4,5}};
        System.out.print(saddlebackSearch(d, 4));
    }
}
```

```
// The rows and columns of rectangular array d are in ascending
// order. x is guaranteed to be in d. Return an index-pair (r,c)
// of an occurrence of x in d
public static Coordinates saddlebackSearch(int[][] d, int x) {
    int r= 0;
    int c= d[0].length-1;
    // invariant: x is in b[r..][0..c]
    while (x != d[r][c]) {
        if (x > d[r][c]) r= r+1;
        else    c= c-1;
    }

    return new Coordinates(r,c);
}
}
```

Draw array d below:	Trace r here	Trace r here	Trace x here
			4

Lesson page 9-3. The Java concept of a multidimensional array

Activity 9-3-1 The Java concept of a multidimensional array

Question 1. Below, draw a picture of array d:

int[][] d= {{1,2,3},{4,5},{6,7,8,9}};

Question 2. For array d of the previous question, write these values:

d.length:

d[0]:

```
d[1]:

d[2]:
```

Activity 9-3-2 The lengths of rows and columns

Question 3. Given array d defined by

```
int[][][] d= {
              { {1,2}, {1,3} },
              { {2,4}, {1,3} }
      };
```

write down the following values:

d.length	d[0][0].length
d[0].length	d[0][1].length
d[1].length	d[1][0].length

Activity 9-3-3 Ragged arrays

Question 4. Define *ragged array*.

Question 5. Programming task: Write a method to print a ragged two-dimensional array of ints. Each row should be on a separate line, and adjacent elements on a line should be separated by a comma.

Activity 9-3-4 Exercises on Java ragged arrays

Be sure to do this exercise!

Lesson page 9-4. Programs that use ragged arrays

Activity 9-4-1 Pascal's triangle

Question 1. Define *combinatorics*.

Question 2. What does the notation "n choose r" mean?

Question 3. Suppose your class has 25 members in it. What expression denotes the number of ways you can choose a set of 10 members from it?

Question 4. Pascal's triangle is a repetitive pattern. Each row starts with a 1 and ends with a 1, and the elements inside the triangle are the sum of the two elements above it.

 The triangle below has a different repetitive pattern. Can you figure out what it is? Show it by completing the next two lines of the triangle.

```
                        1
                    1       1
                1       2       1
            1       2       2       1
        1       2       4       2       1
    1       2       8       8       2       1
```

Activity 9-4-2 Implementing Pascal's triangle

Question 5. Programming task: Wallace Avenue has only 3 houses. Each house has a different number of apartments in it, and each apartment has a renter. Declare a two-dimensional ragged array called `wallaceAve` to contain the name of each renter at the address and house floor. For this exercise, declare the array so that the first house is `wallaceAve[0]` and the first floor of the first house is `wallaceAve[0][0]`.

- House 0 has 2 apartments. Harvey is on floor 0 and Sam is on floor 1.

- House 1 has 1 apartment, and Henry lives there.

- House 2 has 15 apartments, but only 3 tenants. George lives on floor 6, Greg on floor 9, and Geoffrey on the top floor.

Activity 9-4-3 Printing Pascal's triangle

Question 6. Programming task: Write a method d2objPrint that prints its parameter, a two-dimensional array of any object type, one row to a line, with adjacent elements of a row separated by ", ". Test it using the array below. Your method should work with any two-dimensional array of any object type.

```
public static void main(String args[]) {
    String[][] coughy= new String[3][];
    coughy[0]= new String[2];
    coughy[0][0]= "Java";
    coughy[0][1]= "Mocha";
    coughy[1]= new String[1];
    coughy[1][0]= "Joe";
    coughy[2]= new String[4];
    coughy[2][0]= "Latte";
    coughy[2][1]= "Decaf";
    coughy[2][2]= "Expresso";
    d2objPrint(coughy);
}
```

```
Output: Java, Mocha
        Joe
        Latte, Decaf, Expresso, null
```

Chapter 10

Exception handling

Generally, beginning programmers won't write many exception-handling programs. However, a basic knowledge of exceptions will provide some help when a program does throw an exception.

Lesson page 10-1. Output of thrown Exceptions and Errors

Activity 10-1-1 Throwing-an-Exception output

Question 1. Define *exception*.

Question 2. What is the difference between an `Error` and an `Exception`.

Question 3. Define *call stack*.

Question 4. The output from an `Exception` crash consists of method calls that have not completed, listed in the order in which they were called. ☐ `true` ☐ `false`

Lesson page 10-2. The throwable object

Activity 10-2-1 Throwable objects

Question 1. Draw the hierarchy of classes under `Throwable`:

Question 2. If you want to throw an object that should not be caught, throw an _____.

Question 3. If you want to throw an object that is likely to be caught, throw an _____.

Question 4. Classes `Exception`, `RuntimeException`, `ArithmeticException` differ only in their names and what they extend. ☐ true ☐ false

Question 5. List five commonly encountered `Exceptions`.

Lesson page 10-3.   Catching a thrown exception

Activity 10-3-1 The try statement

Question 1. Write the form of a `try` statement.

Question 2. Write the form of a `catch` clause.

Question 3. What might happen during execution of a try block?

1.

2. (a)

    (b)

Activity 10-3-2 Using the try statement in JLiveWindow

Question 4. What two types of `Exceptions` are caught and dealt with in method `getIntField`?

Question 5. How many catch clauses can a `try` statement have?

Activity 10-3-3 Using the try statement in JLiveRead

Question 6. Method `readLineInt` uses a trick. It looks like an infinite loop, but it isn't! Why not?

Activity 10-3-4 Propagation of a thrown object

Question 7. Define *propagation*.

Question 8. If a `try` block doesn't catch an `Exception`, even if it is enclosed in another `try` block, what happens to the `Exception`?

Question 9. When is a `finally` block executed?

Activity 10-3-5 Exercises on exceptions

Participate in this activity to practice your understanding of `Exceptions`.

Lesson page 10-4. The throw statement

Activity 10-4-1 The throw statement

Question 1. Define *throw-statement*.

Question 2. Write a new `ArithmeticException` with the detail message `"Goobers. I just can't do that!"`?

Activity 10-4-2 Catching and throwing an Exception further.

Question 3. If an Exception might occur, it is better to write an if statement to predict it than to write a catch clause to handle it. □ true □ false

Lesson page 10-5. Checked exceptions ...

Activity 10-5-1 The throws clause

Question 1. Which subclasses of Throwable must be explicitly caught if they can be thrown by a program segment?

Question 2. Write the form of a throws clause:

Question 3. How can a tyro programmer avoid having to deal with any Exceptions?

Lesson page 10-6. Hints on using exceptions

Question 1. List the four hints on using exceptions.

1.

2.

3.

4.

Chapter 11
Packages

Lesson page 11-1. Packages

Activity 11-1-1 The `package` and `import` statements

Question 1. Define *package*.

Question 2. What is the form of a `package` statement?

Question 3. What should appear at the top of a file to indicate that the class it contains is in package `myPack`?

Question 4. If class `C` is in package `p1` and class `D` is in package `p2`, how can code inside `D` create instances of class `C`?

Question 5. What statement would you use to import all the classes inside package `myPack`?

Activity 11-1-2 Package names

Question 6. Packages can contain only classes. ☐ `true` ☐ `false`

Question 7. In what package are classes `String`, `Math` and `Integer`?

Activity 11-1-3 The class path

Question 8. Define *classpath*.

Question 9. Name six basic packages that come with Java and state briefly what each contains.

Chapter 12
Interfaces

Lesson page 12-1. Interfaces

Activity 12-1-1 The interface

Question 1. Write down the English meaning of *interface*.

Question 2. Write the form of a Java interface.

Question 3. Consider this interface:

```
interface myInterface {
    public void frooble(String s);
}
```

1. Is `myInterface` abstract or not?

2. Is `frooble` abstract or not?

Question 4. An interface can be instantiated, like a class. ☐ true ☐ false

Activity 12-1-2 Implementing an interface

Question 5. Write the header of a class C that implements interface In.

Question 6. A class that implements an interface must provide an implementation of the methods in that interface. ☐ true ☐ false

Activity 12-1-3 The real use of interfaceActionListener

These questions concern the use of a Button b in a subclass SubFrame of Frame.

Question 7. Write the header of subclass SubFrame.

Question 8. Write the statement that adds b to an instance of SubFrame.

Question 9. Write the statement that registers the instance of SubFrame as a listener of b.

Question 10. Write the method that will be called when button b is clicked by the user. Make it so that the String ''b was pressed.'' is printed in the Java console.

Lesson page 12-2.   The interface as a type

Activity 12-2-1 The interface

Question 1. Define *orthogonal*.

Question 2. Interfaces are just like classes, in that a variable can be defined with an interface as its type, and widening and narrowing casts can be performed on instances of the interface. □ true □ false

Question 3. Fill in the necessary typecasts for the following code. Assume that class A implements interface In.

```
In a= new A();

In i=                    a; // Is a type cast necessary?

A c= new A();

In j=                    c; // Is a type cast necessary?
```

Test these out on your computer to verify your answer.

Question 4. What variables and methods belong to an instance of an interface?

Activity 12-2-2 Implementing more than one interface

Question 5. Write the interface header for a class C that implements interfaces In and Jn.

Question 6. What does class C of the previous question have to define?

Activity 12-2-3 Extending an interface

Question 7. Define *multiple inheritance*.

Question 8. An interface can extend a class. ☐ true ☐ false

Question 9. An interface can extend many interfaces. ☐ true ☐ false

Question 10. An class can extend many classes. ☐ true ☐ false

Activity 12-2-4 Exercises on interfaces

Participate in this activity for further confirmation of your understanding.

Lesson page 12-3. Interface Comparable

Interface `Comparable` was added in Java 1.2. Earlier versions of the Java APIs do not have this interface. Sun API programmers added it when they wrote the `Collections` framework —that is, a bunch of classes and methods useful for dealing with collections of objects. Look in the Java APIs for such classes and interfaces as `Collection`, `Arrays`, `ArrayList`, `List`, and `Vector`.

Activity 12-3-1 Interface `Comparable`

Question 1. Write interface `Comparable` here:

Question 2. List some examples of uses of interface `Comparable`.

Activity 12-3-2 Implementing class Comparable

Question 3. Programming task: Write a method `hasNegative` with one parameter b (an array of `Comparable` objects) that returns the value of "b contains at least one negative value".

Question 4. Write the header of a class C that contains the definition of the method of the previous question.

Question 5. Class `Compares` has two methods that operate on `Comparable` arrays. This means that they will work on any array of `Comparables`, including `Pixels`, `Integers`, and other wrapper classes. (To answer this, you may need to look at the Java APIs to find out how the wrapper classes are defined.) ☐ true ☐ false

Activity 12-3-3 Casting between Pixel and Comparable

Question 6. `Comparables` are automatically cast to `Pixels`. ☐ true ☐ false

Question 7. `Pixels` are automatically cast to `Comparables`. ☐ true ☐ false

Lesson page 12-4. Interface Enumeration

Activity 12-4-1 Interface Enumeration

Question 1. Define *enumeration*.

Question 2. Why can't `StringEnumeration.nextElement` return a **char**?

Question 3. What two methods must be defined in every class that implements `Enumeration`? Write down their specifications, too.

Question 4. Programming task: Use interface `StringEnumeration` to write a method that returns the number of blank characters in its `String` parameter s.

Activity 12-4-2 A neat use of Enumeration

Question 5. Every time we write a new class that implements `Enumeration`, we have to write a new method and a new loop to print its elements. ☐ `true` ☐ `false`

Question 6. Programming task: In Java 1.2, interface `Iterator` was added. It is supposed to replace `Enumeration` because it is more flexible. Rewrite method `print` so that it has an `Iterator` as parameter.

Question 7. Programming task: Write a class `StringIterator` that implements `Iterator`. It will be similar to `StringEnumeration`, and it will have one additional method: `remove`. Method `remove` needs only one line in its body: **throw new** `UnsupportedOperationException()`;

Chapter 13

Programming style

Lesson page 13-1. Good Programming Practices

Question 1. A clear, consistent programming style makes a program easier to read. ☐ true ☐ false

Question 2. When reading someone else's program, you want to see comments. ☐ true ☐ false

Question 3. If a program is readable, you will take less time to understand it. ☐ true ☐ false

Question 4. Different people have different programming styles. They aren't bad just because they are different. ☐ true ☐ false

Question 5. Each programming style has advantages and disadvantages, and it's good to review them when choosing a style to use. ☐ true ☐ false

Question 6. Indentation can make a program difficult to read if not done reasonably. ☐ true ☐ false

Question 7. What does Sun's program `javadoc` do?

Lesson page 13-2. Naming conventions

Question 1. The name of a Java variable or method generally begins with a small letter. ☐ true ☐ false

Question 2. The name of a Java class generally begins with a small letter. ☐ true ☐ false

Question 3. If a name is a sequence of words, capitalize the first character of each of the words (except perhaps the first). ☐ true ☐ false

Activity 13-2-1 Conventions for naming parameters

Question 4. State a good convention for naming parameters of a method if the method is properly specified in a comment.

Question 5. Why is the convention just given reasonable?

Question 6. What is the disadvantage of really long parameter names?

Question 7. You are writing a method that has two parameters: the sides that are adjacent to the 90-degree angle of a right a triangle. What would you name the parameters (there is no single correct answer)?

Activity 13-2-2 Conventions for naming local variables

Question 8. State a good convention for naming a local variable of a method if the variable is properly specified in a comment near its declaration.

Question 9. Why is the convention just given reasonable?

Question 10. Cross out the unnecessary comments.

```
// Used for demonstration only.
public class Test {
    // This is method main
    public static void main(String args[]) {
        int a= 4;             // the number of ants
        int numOfBats= 1; // the number of bats
        int msqu= 500;     // the number of mosquitoes
        // Print out the ratio of bats to ants.
            System.out.println("Ratio of bats to ants is: " +
                numOfBats + ":" + msqu + ".");
    }
}
```

Activity 13-2-3 Conventions for naming instance variables and class variables

Question 11. State a good convention for naming an instance variable or class variable.

Question 12. The name numS is a good name for an instance variable.
□ true □ false

Question 13. When is it okay for a variable to be given a name that is not a description of its meaning?

Activity 13-2-4 Conventions for naming constants

Question 14. In Java, what is considered to be a constant?

Question 15. State the Java convention for naming a constant.

Question 16. Declare a constant for the weight of a bag of chocolate chips (250 grams) as if you were going to use it inside class Fondue. Write the class declaration as well (it contains no methods).

Activity 13-2-5 Review of conventions for variable names

Question 17. Which of the following are good identifiers for constants?

```
height    x    NUM_STAPLES    MINVALUE    PageNum    partNo
```

Question 18. Which of the following are good identifiers for class and instance variables?

```
height    x    NUM_STAPLES    MINVALUE    PageNum    partNo
```

Question 19. Which of the following are good identifiers for parameters and local variables?

```
height   x   NUM_STAPLES   MINVALUE   PageNum   partNo
```

Activity 13-2-6 Conventions for naming methods

Question 20. State two alternatives for naming a procedure.

Question 21. State three alternatives for naming a function.

Question 22. You are designing part of a program that reads information, sorts it, manipulates it, and finally displays it. You could write one method to do all this, but your code would go on for pages —and would look like spaghetti. Instead you will write one control method that calls on four different methods (so there are five methods). Indicate which methods are procedures and which are functions and give them names.

Activity 13-2-7 Conventions for naming classes

Question 23. State the Java convention for naming a class.

Question 24. You are designing a program to analyze the movement of people in and out of the various buildings in a city block. This block has houses, commercial buildings (such as stores), and government buildings. There are also people, bikes, and cars. Make a list of possible classes for this scenario (don't worry about which classes should be subclasses or how they interact.

Lesson page 13-3. Conventions for indentation

Activity 13-3-1 Why indent?

Question 1. Write down the two general principles for indentation.

Question 2. Below is a section from a larger program, which is improperly indented. Can you understand its structure? Rewrite it (on a separate piece of paper) with good indentation.

```
// askQuestions: ask a Professor questions until we're tired
private static void askQuestions (Professor prof)
      throws IOException {
       final String LAST_QUESTION= "bye"; // ends input
      System.out.print("Your question? ('bye' for last) ");
          String question= in.readLine();
          while (! question.equals(LAST_QUESTION)) {
      System.out.print("Your question? ('bye' for last) ");
      System.out.flush(); question= in.readLine();
Prof.answer(question))
          }
          }
```

Activity 13-3-2 Points to watch out for when indenting

Question 3. There is no question to go with this lesson, only a reminder. In the following program segment, the statements x= 3; are not executed, but the statements y= 4; are. Type it in and try it!

```
int x= 4; int y= 4;
if (3 == 4)
    x= 3;
    y= 4;
for (int i= 0; i!=100; i= i+1)
    x= 3;
    y= 4;
if (y < 0)
    x= 3;
    y= 4;
```

Lesson page 13-4. Guidelines for writing methods

Activity 13-4-1 The specification as a logical firewall

Question 1. The specification of a method describes precisely *what* the method does. The body of the method implements the *what* in some fashion; it says *how* to do the *what*. Who is the most important beneficiary of writing the specification first?

Question 2. Write a specification for the following method. Note that it would have been easier to write the spec before writing the method.

```
//
public static boolean match(int a, int b, int c) {
    if (a == b && b == c)
        return true;
    return false;
}
```

Question 3. Rewrite the body of method `match` (above) so that it does not use a conditional statement.

Activity 13-4-2 Consistency of method body and method specification

Follow this principle religiously: if you are going to change a method body so that it does something different, change the method specification first!

Activity 13-4-3 The statement-comment

We treat the statement-comment as a programming language statement, but it is not a Java statement at all. It is a useful mechanism for "abstraction".

Question 4. Describe what is meant by "abstraction".

Question 5. Define *statement-comment*.

Activity 13-4-4 Discussion of the statement-comment

Question 6. What are three benefits of using statement-comments?

Activity 13-4-5 Why indent?

Question 7. Explain why it is useful to indent the implementation of a statement-comment.

Question 8. With the indentation rule given in this activity, how do you find the end of a refinement (or implementation) of a statement-comment?

Question 9. Get out some textbook and investigate its use of indentation. Write down the rules for indentation in that book.

Lesson page 13-5.   Describing variables

Activity 13-5-1 Describing instance variables

Question 1. Variable declarations can be grouped by type, by logical relationship, alphabetically, and perhaps in other ways. Which is the best way to group them, and why?

Question 2. The following variables are used to keep track of the traffic in a mall. Add suitable comments (some of the variables may have more than one possible use! Choose an appropriate one.)

```
private int numShoppers;

private int sumShoppers;

private int numStrollers;

private int numStairs;

private int numStanding;
```

Question 3. Where are parameters described?

Activity 13-5-2 The placement of local-variable declarations

Question 4. What does the "need to know" policy say about the placement of local variable declarations?

Question 5. Can you think of an instance where you would want to declare a local variable at the beginning of a method instead of where it is first used?

Question 6. Programming task: Revisit some of your old programs. Correct the indentation and add comments. You may find it takes some time to figure out what they do if they were not well commented.

Chapter 14

Testing and debugging

You will be testing and debugging throughout your programming career, starting with the very first program you write and run on a computer. You need to study this lesson early in a course in order to get an idea about testing and debugging. However, it is good to return to this lesson several times later in the course, in order to reinforce the concepts and techniques presented.

Lesson page 14-1. Introduction to testing and debugging

Activity 14-1-1 Good programming practices

Question 1. Define *bug*.

Question 2. Define *debugging*.

Question 3. Define *test case*.

Question 4. Fill in the blanks:

1. Don't try to solve a problem until you know what the problem is.

   (a) Write a clear and precise _____ for a method *before* writing the method.

   (b) Use _____ to make code appear shorter and more manageable.

2. Write down the _____ of a variable before you use it.

3. Keep _____ and program consistent, e.g.

   (a) Change the _____ of the method before chang-
       ing its _____.
   (b) Change a statement-comment before changing its _____.
   (c) Change a variable _____ before changing _____
       that use it.

Lesson page 14-2. Testing strategies

Activity 14-2-1 Using GUI JLiveWindow as a test driver

Question 1. Define *test driver*.

Question 2. When writing a test driver using JLiveWindow, what two parts
of JLiveWindow do you have to change?

Activity 14-2-2 Another test driver for a method

Question 3. The previous activity used GUI MyJLiveWindow as a test driver;
this activity uses the Java console. Which one do you prefer, and why?

Question 4. Write a loop to test method TestConvert.KelvFromFahr.

Activity 14-2-3 The test driver for a class

Question 5. What should a test driver for a class do?

   1.

   2.

3.

4.

Question 6. Which instance method will be very helpful in testing any properly-designed class?

Activity 14-2-4 Assertions in testing

Question 7. As a defensive programming strategy, make _____ into tests and leave them in a program.

Lesson page 14-3. Selecting test cases and checking them

Activity 14-3-1 Structural testing

Question 1. Draw lines between the phrases that mean the same thing.

```
blackbox testing
                                    whitebox testing

structural testing
                                    functional testing

exhaustive testing
```

Question 2. List the five guidelines for structural testing:

1.

2.

3.

4.

5.

Activity 14-3-2 Checking test cases automatically

Question 3. Here's a nice mantra for automatic testing:

Silence is beauty.

What does it mean?

Activity 14-3-3 Partial checking done automatically

Question 4. Describe two ideas for doing partially automated testing:

1.

2.

Lesson page 14-4. Debugging

Activity 14-4-1 Tracking down a bug

Question 1. When tracking down a bug, if we suspect that a method has a problem, we can place print statements at its _____ and _____ so we can see what effect the method has.

Activity 14-4-2 Tracking down another bug

Question 2. Write down two guidelines for tracking down a bug within a method:

1.

2.

Chapter 15
Recursion

Lesson page 15-1. Recursion

Recursion is a simple but powerful device. It's neat; it's cool; it rocks. Anything that can be done using a loop can be done using recursion, and often in a simpler fashion.

In these lessons, we take the time to write specifications of methods and some statements, often in English, *before* we write the method bodies, for that is a key to getting recursive methods correct. Do this yourself, and you will find yourself spending less time trying to get your programs right. Don't do this, and you will be continually confused and will spend far more time debugging your programs.

Activity 15-1-1 Recursive definitions

Question 1. Define *recursive definition*.

Question 2. Define *recursive method*.

Question 3. Give a recursive definition of a person's ancestors.

Activity 15-1-2 First recursive method

Question 4. What two cases are there in every recursive method?

Question 5. It is sometimes possible to "hide" the base case. In method `setToZero`, how did we do it, and do we think it's a good idea?

Question 6. Write down the form that we generally use for the body of a recursive method.

Question 7. How did we know what the recursive call should look like? (Hint: it has something to do with the method comment.)

Activity 15-1-3 Second recursive method

Question 8. When removing blanks from a `String`, what is the easiest case to deal with?

Question 9. In the last line of the method, why do we include `p.charAt(0)` in the result?

Activity 15-1-4 Third recursive method

Question 10. What is the product of zero numbers?

Question 11. In the recursive case for `factorial`, how do we know that `n > 0`?

Question 12. Programming task: Write a recursive method that, given an argument n ($>=$ 0) returns the sum 0 + 1 + 2 + $\cdots$ + n. Test it, using GUI JLiveWindow.

Activity 15-1-5 The recursive pattern

Base cases are usually "small" —one or two simple cases, like a parameter being 0 or 1.

In the recursive cases that you have seen, the problem size is 1 smaller than the problem size of the original method call. For example, the first call of a method might have an argument n, and the recursive call might then have the argument n−1. However, there are situations in which the recursive call is *much* smaller, perhaps half the size. We'll see these later.

Question 13. Define *base case*.

Question 14. Define *recursive case*.

Question 15. What's the big idea (behind recursive methods)?

Activity 15-1-6 Exercises on recursion

Participate in this activity for further confirmation of your understanding.

Question 16. Programming task: Complete the following recursive method. Compile and test it, using GUI JLiveWindow.

```
// = the largest value in b[h..k]
public static int largest(int[] b, int h, int k) {
    if (h == k) {
        return /* put some expression here */ ;
    }
```

```
          // {h < k, so b[h..k] has at least two values}
          int large= /* put a recursive call here */ ;

          if (b[h] > large) {
              return /* put some expression here */ ;

          } else {
              return /* put some expression here */ ;

          }
     }
}
```

Lesson page 15-2. Execution of calls on recursive methods

Activity 15-2-1 Execution of a call on a recursive method

Question 1. In tracing execution of recursive calls (that is, executing them by hand, drawing all the frames, etc.), you have to learn a different model of execution. ☐ true ☐ false

Question 2. Execute the statement sequence given below, including drawing frames for method calls. Method setToZero is given in activity 15-1-2.

```
int[] b= 0, 1, 2, 3, 4, 5;
setToZero(b, 3, 4);
```

Question 3. Execute the statement given below, including drawing frames for the method calls. Method deblank is given in activity 15-1-3.

```
String s= deblank(" I am ");
```

Activity 15-2-2 Tail recursion

Question 4. Define *depth of recursion*.

Note that "tail-recursive" applies to method calls, and not to entire methods.

Question 5. Describe when a recursive call is tail-recursive.

Question 6. Below are two methods for computing n!. Circle the tail recursive calls in these methods (if any).

```
// = n! (precondition: n >= 0)
public static int fact1(int n) {
    if (n == 0)
        {return 1;}

    // {n > 0}
    return n*fact1(n-1);
}

// = n!*k (precondition: n >= 0)
public static int fact2(int n, int k) {
    if (n == 0)
        {return k;}

    // {n > 0}
    return fact2(n-1,n*k);
}
```

Activity 15-2-3 Implementation of tail recursion for procedures

Question 7. List the steps to transform a procedure body with tail-recursive calls into a loop:

1.

2.

3.

Lesson page 15-3.   Some interesting recursive methods

This lesson page contains three examples of recursion. They are real nifty, groovy, peachy, corking; they swing. A point of interest is that all three solve the problem in terms of smaller problems that are half the size of the original one, making them really efficient. None of the smaller-by-one stuff here!

We provide no questions on them. We urge you to study them enough so that you *know* them. For example, if someone asks you how to tile Elaine's kitchen, you can explain it to them without looking anything up.

Activity 15-3-1 Tiling a kitchen

Activity 15-3-2 Computing x to the y

Activity 15-3-3 Mergesort

Lesson page 15-4.   Quicksort

This lesson page discusses `quicksort`, one of the most efficient (and famous) sorting algorithms. This is a good algorithm to know by heart —you should be able to explain its least efficient version and then show how to make it more efficient —eliminating the possible linear extra space and removing tail-recursive calls.

Activity 15-4-1 Basic quicksort

Question 1. What is a good base case for quicksort, and what algorithm can be used to sort such small arrays?

Question 2. What does the recursive case do? Write it below —using a call on method `partition` and two recursive calls. Note that this requires you to know what method `partition` does.

Activity 15-4-2 Quicksort at its best

Question 3. In what case does `quicksort` execute most efficiently?

Question 4. Write the formula that gives an upper bound on the number of swaps that `quicksort` makes in the best case.

Question 5. Give an upper bound on the number of frames for recursive calls that `quicksort` has allocated at any one time, in the best case.

Activity 15-4-3 Quicksort at its worst

Question 6. In what case does `quicksort` execute least efficiently?

Question 7. Write the formula that gives an upper bound on the number of swaps that `quicksort` makes in the worst case.

Question 8. Give an upper bound on the number of frames for recursive calls that `quicksort` has allocated at any one time, in the worst case.

Activity 15-4-4 Solving the quicksort space inefficiencies

Question 9. What is done before partitioning the values to increase the chance that the resulting segments are closer in size?

Question 10. After partitioning the array, the two resulting segments have to be sorted. Which one should be sorted first in order to ensure that the recursion depth is at most `n` (if the original array to be sorted has `2**n` elements)?

Chapter 16
Applets

Lesson page 16-1. Applets

Activity 16-1-1 Using applications and applets

Question 1. Define *application*.

Question 2. Define *applet*.

Activity 16-1-2 A first applet

Question 3. What does a browser do to start applet `Apple`?

Question 4. To start an application, the system calls its method _____;
to start an applet, a browser (or applet viewer) calls its method _____.

Activity 16-1-3 The structure of an applet

Question 5. Method _ must be overridden if you want to draw pictures
(paint) in the applet.

Question 6. List five inherited applet methods that are called by the browser
and indicate when each is called.

Question 7. Read the end of the lesson page. What should be imported if you use class `Applet`? `JApplet`?

Lesson page 16-2.   HTML and applet commands

Refer to a footnote of the first activity for a summary of the major HTML tags.

Activity 16-2-1 An overview of HTML

Question 1. What does *HTML* stand for?

Question 2. What tag does every HTML page begin with?

Question 3. Does the <`title`> of a web page go in the head or the body?

Question 4. The sequence   in an HTML file indicates a _____.

Question 5.   Fill in the following table, indicating what each of the tags are for. Write here the two tags <..> for which there is no corresponding tag </..>: _____.

<head > <title> <body >		<h1> <h2> <h6>	
<p>   <center>
    <hr>		<font size=12> <font size=+1> <font size=-1> <font color=red>	
<b> <i> <em> <u>		<a href="..."> <a href="#..."> <a name="..."> <img src="...">	

Activity 16-2-2 The applet command

Question 6. Suppose class `Frooble` extends `JApplet`. Suppose file `Frooble.class` is in subfolder `Java Classes`. Write an HTML tag for the applet so that its window is 400 pixels wide and 200 pixels high.

Question 7. What does *jar* stand for?

Question 8. Suppose class `Frooble` is in jar file `Frooble.jar` instead of subfolder `Java Classes`. Rewrite the HTML tag of the first question for this activity to take care of this change.

Question 9. What is an applet viewer?

Lesson page 16-3. Example of applets

This lesson page contains two examples of applets. Study it to gain a better understanding of applets. No questions are provided for this lesson page.

Activity 16-3-1 Applet: drawing a clock
Activity 16-3-2 Applet: summing two `double` values

Chapter 17
GUIs and event-driven programs

This lesson provides a short introduction to GUIs and event-driven programming. It contains no lectures; only text. However, by reading the lesson pages and the accompanying footnotes, filling in the answers to the questions below, and also trying some of the concepts and techniques in your own programs, you can get a basic understanding of the implementation of GUIs in Java.

Lesson page 17-1. GUIs and event-driven programming

Question 1. What does GUI stand for?

Question 2. The two packages of GUI classes are java.awt and javax.swing. Which is generally best to use?

Question 3. Define *lightweight*.

Question 4. Define *heavyweight*.

Question 5. What is another name for the "Swing" classes?

Question 6. If you want your program to place a window on the monitor, should you use an instance of class JWindow or class JFrame? Why? (See the footnote for this activity.)

Question 7. Write down the sequence of three instructions for creating an instance of a JFrame, storing it in a variable jf, and making it visible on the monitor. (See the footnote for this activity.)

Lesson page 17-2. Components and containers

Question 1. A component is something that can be placed in a JFrame (and in other kinds of frames and windows). Below are some kinds of components. Write down what each is:

1. JButton

2. JLabel

3. JTextField

4. JTextArea

5. JList

Question 2. The statements below create a JButton with title "butt" and add it to JFrame jf, on its east part. What other arguments can you use to place it in other parts of the JFrame? Draw a picture that shows the different areas of a JFrame.

```
JButton jb= new JButton("butt");
jf.getContentPane().add(jb, BorderLayout.EAST);
```

Question 3. Define *container*.

Question 4. A JPanel is a container, so it can contain other components. Using JPanels lets you overcome the limitation of being able to place only 5 components in a JFrame. Below, write statements to (0) create a JPanel named jp, (1) create two JButtons (with titles of your choice), (2) add the buttons to the panel, and finally (3) add the panel to JFrame jf on its south part.

Lesson page 17-3. Layout managers

Question 1. Define *layout manager.*

Question 2. A BorderLayout manager is automatically associated with a JFrame. Draw a picture showing where such a layout manager places components. Then write a statement that will add a component jb to JFrame jf. Describe the five possible arguments that you can use to indicate where the component goes in the JFrame.

   1.

   2.

   3.

   4.

   5.

Question 3. A FlowLayout manager is automatically associated with a JPanel. Write a statement that adds a component jb to JPanel jp.

Question 4. Suppose you add five components to a JPanel that is associated with a FlowLayout manager. Describe how these components appear in the

JPanel; what happens when the JPanel is resized?

Question 5. Write a statement that changes JFrame jf's layout manager from its default to a new FlowLayout manager.

Lesson page 17-4. Listening to a GUI

Question 1. A subclass SubFrame of JFrame that wants to "listen" to a button jb must do three things:

1. Implement interface _____.

2. Define a method _____, with one parameter of type _____, which will be called to process a click of the button.

3. Execute the statement _____
   to register this class, SubFrame, as a listener to button jb.

Question 2. Programming task: Obtain the class that toggled two buttons in a JFrame using *ProgramLive*'s menu Tools item List Programs title GUIs and topic buttons. The name of the file is Applic.java. Run and test the program. Then change the program so that it blanks out the title when a button becomes disabled and puts it back when it becomes enabled. You can use a statement like jb.setText("abc"); to set jb's title to "abc".

Appendix A

Java language summary

This appendix contains summaries of various parts of the Java language. With each part, we give its syntax, its meaning, an example, and possibly some remarks.

This is not a complete language description, but a summary. In places, in the interest of brevity and simplicity, we describe only the major alternatives of a construct. In a few places, we simply illustrate a construct rather than provide a complete definition. See *ProgramLive* for more details and the Sun specification of Java for a complete description.

A syntactic entity is a part of the Java language. Syntactic entities, such as *statementSequence* and *accessModifier*, are written in italics and have entries titled "**Syntactic entity**".

accessModifier: **Syntactic entity**

An *accessModifier* on a declaration or definition indicates the region in which the object being defined (class, field, or method) is visible (can be referenced). The possibilities are:

- **private**: visible in the class in which it is defined.
- default (missing modifier): visible in the class and package in which it is defined.
- **protected**: visible in the class and package in which it is defined and in subclasses of the class.
- **public**: visible everywhere.

applet

See *program*, p. 233.

application

See *program*, p. 233.

arguments: **Syntactic entity**

The arguments of a method call are the expressions in the comma-separated list of expressions that occur between the parentheses of the call. Method definitions have parameters; method calls have arguments. The type of each argument must match the type of the corresponding parameter of the method being called. (If the types of an argument and the corresponding parameter are not the same, the type of the parameter must be wider (see *cast expression*, p. 216) than the type of the argument.) See constructor call (p. 219), function call (p. 224), and procedure call (p. 232).

array

An object that is created by a new expression of the form:

> **new** *type* [*expression*]

The type of this object is *type*[]. It contains *expression* elements, each of type *type*. Suppose the name of the object is stored in a variable b. Then the elements are referenced using the subscripted variables b[0], b[1], ..., b[*expression*-1]. The size of an array, which is the maximum number of elements it can contain, is given by the expression b.length.

Here, we describe only one-dimensional arrays.

array initializer

An array initializer is used to create and initialize an array in a declaration-assignment like

> **int**[] b= {5, 3, 6, 1} ;

Here, the array initializer is {5, 3, 6, 1}. It creates an array of length 4, initializes the elements in the obvious way, and yields the name of the array as its result.

The type of the expressions in the array initializer must be the same as the type that appears before [], in this case, **int**.

Here's an example of a two-dimensional array initializer:

> {{5, 3, 6},{2, 3, 1}}

assignment statement

Syntax: *variable*= *expression* ;
Semantics: To execute an assignment statement, evaluate the *expression* and store the resulting value in variable *variable*.
Example: area= width*height;

Notes: If the types of the *variable* and the *expression* are not the same, the type of the *variable* must be wider (see *cast expression*, p. 216) than the type of the *expression*.

augmented assignment statement

Syntax: *variable binaryOperator*= *expression* ;
Semantics: This statement is equivalent to the assignment

variable = variable binaryOperator expression;
except that the *variable* will be evaluated only once.
Example: The following statement adds 20 to array element b[2*i+4]:
    b[2*i+4] += 20;
Notes: The augmented assignment can be more efficient than its assignment counterpart.

binaryOperator: **Syntactic entity**

An operator with two operands. Generally, a binary operator is written between its two operands. The binary operators in Java:
    * /,
    +, +,
    −,+,
    <<, >>, >>>, <, >, <=, >=,
    ==, &, ^, &&, ||, and **instanceof**.

binary operation

A binary operation has the form
    expression$_0$ *binaryOperator expression*$_1$
where the *binaryOperator* is an operator like + (addition) and < (less than).

block: **Syntactic entity**

A *block* is a block statement (see p. 215).

block statement

Syntax: { *statementSequence* }
Semantics: Execution consists of executing, in the order they appear, the statements in the *statementSequence*.
Example: if (x != 0) {
                z= y/x;
                x= 0;
            }

Notes: The block is used to aggregate a sequences of statement into a single statement. If a block is not all on one line, we suggest indenting it as shown in the example.

boolean

Primitive type **boolean** has the two values (literals) **false** and **true**. The table below defines the **boolean** operators (where b and c have type **boolean**):

op	meaning
!	! b is **false** if b is **true** and **true** if b is **false**.
&&	b && c equals "b and c are **true**".
ǁ	b ǁ c equals "(at least one of) b or c is **true**".
==	b == c equals "b and c are both **true** or both **false**".
!=	b != c equals "one of b and c is **true** and the other is **false**".

break statement

Syntax: break ;   or   **break** *identifier* ;
Semantics: Execution immediately terminates execution of the smallest enclosing loop or switch statement, or the statement that is labeled with label *identifier* (see *labeled statement*, p. 229).
Example: // Process elements b[0..],

```
        // but stop when a zero b[i] is found.
            for (i= 0; i != b.length; i= i+1) {
                if (b[i] == 0) break;
                Process nonzero b[i];
            }
```

Notes: Some programmers feel strongly that break statements should be avoided, because their use means that there is more than one exit point from a loop; this can make loops harder to reason about and understand.

byte

Primitive type **byte** has as its values integers in the range -128..127. Type **byte** has no operations; when necessary, **byte** values are automatically promoted to a wider type like **int**.

cast expression

Syntax: (*type*) *expression*
Semantics: We begin by defining when one type is wider or narrower than another.

   0. Let t1 and t2 be two types in this list: **byte**, **short**, **int**, **long**, **float**, **double**. Type t1 is wider than t2 if it is the same as t2 or occurs later in the list; otherwise, t1 is narrower than t2.

   1. Let t1 and t2 be two types in this list: **char**, **int**, **long**, **float**, **double**. Type t1 is wider than t2 if it is the same as t2 or occurs later in the list, otherwise, t1 is narrower than t2.

   2. A class type is wider than itself. If class SC is a subclass of class C, then SC is narrower than C and C is wider than SC.

We now explain what a cast expression does. There are two cases (in both cases, the type of the result is *type*):

   0. The types involved are primitive types. The result of evaluation is the value of the *expression* converted to the format of *type*. For a narrowing cast,

this may lose information.

    1. The types involved are class types. The result of evaluation is the same object name as the value of *expression* but viewed differently: only the field and method names that are accessible in class *type* are accessible.

Example: (int (x+y))   and   **((Squirrel) animal)**

Notes: In the interests of brevity and simplicity, we have discussed only the major cases of widening and narrowing —e.g. we have not dealt with interface types. Evaluation of a cast expression throws an exception if type *type* is not wider or narrower than the type of *expression*. Generally, if an expression occurs in a context in which a wider type is expected, Java will automatically perform the widening cast.

catenation

Consider the operation b + c, which is usually integer or floating-point addition. If either of the operands b and c is of type String, then the operation is not addition but *catenation*. The other operand is converted to a String, if neccessary, and the result of the catenation is a String that contains the characters of b followed by the characters of c. Note that the expressions are evaluated left-to-right. Here are examples:

    "25" + "32" evaluates to "2532".
    "" + 25+3 evaluates to "258".
    25 + 3 + "" evaluates to "28".

In a catenation, if one of the operands is of a class-type, method toString of that class-type is used to convert it to a String. Catenation is also called concatenation.

char

Primitive type **char** has characters as its values. They are given by literals like 'c' —any character on your keyboard except ' and \ enclosed in single quotes. In addition, the following escape sequences can appear in place of c:

\\	backslash \	\r	carriage return
\"	double quote "	\t	tab
\'	single quote '	\f	form feed
\n	new line	\b	backspace

Finally, Unicode characters like '\u0040' are literals. See lesson page 6-5 of *ProgramLive* for a full description of the Unicode characters.

    Type **char** is actually an integral type and can be cast to and from type **int**. For example, the expression (**int**)'c' yields the integer that represents character 'c', which is 99, and (**char**)99 gives back the character. For more on the integer representation of characters, see lesson page 6-5.

class definition

Syntax: *accessModifier* **class** *identifier* {
              Field declarations and method definitions
          }

Semantics: Class definitions are not executable statements. Instead, think of a class as two things: (1) a repository of the static methods and fields that are defined in it and (2) a template that describes the content of objects of this class —each object of a class contains the nonstatic methods and fields that are defined in the class.

Example: **public class** Example {
              private int x= 0;
              // Constructor: an instance with x set to xp
              public Example **(int** xp)
                  {x= xp;}
              // = the value of field x
              public int getX()
                  {**return** x;}
          }

Notes: A class definition is sometimes called a *class declaration*.

The *accessModifier*, explained on p. 213, is either missing or one of **public**, **private**, and **protected**. It indicates where the class is visible.

For subclasses, see p. 235.

Just after the *accessModifier* can come the keyword **final**; its presence indicates that this class cannot have subclasses.

The class can also implement interfaces (see p. 228), using the syntax shown in the example below. The following class implements interface Comparable, which means that it has to contain definitions of all the methods defined in that interface. (Following keyword **implements** comes a comma-separated list of interface names.)

```
public class Example implements Comparable {
    private int x= 0;
    // Constructor: an instance with x set to xp
    public Example (int xp)
        {x= xp;}
    // = the value of field x
    public int getX()
        {return x;}
    // < 0, 0, or > 0 depending on ...
    public int compareTo(Comparable ob) {
        if (x < ((Example)ob).x) return -1;
        if (x > ((Example)ob).x) return 1;
        return 0;
    }
}
```

comment

> **Syntax:** *// any sequence of characters*
> or
> */* any sequence of characters */*
>
> **Semantics:** A comment is treated as whitespace; it is intended for the reader only and has no effect on the program.
>
> **Example:** `/* this is a comment */`
>
> **Notes:** The first form of comment ends with the end of the line on which `//` appears. The second form of comment may span several lines. There is another special form of comment, called a JavaDoc comment, described in appendix C.

condition: **Syntactic entity**

> A *condition* is an expression of type **boolean**.

conditional expression

> **Syntax:** $expression_b$? $expression_t$: $expression_f$
>
> **Semantics:** Evaluation of a conditional expression proceeds as follows: first, $expression_b$ is evaluated. If it evaluates to **true**, then $expression_t$ is evaluated to yield the result of the conditional expression; otherwise, $expression_f$ is evaluated to yield the result of the conditional expression.
>
> **Example:** `(x > y) ? x : y`
>
> **Notes:** $expression_b$ must be of type **boolean**. The types of $expression_t$ and $expression_f$ must be the same (or they must widen to the same type); the type of the result is the type of these two expressions (or the type to which they widen).

conditional statement

> See *if-statement* (p. 226) and *if-else-statement* (p. 225).

constructor call

> **Syntax:**
>
> > *identifier* (*arguments*) ;
> > or **super**(*arguments*) ;
> > or **this**(*arguments*) ;
>
> **Semantics:** Execution of a constructor call assigns the *arguments* to the *parameters* of the constructor being called and then executes the body of the constructor, which (generally) assigns initial values to a newly created object. No value is returned.
>
> **Example:** `Frame("title of frame")`
>
> **Notes:** A constructor call is used to initialize fields of an object that is being created. The first form of constructor call may appear only as part of a new

expression (p. 230). The second form of constructor call may appear only as the first statement of the body of a constructor (p. 220). It calls a constructor of the superclass. The third form of constructor call may appear only as the first statement of the body of a constructor (p. 220). It calls another constructor of this class. The *arguments* are a possibly-empty comma-separated list of expressions, whose types must match the types of the corresponding *parameters* of the constructor being called —the number of *arguments* must equal the number of *parameters*.

constructor definition

Syntax: *accessModifier identifier (parameterDeclarations)*
            { statementSequence }

Semantics: This is not an executable statement but simply a definition of a constructor with parameters *parameters* and body *statementSequence*.

Example: `// Initialize field x to xp`
            `public Example(int xp)`
                `{x= xp;}`

Notes: The *accessModifier*, explained on p. 213, is either missing or one of **public**, **private**, and **protected**. It indicates where the constructor is visible.

The *identifier* is the name of the class in which this constructor definition appears.

The *parameters* are a possibly-empty comma-separated list of declarations of the form *type identifier*.

A constructor definition should be preceded by a comment that gives its specification, i.e. that explains what a call on the constructor does.

If a class does not contain a constructor definition, then a default constructor with no parameters and an empty *statementSequence* is automatically present in the class.

If a constructor definition appears in a subclass, then the first statement in its body should be a call **super** (*parameters*) ; on a constructor of its superclass. This is the preferred way to initialize inherited fields. If such a call is not present, the call **super** () ; is automatically inserted.

continue statement

Syntax: continue ;   or   **continue** *identifier* ;

Semantics: Execution immediately terminates execution of the repetend of the smallest enclosing loop, or of the loop that is labeled with label *identifier* (see *labeled statement*, p. 229).

Example: `// Process all nonzero elements b[0..].`
            `for (i= 0; i != b.length; i= i+1) {`
                `if (b[i] == 0) continue;`
                `Process nonzero b[i];`
            `}`

Notes: Some programmers feel strongly that continue statements should be avoided, because their use can make loops harder to reason about and understand.

declaration

See *parameter declaration* (p. 231), *local variable declaration* (p. 229), and *field declaration* (p. 223).

decrement statement

Syntax: --*variable*; or *variable*--;
Semantics: This statement is equivalent to the assignment *variable*= *variable* - 1;, except that the *variable* will be evaluated only once.
Example: int i= b.length;
```
while (i != 0) {
    Process b[i];
    --i;
}
```

Notes: The decrement statement can be more efficient than its assignment-statement counterpart.

double

Primitive type **double** has as its values floating-point numbers like $32.5 * 10^{23}$. In Java, this number would be written as **32.5e23D**. See *ProgramLive* lesson page 6.3 for full details on writing **double** literals.

The table below gives the **double** operators (where b and c have type **double**):

op	meaning
−	− c is unary minus, or "negative c".
+	+ c is the same as c.
−	b − c is subtraction.
+	b + c is addition.
*	b * c is multiplication.
/	b / c is division.
==	b == c is equality.
!=	b != c is inequality —the same as !(b == c).

Further, the relations <, <=, >, and >= have their usual meaning.

do-while loop

Syntax: do *repetend* **while** (*condition*) ;
Semantics: This loop is equivalent to the following program segment:

> *repetend*
> **while** (*condition*) {
>   *repetend*
> }

Example: do {
            System.out.println("Type an integer");
            i= JLiveRead.readInt();
            Process i;
        } **while** (i != 0);

Notes: The *repetend*, the body of the loop, is any sequence of statements. We prefer not to use this statement, because its use often leads to errors. See the discussion of the do-while loop in *ProgramLive*.

empty statement

Syntax: ;   (it is just a semicolon!)
Semantics: Execution of an empty statement does nothing (but very fast).
Example: // Set i to the index of the last
        // nonzero element of b (-1 if none)
            i= b.length;
            while (i != -1 && b[--i] != 0) ;

Notes: The empty statement is also called the null statement.

exit statement

Syntax: System.exit(0);
Semantics: Execution of an exit statement terminates execution of the program.
Example: if (x == 0) {
            // Terminate the program!! x is 0!!
                System.exit(0);
        }

Notes: The exit statement is actually a call of static method **exit** in class System.

expression: Syntactic entity

An *expression* is a construct that is evaluated to yield a value. For example, if variable x has the value 3, then:

    0. *expression* x evaluates to the value 3,
    1. *expression* $2 * x$ evaluates to the value 6, and
    2. *expression* 72 evaluates to the value 72.

Each *expression* has a type, which is a syntactic property —it is determined from the text of the program, without evaluating the program. Here are the kinds of expressions in Java:

0. A literal, like 3 and `"abc"`,
1. A *variable* (see p. 237),
2. A function call (see p. 224),
3. A new expression (see p. 230),
4. A cast expression (see p. 216),
5. A parenthesized expression (see p. 231).
6. A unary operation (see p. 237),
7. A binary operation (see p. 215), and
8. A conditional expression (see p. 219).

If operators are adjacent to each other in an expression, as in

    -x + y * z

precedence rules are used to determine the order of evaluation (see p. 231). If two operators have the same precedence, the expression is evaluated left to right.

field declaration

Syntax: *accessModifier type identifier* ;

    or

    accessModifier **static** *type identifier* ;

Semantics: A field declaration occurs in a class. In the first version, it indicates that variable *identifier* belongs to (is a field of) each instance of the class. In the second version, variable *identifier* is termed a static variable, and it belongs to the class itself.

The default initial values for fields are: 0 for types **byte**, **short**, **int**, **long float**, and **double**; '\u0000' for type **char**; **false** for type **boolean**; and **null** for class types.

Example: **public class** Example3 {

        `// Below are three field declarations`

            public int[] b;

            private int y= 53;

            public static final int TWO= 2;

        }

Notes: The *accessModifier*, explained on p. 213, is either missing or one of **public**, **private**, and **protected**. It indicates where the field is visible.

See p. 213 for an explanation of the *type* of the field.

A field declaration can have "= *expression*" after the *identifier*. The value of the *expression* is the initial value of the variable.

If the above-mentioned addition is present, keyword **final** can appear before the *type*; its presence means that no other assignment to the variable is allowed, so the variable is effectively a constant.

A nonstatic field is also known as an instance variable; a static field is also known as a class variable.

float

Primitive type **float** has as its values floating-point numbers like $32.5 * 10^{23}$. In Java, this number would be written as `32.5e23`. A value of type **float** takes half the space (4 bytes) as a value of type **double**. Because of this, there are fewer **float** numbers and they have less precision. The operations of this type are similar to those of type **double**. For the kinds of programs you write as a beginner, instead of type **float** use type **double** (see p. 221).

for-loop

Syntax: for (*initialization* ; *condition* ; *increment*)
             repetend
Semantics: The for-loop is equivalent to the following while-loop, except that in the for-loop, variables declared in the *initialization* are accessible only in the *repetend*.

```
    initialization ;
    while ( condition ) {
        repetend ;
        increment ;
    }
```

Example: `// Add 2 to each element of array b`
```
        for (int i= 0; i != b.length; i= i+1)
            {b[i]= b[i] + 2;}
```

Notes: The *initialization* is typically an assignment statement, but without a semicolon. The *increment* is typically an assignment, but without a semicolon, that increments or decrements a variable. And the *repetend* is any statement.

function call

Syntax: *identifier* (*arguments*)
Semantics: Evaluation of the function call assigns the *arguments* to the *parameters* of the function named *identifier* and then executes the body of the function; the value of the function call is the value returned by execution of a return statement within the method body.
Example: `Math.max(x,y)`
Notes: A function call is an expression, not a statement. The *arguments* are a possibly-empty comma-separated list of expressions, whose types must match the types of the corresponding *parameters* of the function being called —the number of *arguments* must equal the number of *parameters*.

Above, we stated that the first item of a function call is an *identifier* that is the function name. Actually, a prefix may be needed:

- For a function call that appears in the same class in which the function is defined, use either *identifier* or `this.`*identifier*.

- For a static function that is defined in a class `C`, use `C.`*identifier*.

- For a nonstatic function that appears in an object named `obj` (say), use *expression.identifier*, where *expression* is an expression that evaluates to `obj`.

function definition

Syntax: *accessModifier type identifier(parameterDeclarations)*
{ *statementSequence* }

Semantics: This is not an executable statement but simply a definition of a function named *identifier* with parameters *parameters*, return type *type*, and body *statementSequence*. Execution of the body must end with execution of a statement of the form **return** *expression*;, where the *expression* has type (or can be widened to type) *type*.

Example: `// = the maximum of x and y`
```
public int printMax(int x, int y) {
    if (x >= y)
        {return x;}
    else {return y;}
}
```

Notes: A function definition is sometimes called a function declaration.

The *accessModifier*, explained on p. 213, is either missing or one of **public**, **private**, and **protected**. It indicates where the function is visible.

The *parameters* are a possibly-empty comma-separated list of declarations of the form *type identifier*.

Keyword **final** may appear after the *accessModifier*; its presence indicates that this function cannot be overridden in a subclass.

A function definition should be preceded by a comment that gives its specification —i.e. that explains what a call on the function does.

Some programmers feel strongly that functions should not modify the values of fields, that their purpose is only to produce values. Only procedures should modify the values of fields. Otherwise, expressions such as `r.f() == r.f()` might not always evaluate to `true`!

identifier: **Syntactic entity**

An identifier is a sequence of characters with the following properties:
(0) The first character is a letter, "_", or "$".
(1) The other characters are letters, digits, "_", or "$".
(2) No whitespace may occur between characters of the identifier.
(3) Keywords are not identifiers.
(4) It is best not to use "$" in an identifier.

if-else-statement

Syntax: **if** (*condition*) *statement*$_1$
else *statement*$_2$

Semantics: To execute an if-else-statement, evaluate its *condition*; if it was true, execute *statement₁*, otherwise execute *statement₂*.

Example: if (amt > balance) {
                        amt= amt-balance;
                } else {
                        System.out.println("Negative money!");
                }

Notes: The *condition* is any boolean *expression*. It is best to always use a block for the *statement*s, as in the example. *statement₁* is called the "then-part" of the if-else-statement; *statement₂*, the "else-part".

if-statement

Syntax: if (*condition*) *statement*

Semantics: To execute an if-statement, evaluate its *condition* and, if it was true, execute the *statement*.

Example: if (amt > balance) {
                        amt= amt-balance;
                }

Notes: The *condition* is any boolean *expression*. It is best to always use a block for the *statement*, as in the example. Part *statement* is called the "then-part" of the if-statement.

import directive

Syntax: import *packageName* . *className* ;
            or
            import *packageName* . * ;

Semantics: This is a directive, not a statement. It is placed just before the class definition in a .java file. It directs that class *className* (or all the classes in the named package if "*" is used) be referenceable in the class being defined in this .java file.

Example: import java.swing.*;
                import java.util.GregorianCalendar;

Notes: The *packageName* is a list of directories (separated by ".") that leads from some directory in the CLASSPATH environment variable to a directory that contains the desired classes.

increment: **Syntactic entity**

See *for-loop*, p. 224.

TABLE A.1. BITWISE OPERATIONS ON ints

~   ~ c is bitwise complement —the same as (-c)-1 (the bits of c are complemented).

&   b & c is bitwise and —the bits of b and c are "anded" together.

| b | c is bitwise or —the bits of b and c are "ored" together.

^   b ^ c is bitwise exclusive or —the bits of b and c are "exclusively ored" together. The exclusive or of two bits is the bit 1 if they are different and 0 if they are the same.

Above, b and c are of type int

TABLE A.2. SHIFTING OPERATORS ON ints

<<   b << s shifts b's bits s bits to the left. It is equivalent to $b * 2^s$.

>>   b >> s shifts b's bits s bits to the right, with sign extension. For non-negative values of b, it is equivalent to the integer division $b/(2^s)$.

>>>   b >>> s shifts b's bits s bits to the right, with zero extension. For b>=0, the result is the same as b >> s. For b<0, it is (n>>s) + (2<<~s) .

Above, b and c are of type int and 0≤c<32.

---

increment statement

Syntax: ++*variable*; or *variable*++;

Semantics: This statement is equivalent to the assignment *variable*= *variable* + 1;, except that the *variable* will be evaluated only once.

Example: int i= 0;
```
while (i != b.length) {
    Process b[i];
    ++i;
}
```

Notes: The increment statement can be more efficient than its assignment-statement counterpart.

instanceof expression

Syntax: *expression*$_0$ **instanceof** *expression*$_1$

Semantics: Evaluation yields the value of "object *expression*$_0$ is an instance of class *expression*$_1$".

Example: if (animal **instanceof** Squirrel) ...

Notes: Use this test to see whether a narrowing cast (see p. 216) is legal.

initialization: **Syntactic entity**

See *For-loop*, p. 224.

int

Primitive type **int** has as its values the integers in the range $-2^{31}..+2^{31} - 1$ (2^{31} = 2147483648). Do *not* write an **int** literal with a preceding 0 for it means something else (see *ProgramLive* lesson page 6-2). For example, 010 is not the same integer as 10.

The table below gives the **int** operators (where b and c have type **int**):

op	meaning
−	− c is unary minus, or "negative c".
+	+ c is the same as c.
−	b − c is subtraction.
+	b + c is addition.
∗	b ∗ c is multiplication.
/	b / c is integer division: if conventional division would yield a number that is not an integer, the result is rounded down to the nearest integer, e.g. 5/3 is 1.
%	b % c is the remainder when b is divided by c, e.g. 5/3 is 2.
==	b == c is equality.
!=	b != c is inequality —the same as !(b == c).

Further, the relations <, <=, >, and >= have their usual meaning. See Table A.1 for the bitwise operations and Table A.2 for the shift operations.

An operation like addition may produce a result that is outside the range of type **int**. This is called "overflow". You are not given a warning about this, and the answer is incorrect.

integer: **Syntactic entity**

By an *integer*, we mean an integer literal, e.g. 0, -5, or 42639.

interface definition

Syntax: public interface *identifier* {
        field definitions (constants only) and
        method definitions (abstract)
    }

Semantics: The *identifier* is the name of the interface.

An interface is not an executable statement; it is simply a template that describes a number of abstract methods and constants. A class that implements an interface (see *class definition* on p. 218) must provide implementations of all the methods of the interface, and it has access to the constants defined in the interface.

Example: interface `Comparable {`

```
            // < 0 if b < this object, 0 if b = this
            // object, and > 0 if b > this object
            int compareTo(Comparable b);
      }
```

Notes: The methods should not have an access modifier; the methods are automatically **public**. The methods are abstract —they have semicolons instead of bodies. Otherwise, they look like normal method definitions. The only fields that can be defined in an interface are static constants, e.g. **static final int** `NUM_SHOES= 5;`.

labeled statement

Syntax: *identifier* : *statement*
Semantics: Execution of a labeled statement consists of executing the *statement*.
Example: `lp:` **for** `(i= 0; i != b.length; i= i+1) {`

```
            if (b[i] == 0) continue lp;
            Process b[i];
      }
```

Notes: The purpose of a labeled statement is to be able to put a name —the *identifier*— on a statement, so that it can be referred to in a break statement or a continue statement.

local variable declaration

Syntax: *type identifier* ;
Semantics: A local variable declaration can appear within a method body in any *statementSequence*. It declares *identifier* to be a variable of type *type* whose scope —the region where it can be referenced— is the part of the *statementSequence* that follows the local variable declaration.
Example: `// = index of last occurrence of x in b (-1 if none)`

```
      public int search(int x, int[] b) {
            int i; // This is a local-variable declaration
            i= b.length-1;
            // inv: x does not occur in b[i+1..]
            while (i != -1)
                {if (x == b[i]) return i;}
            return -1;
      }
```

Notes: See p. 237 for an explanation of *type*.

A local-variable declaration and its initializing assignment can be abbreviated in one statement. For example, the first two lines of the method body in the example can be written as the single line **int** `i= b.length-1;`.

Keyword **final** can be placed at the beginning of the declaration; its presence means that only one assignment to the variable is allowed. That assignment does not have to occur immediately.

long

Primitive type **long** has as its values the integers in the range $-2^{63} \; .. \; +2^{63} - 1$. To turn any **int** literal (e.g. **45**) into a **long**, follow it by L (e.g. **45L**). The operations of this type are similar to those of type **int** (see p. 228), except they work on operands of type **long** instead of operands of type **int**.

loop

See *do-while loop* (p. 221), *for-loop* (p. 224), and *while-loop* (p. **??**).

method

See *function definition* (p. 225), *procedure definition* (p. 232), and *constructor definition* (p. 220).

method call

Either a function call (p. 224), procedure call (p. 232), or constructor call (p. 230)

new expression

Syntax: new *identifier* (*arguments*)
Semantics: Evaluation of a new expression first creates a new instance (or object) of class *identifier* and then executes the constructor call *identifier* (*arguments*). The result of evaluation is the name of the new instance.
Example: new `Example2(0, 15)`
Notes: There are two other ways to call a constructor. They are explained in *constructor definition*, p. 220.

null

The value that denotes the absence of the name of (or pointer to) an object. It can be assigned to class-type variables.

null statement

Syntax: ;   (it is just a semicolon!)
Semantics: Execution of an empty statement does nothing (but very fast).
Example:
```
// Set i to the index of the last
// nonzero element of b (-1 if none)
    i= b.length;
    while ( i != -1 && b[--i] != 0) ;
```

Notes: The null statement is also called the empty statement.

parameter: **Syntactic entity**

> A *parameter* is a variable that is declared in the *parameterDeclarations* of a method definition. The scope of the *parameter* is the method body. Methods definitions have parameters; method calls have arguments.

parameterDeclarations: **Syntactic entity**

> A parameter declaration is a declaration, of the form *type identifier*, that occurs within the parentheses of a method (i.e. method definition). The declarations in a method are separated by commas. A parameter declaration declares the *identifier* to be a parameter of type *type* whose scope —the region where it can be referenced— is the body of the method. Method definitions have parameters; method calls have arguments.

parenthesized expression

> **Syntax:** (*expression*)
> **Semantics:** The result of evaluation of a parenthesized expression is the value of the *expression*.
> **Example:** (x+y)*z
> **Notes:** Parentheses are used around an expression to help indicate the order of evaluation of the operations of the expression.

precedence

> To reduce the number of parentheses needed in expressions, precedences are assigned to operators. The table of precedences of operators in Java is shown below, beginning with operators with highest precedence.
>
> Component selection and function call (e.g. `Pair.x` and `Math.max(b,c)`)
> Unary operators: $+ \ - \ ++ \ -- \ ! \ \sim$
> Binary arithmetic operators: $* \ /$
> Binary arithmetic operators: $+ \ -$
> Shifts: $<< \ >> \ >>>$
> Relations: $< \ > \ <= \ >=$ **instanceof**
> Relations: $== \ !=$
> Bitwise and: &
> Bitwise exclusive or: ^
> Bitwise or: |
> Logical and: &&
> Logical or: ||
> Conditional expression: ? :
> Assignment: $= \ += \ =*= \ *= \ /=$ etc.

procedure call

Syntax: *identifier* (*arguments*) ;

Semantics: Execution of the procedure call assigns the *arguments* to the *parameters* of the procedure named *identifier* and then executes the body of the procedure. No value is returned (as opposed to a function call, which returns a value).

Example: `System.out.println("x+y is: " + (x+y));`

Notes: The identifier is the name of a procedure. The *arguments* are a possibly-empty comma-separated list of expressions, whose types must match the types of the corresponding *parameters* of the procedure being called. The number of *arguments* must equal the number of *parameters*.

Above, we stated that the first item of a procedure call is an *identifier* that is the procedure name. Actually, a prefix may be needed:

- For a procedure call that appears in the same class in which the procedure is defined, use either *identifier* or `this.`*identifier*.

- For a static procedure that is defined in a class `C`, use `C.`*identifier*.

- For a nonstatic procedure that appears in an object named `obj` (say), use *expression.identifier*, where *expression* is an expression that evaluates to `obj`.

procedure definition

Syntax: *accessModifier* **void** *identifier* (*parameterDeclarations*)
                       { *statementSequence* }

Semantics: This is not an executable statement; it is a definition of a procedure *identifier* whose parameters are given by the *parameterDeclarations* and whose body is the *statementSequence*.

Example:
```
// Print the maximum of x and y
public void printMax(int x, int y) {
    if (x >= y)
        {System.out.println(x);}
    else {System.out.println(y);}
}
```

Notes: The *accessModifier*, explained on p. 213, is either missing or one of **public**, **private**, and **protected**. It indicates where the procedure is visible.

The *parameterDeclarations* is a possibly-empty comma-separated list of variable declarations of the form *type identifier*. Each such declaration declares the *identifier* to be a parameter, whose scope is the method body —the *statementSequence*.

Keyword **final** may appear after the *accessModifier*; its presence indicates that this function cannot be overridden in a subclass.

A procedure definition should be preceded by a comment that gives its specification, i.e. that explains what a call on the procedure does.

program

A Java program is a collection of classes.

If the program is used as an application, then one of the classes contains a method of the form shown below; this method is called to begin execution of the program.

public static void main(String[] pars) { ⋯ }

If the program is used as an applet, then it has a class that extends class Applet; this class can override (at least) the following four methods:

init(): Called just before starting the applet.

start(): Called to start or continue (after pausing) the applet.

stop(): Called to pause the applet.

destroy(): Called just before destroying the applet.

repeat loop

See *do-while loop* (p. 221).

repetend: **Syntactic entity**

The body of a loop (see pp. 224, **??**, and 221). "Repetend" means "the thing repeated".

return statement

Syntax: return ;   or   **return** *expression* ;

Semantics: Execution terminates execution of the method body and of the method call that caused the method body to execute. The first form of the return statement is used in a procedure or constructor body. The second form is used in a function body; the value of the function call is the value of the *expression*.

Example:
```
// = the index of the last occurrence
// of x in b[0..] (-1 if none)
public static int lastocurr(int x, int[] b) {
    for (i= b.length-1; i != -1; i= i-1) {
        if (b[i] == x)
            {return i;}
    }
    return -1;
}
```

Notes: The type of the expression (in the second form of the return statement) must match the return type of the function.

short

Primitive type **short** has values in the range −32768..32767. Type **short** has no operations; when necessary, **short** values are automatically promoted to a wider type like **int**.

statement: **Syntactic entity**

By a *statement* we mean any of the Java executable statements. They can be found in *ProgramLive*'s glossary under entry "statement". In this Appendix, they are the entries of the form "*. . . statement*" and "*. . . loop*".

statement-comment

Syntax: // A statement written in English; with its
             // implementation indented underneath.
Semantics: Execution consists of executing the statements indented underneath the comment.
Example: // Set z to the larger of x and y
              if (x > y)
                  {z= x;}
              else {z= y;}

Notes: This is not a Java statement but a convention for using comments and indentation to achieve a level of abstraction. One can read a statement-comment in two ways. First, forget about the indented sequence of statements and understand what is happening in terms of the English statement. Second, to find out how the English statement is implemented, read the indented sequence of statements underneath it. See *ProgramLive* for a description of why it is important to indent the statements underneath the comment.

statementSequence: **Syntactic entity**

A sequence of statements and local variable declarations (see p. 229). Execution of a *statementSequence* consists of executing the statements in it, in the order given (unless execution is changed by executing a **return**, **break**, or **continue** statement) or unless an exception is thrown). The scope of a local variable declared in the *statementSequence* is the statements that follow its declaration.

String

This class appears in package `java.lang`. It occupies a unique place in Java in that it is a class but it is also integrated into the core of the language, in two ways. First, its literals consist of a sequence of characters enclosed in double-quote signs ". See p.106 or *ProgramLive* for a description of `String` literals. Second, the operator + means catenation if either of its operands are `String`s.

subclass definition

> **Syntax:** *accessModifier* **class** *identifier* **extends** *identifier*$_1$ {
>   Field declarations and method definitions
> }

Semantics: A subclass definition is just like a class definition (see p. 218) and has the same meaning, except for the following. Class *identifier* is a subclass of class *identifier*$_1$, and *identifier*$_1$ is a superclass of *identifier*. This means that in addition to the fields and methods that it defines, class *identifier* inherits the fields and methods of class *identifier*$_1$. If the subclass contains a new definition of an inherited method, the new definition is said to override the inherited one.

Example:
```
public class Example1 {
    private int x= 0;
    // Constructor: an instance containing xp
    public Example (int xp) {x= xp;}
    // = the value of field x
    public int getX() {return x;}
}
public class Example2 inherits Example1 {
    private int y= 0;
    // Constructor: an instance containing xp and yp
    public Example2 (int xp, int yp) {
        super(xp);
        y= yp;
    }
    // = the y value
    public int getY() {return y;}
}
```

Notes: A subclass can also implement interfaces, as explained in *class definition* (see p. 218).

switch statement

> **Syntax: switch** (*expression*) {
>   **case** *integer* : *statementSequence*
>   ...
>   **case** *integer* : *statementSequence*
>   **default** : *statementSequence*
> }

Semantics: To execute a switch statement, evaluate the *expression* to obtain an integer i (say) and then execute *all* the statements beginning at the *statementSequence* labeled "case i". Execution of statements continues until a break statement (p. 216) is executed or until the last statement is executed. If there is no "case i", the default *statementSequence* is used instead, but if the default is also missing, nothing is executed.

Example: switch (e) {

```
        case 0: System.out.println("e was 0");
        case 1: System.out.println("e was 1");
                break;
        case 2:
        case 4: System.out.println("e was 2 or 4");
                break;
        default: System.out.println(
                    "e wasn't 0, 2, or 4");
    }
```

Notes: The *expression* must be of some integral type. The default case is optional. The switch statement is tricky to use properly, because it is easy to omit necessary break statements. In the example, if e evaluates to 0, both "e was 0" and "e was 1" are printed, because all following statements are executed until a break statement is executed (or the last statement is executed). This, many people feel, was a bad language-design decision, because in 95% or more of the cases, a break is needed with each case part. Rarely does a case part not end with a break statement.

throw statement

Syntax: throw *expression* ;
Semantics: Execution of a throw statement "throws" the value of the *expression*, causing "propagation" of it to a catch block (see p. 237) that catches it. See *ProgramLive* for full details.
Example: if (y == 0)

```
        {throw new ArithmeticException("x mod 0");}
    return x % Math.abs(y);
```

Notes: The type of *expression* must be (a subclass of) class Throwable — usually a subclass of Exception or Error.

try statement

Syntax: try *block*$_0$
         catch (*expression*) *block*$_1$
             . . .
         catch (*expression*) *block*$_2$
         finally *block*$_3$
Semantics: Execution begins by executing *block*$_0$, called the *try block*; if no exception is thrown, that's it. If an exception is thrown while executing *block*$_0$, then the exception is *propagated*. See *ProgramLive* for a discussion of propagation.

Example: // Calculate x;
        try { y= 5/x; }
        catch (ArithmeticException ae) {
           System.out.println(
               "x=0; using 0 for 5/x'');
           y= 0;
        }

Notes: Each phrase catch (*expression*) *block* is called a catch clause; its *block* is called the catch block.

The **finally** clause is optional; if it is not present, then there must be at least one catch clause.

type: Syntactic entity

A *type* is either (0) one of the primitive types **boolean**, **byte**, **short**, **int**, **long**, **char**, **float**, and **double**, (1) a class type (the name of a class or interface), (2) an array type of the form *t* [], where *t* is any type, or (3) void.

A *type* defines a set of values and a set of operations that can be performed on the values. A *type* is used to indicate the type of a variable (field, parameter, or local variable) and the return type of a function.

variable: Syntactic entity

By a *variable*, we mean a reference to a variable that is declared in a field declaration, local variable declaration, or parameter declaration (see pp. 223, 229, or 231) or subscripted variable.

A reference to a local variable or parameter v is given by the name: v.

A reference to a static field f of a class C generally takes one of two forms:

    0. f —can be used only in the class and its subclasses.

    1. C.f —can be used anywhere where C and f can be accessed.

A reference to a nonstatic field f of an instance obj of a class generally takes one of two forms:

    0. f —can be used only in the class and its subclasses.

    1. obj.f —can be used anywhere where obj and f can be accessed.

A subscripted variable, a reference to element number i of an array b, is written as b[i]. Integer i must satisfy 0 <= i < b.length.

unary operation

A unary operation has the form
    unaryOperator expression
where the *unaryOperator* is one of + − ++ −− ! . A cast like
    (Squirrel) animal
can also be considered to be a unary operation, with (Squirrel) being the unary operator.

variable declaration

See *parameter declaration* (p. 231), *local variable declaration* (p. 229), and *field declaration* (p. 223).

while loop

Syntax: while (*condition*) *repetend*
Semantics: To execute the while loop, do the following until evaluation of the *condition* yields false: evaluate the *condition* and then (if the *condition* was true) execute the *repetend*.
Example: // Add 2 to each element of array b

```
i= 0;
while(i != b.length) {
    b[i]= b[i] + 2;
    i= i+1;
}
```

Notes: The *repetend* is any statement; it is best to make it a block (p. 215).

whitespace

A sequence of characters that is made up of blanks, tabs, end-of-lines, carriage returns, and comments. Whitespace has no effect on a program, except that:

0. Whitespace cannot appear between characters of a Java symbol. For example, "//" cannot be written as "/ /", and the identifier abc must be written completely on one line.

2. Whitespace must appear between adjacent keywords and identifiers. For example, **public void** cannot be written as **publicvoid**.

Appendix B

Installing and running Java

Several IDEs are available for developing and running Java programs —BlueJ, CodeWarrior, Forte, JBuilder, Oracle JDeveloper, and Visual Cafe, to name a few. Your instructor will probably tell you which one to use and give you instructions on using it.

In this appendix, we give brief instructions for downloading and installing the Sun Java Software Development Kit, or SDK, and using it with command-line instructions —for example, in a UNIX or DOS command-line window. We also give brief instructions for downloading Sun's IDE for Java, Forte, one version of which is currently free.

Here are the URLs for the above-mentioned IDEs:

BlueJ	http://www.bluej.org/
CodeWarrior	http://www.metrowerks.com/
Forte	http://www.sun.com/forte/
JBuilder	http://www.borland.com/jbuilder/
JDeveloper	http://www.oracle.com/tools/jdeveloper/
Visual Cafe	http://www.visualcafe.com/Products/
	VisualCafe_Overview.html

B.1 The Java Software Development Kit

If you are using an IDE, or if you are using a command-line system on a computer that is maintained by others (e.g. in a CS department computer lab), you need not read this part. However, if you want to install a barebones Java system on your computer, without an IDE, then continue reading.

You want the latest Java Software Development Kit, or SDK, which at the time of this writing is the:

> Java 2 platform, Standard Edition (J2SE), version 1.3, known as SDK 1.3.

You can download this from the Sun web page; `http://java.sun.com`; just follow the links to the download site, download it, and follow directions for installing it. The installed software contains, among other things, the following (we give the directory structure in a Windows system; the structure and contents are similar but slightly different in Unix systems):

Item	About	Directory
javac.exe	A compiler that translates Java programs into the Java Virtual Machine language	c:\jdk1.3\bin
java.exe	A program that runs applications that have been compiled into the Java Virtual Machine language	c:\jdk1.3\bin
applet-viewer.exe	A program for viewing applets	c:\jdk1.3\bin
javadoc.exe	A program that extracts documentation from Java programs	c:\jdk1.3\bin
src.jar	A compressed version of the source for all the API classes, e.g. java/lang/String.java	c:\jdk1.3
Example programs	Used to illustrate parts of Java	c:\jdk1.3\demo

We have shown directory jdk1.3 placed under the root of the C drive; you may place it elsewhere when you install it. Do take a look at some of the example programs, for they are quite interesting and illuminating.

File src.jar contains the source for all the classes. Don't change the source, but you might want to browse through it to see how various classes and methods are implemented. You can extract all the source files into a directory using the following command.

```
jar  xvf  src.jar
```

You can get a list of all the files using the following command.

```
jar  tvf  src.jar
```

B.2   Setting path and classpath (Windows)

In a Windows system, you have to let the system know two things: (0) where the programs (such as javac) are, and (1) where certain class files are. We outline how to do this here; you can find more information on the following site:

http://java.sun.com/j2se/1.3/install-windows.html

Below, we assume that Java has been installed so that its root directory is C:\jdk1.3.

Setting variable PATH

Variable PATH is used to find executable programs, like javac. You tell the system where the Java programs are by adding to system variable PATH the following path:

```
C:\jdk1.3\bin
```

You can see the contents of variable `PATH` by using the DOS command

```
set
```

A list of variables and their values will appear; if `PATH` is not on it, it has never been set.

In Windows NT or Windows 2000, do the following. Start the Control panel and select System and then Environment. In the User Variables and System Variables, add

```
;C:\jdk1.3\bin
```

at the end of the path list for variable `PATH`. The semicolon is used to separate paths in such a path list. (If there is no variable `PATH`, add one with value `C:\jdk1.3\bin`.)

If you previously had an older version of Java on your computer, there might already be a path to its bin directory; delete any old ones.

After setting variable `PATH`, the new path will be in effect in any MSDOS window that you create.

In Windows95 or Windows98, do the following. Choose Start, choose Run, enter `sysedit`, and click OK. Several system-editor windows will be created; select the one that displays `AUTOEXEC.BAT`. Add

```
;C:\jdk1.3\bin
```

to the end of the `PATH` statement. The semicolon is used as a path separator. If there is no `PATH` statement, add one that looks like this:

```
PATH C:\jdk1.3\bin
```

If you previously had an older version of Java on your computer, there might already be a path to its bin directory; delete any old ones.

After setting variable `PATH`, the new path will be in effect in any MSDOS window that you create. You can make the new path take effect in any existing MSDOS window by executing the following command:

```
c:\autoexec.bat
```

Setting variable `CLASSPATH`

Java has to know where user classes are —classes that you have written, for example. The paths of directories in which such classes are stored appears in variable `CLASSPATH`; the procedure for changing `CLASSPATH` is similar to the procedure for changing `PATH`.

The only path that must be in CLASSPATH is the path consisting of a period, ".", which refers to the current directory, i.e. the directory in which a command is being typed and executed. Check this variable and make sure the current directory is on it.

If you were using an older version of Java, variable CLASSPATH may contain a path of the form ...\classes.zip. It's a good idea to remove such paths from variable CLASSPATH, if you are going to stick with Java 2 now.

For more information on how Java finds classes, see the site:

```
http://java.sun.com/j2se/1.3/docs/tooldocs/findingclasses.html
```

B.3   Setting path and classpath (Linux)

You have to let Linux know two things: (0) where the programs (like javac) are, and (1) where certain class files are. We outline how to do this here; you can find more information on the following site:

> http://java.sun.com/products/jdk/1.2/install-linux.html

The following instructions are given under the assumption that Java was installed so that its root is /usr/local/jdk1.3.

Setting variable path

Variable path is used to find executable programs, like javac. To make the Java programs permanently available, you can place in variable path the following path:

```
/usr/local/jdk1.3/bin
```

In any directory, execution of the command shown below will print the known path to program java. If the command is not found, you have to change variable path; if a path is found, make sure it is the one you want (listed above).

```
which java
```

How you set variable path depends on what shell you use. For the C shell (csh) edit file /.cshrc and place at the end of it the command

```
set path=(/usr/local/jdk1.3/bin $path)
```

For the shells ksh, bash or sh, edit file /.profile and place at the end of it the command

```
PATH=/usr/local/jdk1.3/bin:$PATH
```

Now you have to reload the file that was edited; at the same time, you can verify that the path was set correctly. In the C shell, issue the commands

```
source  /.cshrc
which java
```

In the other shells, issue the commands

```
. $HOME/.profile
which java
```

Setting variable CLASSPATH

Java has to know where user classes are —classes that you have written, for example. The paths of directories in which such classes are stored appears in variable CLASSPATH; the procedure for changing CLASSPATH is similar to the procedure for changing PATH.

The only path must be in CLASSPATH is the path consisting of a period, ".", which refers to the current directory, i.e. the directory in which a command is being typed and executed. Check this variable and make sure the current directory is on it.

If you were using an older version of Java, variable CLASSPATH may contain a path of the form ...\classes.zip. It's a good idea to remove such paths from variable CLASSPATH, if you are going to stick with Java 2 now.

For more information on how Java finds classes, see the site:

```
http://java.sun.com/j2se/1.3/docs/tooldocs/findingclasses.html
```

B.4   Compiling and running programs

You can use any editor you wish to write and modify Java programs, which should be in files with the extension .java.

To compile a program Prog.java that appears in directory dir, make dir the current directory and execute the following command.

```
javac  Prog.java
```

If the directory contains several files that you would like to compile, then use the following command.

```
javac  *.java
```

If the program has errors in it, error messages will be printed in the DOS or Unix window. If there are no errors in the program, then it can be executed.

If the program is an application, execute it using the command

```
java  Prog.java
```

where class Prog is the class that contains method main.

Suppose class Prog is an applet —it is a subclass of Applet. Then execute the command

```
appletviewer  f.html
```

where html file f.html contains an applet tag that calls on applet Prog.

B.5   Java API documentation

Appendix D (p. 249) of this *Companion* contains our versions of specifications of many classes of the Java API. This documentation should be sufficient for beginner and intermediate programmers. However, in order to save space, the specifications have been made terse (though still precise), the specifications of many classes have been omitted, and some methods and fields within a class may not appear at all. In order to save space, much has been omitted. You can download an html version of our specs from Wiley's web page.

The complete Sun Java API specification is available on the web at the site given below; it's easy to use, easy to find your way around the multitude of classes —though we prefer our style of specification.

```
http://java.sun.com/j2se/1.3/docs/api/index.htm
```

You can download the Sun Java API Specification onto your own computer, so that you can view it when your computer is not attached to the Internet. But you may not redistribute it. See site

```
http://java.sun.com/docs/redist.html
```

for Sun's distribution policy.

To download the specification, bring up site

```
http://java.sun.com/j2se/1.3/docs.html
```

and follow the instructions. As the instructions say, it is best to put the documentation, as a bunch of directories and html files, in the same directory as the JDK. For example, on a Windows system, the documentation for class `String` will have the following path.

```
C:\jdk1.3\doc\lang\String.html
```

Appendix C
Javadoc

Introduction

To use some methods of a class, you need to study the specification of the class and the specification of those methods. The Java code in the class is of no help. However, specifications are usually given just before the class and before the methods; that is, the specifications and programs are intertwined. So how can you view the specifications without viewing the program?

The Java system has a program, called `javadoc`, that will extract specifications from a program and produce HTML files for them. This program was used by Sun to create the Java API specifications, and we used a version of this program to create Appendix D (p. 249). Using the "doclet" feature of application `javadoc`, we produced LaTeX[1] instead of HTML.

Below, we show you how to write specifications, as comments, that can be extracted from your program by `javadoc` and turned into HTML files.

The basic form of javadoc comments

Fig. C, at the end of this appendix, shows part of class `Integer`. The class itself and each method and field within it is preceded by a comment that begins with "/**", rather than simply "/*".

For each such .java file that `javadoc` is given to process, `javadoc` produces an HTML file (or set of files) that contains the specification part of the class. There is absolutely no code —no method bodies, for example. To illustrate, Fig. C presents the main content of the output produced by `javadoc` for the class in Fig. C.

The class specification appears just after the class header. Also, the header of each public field and method is given, followed by its extracted specification. Private items are not extracted, because they cannot be accessed by the user of the class and hence cannot be considered part of the class specification. For example, field `value` of class `Integer`, which is defined in Fig. C, does not appear in Fig. C.

A comment that directly precedes a method or field and that begins only

---

[1] LaTeX is a typesetting system. It is built on top of the typesetting system TeX). Many computer scientists and mathematicians —and even some journals— use LaTeX to typeset their papers and books.

with "/*" rather than with "/**" will not be extracted by `javadoc`. To be extracted, a comment must directly precede the method or field and must start with "/**".[2]

The real javadoc output

Fig. C shows the basic content of the output of `javadoc` (not the actual output). The actual HTML output is quite elaborate, requiring over 10 files! To see the output for the little class of Fig. C, start *ProgramLive*, turn to lesson 13 (Programming style), and click the web icon in *ProgramLive*'s menu bar. Your browser will open, and you will be able to click one link to look at the .java file and another link to look at the HTML that `javadoc` produced for it. It is quite elaborate. It has a Frames version and a No-Frames version. There is a Help link, which brings up a page that explains how this API document is organized. All this is produced automatically by `javadoc`.

Javadoc tags

Consider the following method:

```
/** = true if and only if argument b is not null and is an
      Integer that contains the same int value as this object
      @param b the object to compare this object with
      @return true if the objects are the same; false otherwise.
   */
public boolean equals(Object b) {
    if (b instanceof Integer)
        return value == ((Integer)b).intValue();
    return false;
}
```

Phrases of the form "`@param` *name description*" and "`@result` *description*" are called *tags*. They are formatted in a special style by `javadoc`. This specification would be extracted and formatted as follows:

```
true if and only if argument b is not null and is an Integer that
contains the same int as this object
Parameters:
    b - the object to compare this object with
Returns:
    true if the objects are the same; false otherwise.
```

---

[2]An earlier version of `javadoc` required that each line of an extracted comment, except the first, start with "* ". This obligation has been removed.

There are a dozen other "tags", besides @param and @result. Look at the web page for *ProgramLive*'s lesson 13; it contains a link that will get you to good documentation for javadoc.

How to use javadoc

In a command-line system, like Unix (or DOS), you run javadoc to extract a specification of a class C1 using a command like

```
javadoc -classpath /usr/java/lib/tools.jar C1.java
```

You can extract the specifications for all classes in the current directory using:

```
javadoc -classpath /usr/java/lib/tools.jar *.java
```

The classpath argument tells javadoc where file tools.jar is. You won't need this argument if variable classpath is initialized suitably. For example, on a Windows system, you should be able to use the command

```
javadoc *.java
```

The LaTeX source for Appendix D was produced using the command

```
javadoc -doclet TexDoclet -classpath /usr/java/lib/tools.jar
        java/*/*.java java/*/*/*.java javax/swing/*.java
```

TexDoclet is a program that we modified to produce LaTeX source files instead of HTML files. The specifications for all the classes in all eight packages were created by running javadoc once.

See Appendix B for information on setting up your system to use javadoc (and the Java compiler javac).

FIGURE C.1. **Part of class Integer**

```
package java.lang;
/** An instance "wraps" a value of primitive type int. */
public final class Integer extends Number implements Comparable {
    /** The value of this Integer */
    private int value;

    /**
      The smallest value of type int
      */
    public static final int MIN_VALUE= 0x80000000;

    /** Constructor: an object that wraps value v */
    public Integer(int v)
        { this.value = v; }

    /** = a positive integer, 0, or a negative integer, depending on
      whether this Integer is greater than, equal to, or less than
      i. A ClassCastException is thrown if i is not an Integer.
      */
    public int compareTo(Integer i) {
        int thisV = this.value;
        int thatV = i.value;
        return (thisV<thatV ? -1 : (thisV==thatV ? 0 : 1));
    }
}
```

FIGURE C.2. **Partial content of the javadoc output**

```
public class Integer, extends Number, implements Comparable;
    An instance ''wraps'' a value of primitive type int.

    public static final int MIN_VALUE
        The smallest value of type int

    public Integer(int v)
        Constructor: an object that wraps value v

    public int compareTo(Integer i)
        = a positive integer, 0, or a negative integer, depending on
        whether this Integer is greater than, equal to, or less than
        i. A ClassCastException is thrown if i is not an Integer.
```

Appendix D

Java API Specifications

This appendix contains specifications of the Java API packages and classes that students in a first-year course on Java might use (or just look at).

We have written our own specifications for two reasons: (1) Sun does not allow their specifications to be distributed in this fashion, and (2) the specs had to be short enough to appear in this book.

We have saved space in several ways.

1. Not all classes are shown.

2. Not all methods within each class are shown.

3. Most deprecated methods are not shown.

4. When displaying a list of inherited methods, we show the length of the list instead of the list if more than 15 methods are inherited.

5. Adjacent methods or fields with similar specifications are described by a single specification.

In the specs, we use notations this[i], this[i..], and this[i..j] to refer to an element or a subpart of this. Here, this may refer to an array, a String, a list, or any similar data structure. The first element is always this[0].

Generally, the presence of this notation in a specification of a method means that the method throws an IndexOutOfBounds-Exception if one of the indices i and j is out of range.

The packages described here are:

- Appendix D.1 java.applet, p. 249

- Appendix D.2 java.awt, p. 250

- Appendix D.3 java.awt.event, p. 268

- Appendix D.4 java.io, p. 271

- Appendix D.5 java.lang, p. 281

- Appendix D.6. java.text, p. 294

- Appendix D.7 java.util, p. 296

- Appendix D.8. javax.swing, p. 311

D.1 Package java.applet

D.1.1 CLASSES

D.1.1.1 CLASS **Applet**

public class Applet extends Panel
   A program embedded in a web page.

CONSTRUCTORS
public Applet()

METHODS
public void destroy()
   Destroy this Applet. Called (only) by the system.
public String getAppletInfo()
   = information about this Applet. Returns null; override to return author, version, etc.

public URL getCodeBase()
   = the URL of this Applet.
public URL getDocumentBase()
   = the URL of the file containing this Applet.
public Locale getLocale()
   = the Locale for this Applet.
public String getParameter(String n)
   = the value of parameter n in the HTML tag. n is case insensitive.
public void init()
   Initialize this Applet. Called by the system when the web page containing this Applet is first visited.
public boolean isActive()
   = "this applet is active": it is active between calls on methods start and stop.
public void resize(int w, int h)
   Set this Applet's width and height to w and h.
public void showStatus(String msg)
   Display msg in the status window of the browser in which this Applet is running.
public void start()
   Start this Applet. Called by the system whenever this Applet's web page is visited.
public void stop()
   Stop this Applet. Called by the system whenever this Applet's web page is exited.

INHERITED FROM Panel (in D.2.2.26, p. 264) : addNotify, getAccessibleContext
INHERITED FROM Container (in D.2.2.10, p. 256) : 52
INHERITED FROM Component (in D.2.2.9, p. 255) : 165

D.2   Package java.awt

Controls the layout of components in a grid of cells.

D.2.1   INTERFACES

D.2.1.1   INTERFACE **Adjustable**

public interface Adjustable
A value from an integer range with discrete increments.

FIELDS

public static final int HORIZONTAL
public static final int VERTICAL
Constants: the horizontal and vertical orientation.

METHODS

public void addAdjustmentListener(AdjustmentListener l)
Register l to respond to this Adjustable's adjustment events.

public int getBlockIncrement()
= this Adjustable's block value increment.

public int getMaximum()
public int getMinimum()
= this Adjustable's maximum (minimum) value.

public int getOrientation()
= this Adjustable's orientation (HORIZONTAL or VERTICAL).

public int getUnitIncrement()
= this Adjustable's unit value increment.

public int getValue()
= this Adjustable's value.

public int getVisibleAmount()
= this Adjustable's proportional indicator length.

public void removeAdjustmentListener(AdjustmentListener l)
Deregister l: it will no longer respond to this Adjustable's events.

public void setBlockIncrement(int b)
Set this Adjustable's block value increment to b.

public void setMaximum(int m)
public void setMinimum(int m)
Set this Adjustable's maximum (minimum) value to m.

public void setUnitIncrement(int u)
Set this Adjustable's unit value increment to u.

public void setValue(int u)
Set Adjustable's value to u.

public void setVisibleAmount(int v)
Set this Adjustable's proportional indicator length to v.

D.2.1.2   INTERFACE **Shape**

public interface Shape
A geometric 2D shape.

METHODS

public boolean contains(double x, double y)
= "this Shape contains (x,y)".

public boolean contains(double x, double y,
double w, double h)
= "this Shape contains the rectangle given
by (x,y,w,h)".

public Rectangle getBounds()
= a rectangle that contains this Shape.

public boolean intersects(double x, double y,
double w, double h)
= "this Shape intersects the rectangle
given by (x,y,w,h)".

D.2.2 CLASSES

D.2.2.1 CLASS **AWTEvent**

public abstract class AWTEvent extends
EventObject
The superclass of all events in the Abstract Window Toolkit.

FIELDS

public static final long
COMPONENT_EVENT_MASK
public static final long
CONTAINER_EVENT_MASK
public static final long
FOCUS_EVENT_MASK
public static final long KEY_EVENT_MASK
public static final long
MOUSE_EVENT_MASK
public static final long
MOUSE_MOTION_EVENT_MASK
public static final long
WINDOW_EVENT_MASK
public static final long
ACTION_EVENT_MASK
public static final long
ADJUSTMENT_EVENT_MASK
public static final long ITEM_EVENT_MASK
public static final long TEXT_EVENT_MASK
public static final long
INPUT_METHOD_EVENT_MASK
public static final long PAINT_EVENT_MASK
public static final long
INVOCATION_EVENT_MASK
public static final long
HIERARCHY_EVENT_MASK
public static final long

HIERARCHY_BOUNDS_EVENT_MASK
public static final int RESERVED_ID_MAX
Event masks, useful for determining which
event happened.

CONSTRUCTORS

public AWTEvent(Event ev)
An AWTEvent based on ev.

public AWTEvent(Object so, int id)
An AWTEvent associated with so and of
type id, one of the class constants.

METHODS

public int getID()
= This AWTEvent's type (one of the class
constants).

public String toString()
= this AWTEvent's String representation.

INHERITED FROM EventObject : getSource,
toString

D.2.2.2 CLASS **BorderLayout**

public class BorderLayout extends Object
implements LayoutManager2,
Serializable
Controls the layout of a container in five
regions: NORTH, SOUTH, EAST, WEST,
and CENTER.

FIELDS

public static final String NORTH
public static final String SOUTH
public static final String EAST
public static final String WEST
public static final String CENTER
Constants: the location of a component in
this BorderLayout.

CONSTRUCTORS

public BorderLayout()
A BorderLayout with no gaps between
components.

public BorderLayout(int hg, int vg)
A BorderLayout with horizontal and vertical gaps hg and vg between components.

METHODS

public int getHgap()
public int getVgap()

= the horizontal or vertical gap between components.

public void setHgap(int g)
public void setVgap(int g)
Set this BorderLayout's horizontal (H) or vertical (V) gap between components to g.

public String toString()
= this BorderLayout's String representation.

D.2.2.3   Class **Button**

public class Button extends Component
implements Accessible
A labeled clickable button.

CONSTRUCTORS

public Button()
public Button(String s)
A Button with an empty text label (or with label s).

METHODS

public synchronized void
addActionListener(ActionListener l)
Register l to respond to this Button's action events.

public String getLabel()
= this Button's text label.

public synchronized void
removeActionListener(ActionListener l)
Deregister l: it will no longer respond to this Button's events.

public void setLabel(String s)
Set this Button's text label to s.

INHERITED FROM Component (in D.2.2.9, p. 255) : 165

D.2.2.4   Class **Canvas**

public class Canvas extends Component
implements Accessible
A rectangular area on which to draw. Extend Canvas and override method paint to draw on the area.

CONSTRUCTORS

public Canvas()
A blank Canvas.

METHODS

public void paint(Graphics g)
Repaint this Canvas. This method is called by the system, not the application.

INHERITED FROM Component (in D.2.2.9, p. 255) : 165

D.2.2.5   Class **Checkbox**

public class Checkbox extends Component
implements ItemSelectable, Accessible
A clickable component. Clicking toggles between on (checked) and off (unchecked).

CONSTRUCTORS

public Checkbox()
An unchecked CheckBox with no text label.

public Checkbox(String s)
An unchecked Checkbox with text label s.

public Checkbox(String s, boolean st)
A Checkbox with text label s that is checked iff st).

public Checkbox(String s, boolean st,
CheckboxGroup g)
A Checkbox with text label s that is checked iff st and that is part of g.

METHODS

public synchronized void
addItemListener(ItemListener l)
Register l to respond to this Checkbox's item events.

public CheckboxGroup getCheckboxGroup()
= this Checkbox's group.

public String getLabel()
= this Checkbox's text label (null if none).

public boolean getState()
= "this Checkbox is on".

public synchronized void
removeItemListener(ItemListener l)
Deregister l: it will no longer respond to this Checkbox's events.

public void
setCheckboxGroup(CheckboxGroup g)
Set this Checkbox's group to g.

public void setLabel(String s)
Set this Checkbox's text label to s.

public void setState(boolean st)
Set this Checkbox's state to checked iff st.

INHERITED FROM Component (in D.2.2.9,
p. 255) : 165

D.2.2.6   CLASS **CheckboxGroup**

public class CheckboxGroup extends Object
implements Serializable
A set of related Checkboxes. Clicking one
of them checks it and unchecks the others.

CONSTRUCTORS
public CheckboxGroup()
An empty CheckboxGroup.

METHODS
public Checkbox getSelectedCheckbox()
= the Checkbox that is on (null if all off).
public void setSelectedCheckbox(Checkbox b)
Check b and uncheck all other Checkboxes
in this CheckBoxGroup.
public String toString()
= this CheckboxGroup's String representation.

D.2.2.7   CLASS **Choice**

public class Choice extends Component
implements ItemSelectable, Accessible
A pop-up menu of selectable items. Clicking on the menu allows selection of a particular item.

CONSTRUCTORS
public Choice()
A Choice with no items in it.

METHODS
public void add(String s)
public void addItem(String s)
Append s to this Choice's list of items.
public synchronized void
addItemListener(ItemListener l)
Register l to respond to this Choice's item
events.
public String getItem(int ind)
= item this[ind].
public int getItemCount()
= this Choice's number of items.
public int getSelectedIndex()
= the index of the currently selected item.

public synchronized String getSelectedItem()
= a String representation of the currently
selected item.
public synchronized Object[]
getSelectedObjects()
= an array of length 1 that contains the
selected item (null if none).
public void insert(String s, int ind)
Insert item s at this[ind], shifting this[ind..]
to make room.
public void remove(int ind)
Remove item this[ind], shifting
this[ind+1..] to fill the hole.
public void remove(String item)
Remove item from this Choice.
public void removeAll()
Empty this Choice.
public synchronized void
removeItemListener(ItemListener l)
Deregister l: it will no longer respond to
this Choice's events.
public synchronized void select(int ind)
public synchronized void select(String s)
Select item this[ind] (or the one whose
name is s).

INHERITED FROM Component (in D.2.2.9,
p. 255) : 165

D.2.2.8   CLASS **Color**

public class Color extends Object
implements Paint, Serializable
A color.

FIELDS
public static final Color white
public static final Color lightGray
public static final Color gray
public static final Color darkGray
public static final Color black
public static final Color red
public static final Color pink
public static final Color orange
public static final Color yellow
public static final Color green
public static final Color magenta
public static final Color cyan
public static final Color blue
Constants: colors in the sRGB space.

CONSTRUCTORS

public Color(int r, int g, int b)
   A Color with components r (red), g (green), and b (blue), all in the range 0..255.

METHODS

public Color brighter()
public Color darker()
   = a brighter (darker) version of this Color.
public boolean equals(Object b)
   = "b represents the same color as this Color".
public int getBlue()
public int getGreen()
public int getRed()
   = this Color's blue, green, and red components.
public String toString()
   = this Color's String representation.

D.2.2.9   CLASS **Component**

public abstract class Component extends Object implements ImageObserver, MenuContainer, Serializable
Any graphical AWT object on the screen, except for menu-related items. A Component has the following properties:
It can be *enabled*: it responds to events.
It can be *visible*: when its parent Container is visible, it is.
It can be *showing*: when it is visible and its parent container is showing, this Component is showing.
It can be *valid*: it is laid out correctly.

FIELDS

public static final float TOP_ALIGNMENT
public static final float CENTER_ALIGNMENT
public static final float BOTTOM_ALIGNMENT
public static final float LEFT_ALIGNMENT
public static final float RIGHT_ALIGNMENT
   Constants: component alignment.

CONSTRUCTORS

protected Component()
   A generic Component.

METHODS

public synchronized void add(PopupMenu p)
   Add p to this Component.
public synchronized void addComponentListener(ComponentListener l)
public synchronized void addFocusListener(FocusListener l)
public synchronized void addKeyListener(KeyListener l)
public synchronized void addMouseListener(MouseListener l)
public synchronized void addMouseMotionListener(MouseMotionListener l)
   Register l to respond to this Component's events.
public boolean contains(int x, int y)
public boolean contains(Point p)
   = "this Component contains point (x,y) or p".
public Color getBackground()
public Rectangle getBounds()
public Font getFont()
public Color getForeground()
   = this Component's background color, bounds, font, and foreground color.
public int getHeight()
public Locale getLocale()
public Point getLocation()
   = this Component's height, locale, and top-left corner within its parent Container.
public Container getParent()
public Dimension getSize()
public int getWidth()
   = this Component's parent, size or width
public int getX()
public int getY()
   = this Component's x- and y-coordinate.
public void invalidate()
   Mark this Component and its ancestors as laid out incorrectly.
public boolean isEnabled()
public boolean isShowing()
public boolean isValid()
public boolean isVisible()
   = "this Component is enabled (showing, valid, or visible)".
public void paint(Graphics g)
   Paint this Component using g. Never call this method: call repaint instead.
public synchronized void remove(MenuComponent p)

Remove p from this Component.

public synchronized void removeComponentListener(ComponentListener l)

public synchronized void removeFocusListener(FocusListener l)

public synchronized void removeKeyListener(KeyListener l)

public synchronized void removeMouseListener(MouseListener l)

public synchronized void removeMouseMotionListener(MouseMotionListener l)

Deregister l: it will no longer respond to this Component's events.

public void repaint()

public void repaint(int x, int y, int w, int h)

Repaint this component (or the subrectangle at (x,y), width w, height h).

public void setBackground(Color c)

Set Component's background color to c.

public void setBounds(int x, int y, int w, int h)

public void setBounds(Rectangle r)

Move this Component to (x,y) (or (r.x,r.y)) and change its width and height to w and h (or r.width and r.height).

public void setEnabled(boolean b)

Enable this Component iff b.

public void setFont(Font f)

Set this Component's font to f.

public void setForeground(Color c)

Set this Component's foreground color to c.

public void setLocale(Locale l)

= this Component's height, locale, and top-left corner within its parent Container.

public void setLocation(int x, int y)

public void setLocation(Point p)

Move this Component to (x,y) (or p) within its parent Container.

public void setSize(Dimension d)

public void setSize(int w, int h)

Set this Component's size to (w,h) (or d).

public void setVisible(boolean b)

Show this Component if b; hide it if not b).

public String toString()

= this Component's String representation.

public void validate()

Lay out Component, if not yet laid out.

D.2.2.10   CLASS **Container**

public class Container extends Component

A list of Component, e.g. Frame. The order is important: earlier Components may obscure later ones.

CONSTRUCTORS

public Container()

An empty Container.

METHODS

public Component add(Component comp)

Append comp to this Container. Return comp.

public Component add(Component comp, int ind)

Insert comp at this[ind], shifting this[ind..] to make room. Return comp.

public synchronized void addContainerListener(ContainerListener l)

Register l to respond to this Container's container events.

public Component getComponent(int n)

= this[n].

public Component getComponentAt(int x, int y)

public Component getComponentAt(Point p)

= the Component of this Container that contains (x,y) or p.

public int getComponentCount()

= this Container's number of Components.

public Component[] getComponents()

= this Container's Components.

public LayoutManager getLayout()

= this Container's layout manager.

public void paint(Graphics g)

Paint this component. (If paint is overridden, be sure to call super.paint(g).)

public void remove(Component comp)

Remove comp from this Container.

public void remove(int index)

Remove this[ind], shifting this[ind+1..] to fill the hole.

public void removeAll()

Empty this Container.

public synchronized void removeContainerListener(ContainerListener l)

Deregister l: it will no longer respond to this Container's events.

public void setFont(Font f)
  Set this Container's font to f.

public void setLayout(LayoutManager m)
  Set this Container's layout manager to m.

INHERITED FROM Component (in D.2.2.9, p. 255) : 165

D.2.2.11   CLASS **Cursor**

public class Cursor extends Object
    implements Serializable
  A cursor on the screen.

FIELDS

public static final int DEFAULT_CURSOR
public static final int CROSSHAIR_CURSOR
public static final int TEXT_CURSOR
public static final int WAIT_CURSOR
public static final int SW_RESIZE_CURSOR
public static final int SE_RESIZE_CURSOR
public static final int NW_RESIZE_CURSOR
public static final int NE_RESIZE_CURSOR
public static final int N_RESIZE_CURSOR
public static final int S_RESIZE_CURSOR
public static final int W_RESIZE_CURSOR
public static final int E_RESIZE_CURSOR
public static final int HAND_CURSOR
public static final int MOVE_CURSOR
  Constants: cursor types.
public static final int CUSTOM_CURSOR
  The type associated with all custom cursors.

CONSTRUCTORS

public Cursor(int t)
  A Cursor of type t (one of the static constants).

METHODS

public static Cursor getDefaultCursor()
  = the default system Cursor.
public String getName()
  = this Cursor's name.
public static Cursor getPredefinedCursor(int t)
  = a Cursor of type t (one of the class constants).
public int getType()

= this Cursor's type.
public String toString()
  = this Cursor's String representation.

D.2.2.12   CLASS **Dimension**

public class Dimension extends
    Dimension2D implements Serializable
  A width and height.

FIELDS

public int width
public int height
  this Dimension's width and height.

CONSTRUCTORS

public Dimension()
public Dimension(int w, int h)
  A Dimension with width and height 0 (or w and h).

METHODS

public boolean equals(Object b)
  = "b is equal to this Dimension".
public double getHeight()
public Dimension getSize()
public double getWidth()
  = this Dimension's height, size, and width.
public void setSize(Dimension d)
public void setSize(double w, double h)
public void setSize(int w, int h)
  Set this Dimension's size to (w,h) or to (d.width,d.height).
public String toString()
  = this Dimension's String representation.

INHERITED FROM Dimension2D : clone, getHeight, getWidth, setSize

D.2.2.13   CLASS **FileDialog**

public class FileDialog extends Dialog
  A window that prompts the user to select a file.

FIELDS

public static final int LOAD
public static final int SAVE
  Constants: whether the selected file is to be read or written.

CONSTRUCTORS

public FileDialog(Frame parent)
public FileDialog(Frame parent, String s)
> A FileDialog owned by parent, with an empty title or title s, for loading (reading) a file.
public FileDialog(Frame parent, String s, int mode)
> A FileDialog owned by parent with title s; mode is either LOAD or SAVE.

METHODS

public String getDirectory()
> = this FileDialog's current directory.
public String getFile()
> = this FileDialog's selected file (null if none).
public int getMode()
> = LOAD or SAVE, depending on file mode.
public void setDirectory(String d)
> Set this FileDialog's directory to d.
public void setFile(String f)
> Set this FileDialog's selected file to f. (Should be called before FileDialog is shown.)
public void setMode(int m)
> Set this FileDialog's mode to m (LOAD or SAVE).

INHERITED FROM Dialog : addNotify, dispose, getAccessibleContext, getTitle, hide, isModal, isResizable, paramString, setModal, setResizable, setTitle, show
INHERITED FROM Window (in D.2.2.35, p. 268) : 27
INHERITED FROM Container (in D.2.2.10, p. 256) : 52
INHERITED FROM Component (in D.2.2.9, p. 255) : 165

D.2.2.14   CLASS **FlowLayout**

public class FlowLayout extends Object implements LayoutManager, Serializable
> Controls the layout of components in a container: left to right in the order the components were added. If there is no room on a row, a new row is started.

FIELDS

public static final int LEFT
public static final int CENTER
public static final int RIGHT
> Constants: whether rows should be left, center (default), or right justified.

CONSTRUCTORS

public FlowLayout()
public FlowLayout(int al)
> A FlowLayout with centered alignment or alignment al (one of the class constants).

METHODS

public int getAlignment()
> = this FlowLayout's alignment.
public void setAlignment(int al)
> Set this FlowLayout's alignment to al.
public String toString()
> = this FlowLayout's String representation.

D.2.2.15   CLASS **Font**

public class Font extends Object implements Serializable
> A font. You can get 3 different names from a Font: its logical name, as used in JDK1.1, the font face name (e.g. Helvetica Bold), and the family name (e.g. Helvetica).

FIELDS

public static final int PLAIN
public static final int BOLD
public static final int ITALIC
> Constants: the font style.

CONSTRUCTORS

public Font(String n, int s, int i)
> A Font with name n, style s, and size i. See the SUN API spec for full details.

METHODS

public boolean equals(Object b)
> = "b != null and b represents the same font as this Font".
public String getFamily()
public String getFamily(Locale loc)
> = this Font's family name, e.g. Helvetica (localized for locale loc).

public String getFontName()
public String getFontName(Locale loc)
= this Font's font face name (localized for locale loc).
public String getName()
= this Font's logical name.
public int getSize()
public float getSize2D()
= this Font's point size.
public int getStyle()
= this Font's style (PLAIN, BOLD, ITALIC, or BOLD+ITALIC).
public boolean isBold()
public boolean isItalic()
public boolean isPlain()
= "this Font's style is BOLD, ITALIC, or PLAIN".

D.2.2.16 CLASS **Frame**

public class Frame extends Window
        implements MenuContainer
A window with a border and title. The default layout is BorderLayout.

FIELDS

public static final int NORMAL
public static final int ICONIFIED
Constants: normal or iconified window state.

CONSTRUCTORS

public Frame()
public Frame(String s)
An empty Frame with no title (or title s), not yet visible on the screen.

METHODS

public MenuBar getMenuBar()
public synchronized int getState()
public String getTitle()
= this Frame's menu bar (null if none) or NORMAL/ICONIFIED state or title
public boolean isResizable()
= "this Frame is resizable by the user".
public void remove(MenuComponent m)
Remove menu bar m from this Frame.
public void setMenuBar(MenuBar mb)
Set this Frame's MenuBar to mb.
public void setResizable(boolean b)

Set this Frame's resizable attribute to b.
public synchronized void setState(int s)
Set this Frame's state to s (ICONIFIED or NORMAL).
public synchronized void setTitle(String s)
Set this Frame's title to s.

INHERITED FROM Window (in D.2.2.35, p. 268) : 27
INHERITED FROM Container (in D.2.2.10, p. 256) : 52
INHERITED FROM Component (in D.2.2.9, p. 255) : 165

D.2.2.17 CLASS **Graphics**

public abstract class Graphics extends
        Object
A drawing area associated with a Component.

METHODS

public abstract void clearRect(int x, int y, int w, int h)
Fill the rectangle (top-left corner (x,y), width w, height h) with the background color.
public void draw3DRect(int x, int y, int w, int h, boolean b)
Draw the outline of a 3-D highlighted rectangle (top-left corner (x,y), width w, height h). If b, the rectangle appears to be raised above the surface.
public abstract void drawArc(int x, int y, int w, int h, int start, int ang)
Draw the outline of an elliptical arc beginning at angle start. (0 degrees indicates the positive x-axis.) ang is the counter-clockwise angle of the sweep of the arc. The arc fits in the rectangle (top-left corner (x,y), width w, height h).
public abstract void drawLine(int x1, int y1, int x2, int y2)
Draw a line from (x1,y1) to (x2,y2).
public abstract void drawOval(int x, int y, int w, int h)
Draw the outline of the oval that fits in the rectangle (top-left corner (x,y), width w, height h).
public abstract void drawPolygon(int[] xP, int[] yP, int nP)
Connect the points (xP[i],yP[i]), 0 <= i

<nP, including a segment connecting the first and last points.

public abstract void drawPolyline(int[] xP, int[] yP, int nP)
Connect the points (xP[i],yP[i]), 0 <= i <nP.

public void drawRect(int x, int y, int w, int h)
Draw the outline of the rectangle (top-left corner (x,y), width w, height h).

public abstract void drawRoundRect(int x, int y, int w, int h, int aw, int ah)
Draw the outline of the rounded rectangle (top-left corner (x,y), width w, height h); aw and ah give the horizontal and vertical widths of the arcs.

public abstract void drawString(String s, int x, int y)
Draw s, with its baseline at (x,y).

public void fill3DRect(int x, int y, int w, int h, boolean b)
Fill a 3-D highlighted rectangle (top-left corner (x,y), width w, height h). If b, the rectangle appears to be raised above the surface.

public abstract void fillArc(int x, int y, int w, int h, int start, int ang)
Fill an elliptical arc beginning at angle start. (0 degrees indicates the positive x-axis.) ang is the counter-clockwise angle of the sweep of the arc. The arc fits in the rectangle (top-left corner (x,y), width w, height h).

public abstract void fillOval(int x, int y, int w, int h)
Fill the oval that fits in the rectangle (top-left corner (x,y), width w, height h).

public abstract void fillPolygon(int[] xP, int[] yP, int nP)
Fill in the region defined by the points (xP[i],yP[i]), 0 <= i <nP, including a segment connecting the first and last points.

public void fillPolygon(Polygon p)
Fill the interior of p.

public abstract void fillRect(int x, int y, int w, int h)
Draw the outline of the rectangle (top-left corner (x,y), width w, height h).

public abstract void fillRoundRect(int x, int y, int w, int h, int aw, int ah)
Fill the rounded rectangle (top-left corner (x,y), width w, height h); aw and ah give the horizontal and vertical widths of the arcs.

public abstract Color getColor()
public abstract Font getFont()
= this Graphics's color and font.

public abstract void setColor(Color c)
Set this Graphics's color to c.

public abstract void setFont(Font f)
Set this Graphics's font to f.

public String toString()
= this Graphics' String representation.

public abstract void translate(int x, int y)
Translate this Graphics's origin by (x,y).

D.2.2.18 CLASS GridBagConstraints

public class GridBagConstraints extends Object implements Cloneable, Serializable
Constraints for a single component in a GridBagLayout. See Sun's APIs for more details.

FIELDS

public static final int NONE
public static final int BOTH
public static final int HORIZONTAL
public static final int VERTICAL
Constants: how to resize the component horizontally and vertically.

public static final int CENTER
public static final int NORTH
public static final int NORTHEAST
public static final int EAST
public static final int SOUTHEAST
public static final int SOUTH
public static final int SOUTHWEST
public static final int WEST
public static final int NORTHWEST
Constants: the component's justification.

public int gridx
public int gridy
public int gridwidth
public int gridheight
The visible part of this GridBag spans this[gridy .. gridy + gridheight - 1, gridx .. gridx + gridwidth - 1].

public double weightx
public double weighty
Proportional distribution of surrounding horizontal or vertical space.

public int anchor
  Where to place the component (one of the
  justification constants).
public int fill
  How to resize the component (one of the
  resizing constants).
public Insets insets
  The amount of space around the component.

CONSTRUCTORS

public GridBagConstraints()
  A centered instance with width and height
  1.

METHODS

public Object clone()
  = a copy of this GridBagConstraints.

D.2.2.19 CLASS GridBagLayout

public class GridBagLayout extends Object
    implements LayoutManager2,
    Serializable
  Controls the layout of Components in a
  grid of cells of (perhaps) different sizes.
  Each Component can occupy one or more
  cells, and each is controlled by an instance
  of GridBagConstraints that indicates how
  the Component is laid out.
    See Sun's APIs for more details.

CONSTRUCTORS

public GridBagLayout()
  A GridBag with a default GridBagConstraints that will apply to all Components,
  unless otherwise specified.

METHODS

public GridBagConstraints
    getConstraints(Component comp)
  = a clone of comp's constraints.
protected GridBagLayoutInfo
    GetLayoutInfo(Container parent, int
    sizeflag)
  Print the layout constraints. Useful for debugging.
public Point location(int x, int y)
  = the index of the cell that contains point
  (x,y).

protected GridBagConstraints
    lookupConstraints(Component comp)
  = comp's constraints.
public void setConstraints(Component comp,
    GridBagConstraints cons)
  Set the constraints for component comp to
  cons.
public String toString()
  = this GridBagLayout's String representation.

D.2.2.20 CLASS GridLayout

public class GridLayout extends Object
    implements LayoutManager,
    Serializable
  Controls the layout of components in a
  grid of cells. Components appear in the order in which they were added, left to right,
  top to bottom. If the number of rows (or
  columns) is initially 0, rows (or columns)
  are created as they are needed. The numbers of rows and columns can't be zero at
  the same time.

CONSTRUCTORS

public GridLayout(int r, int c)
  A GridLayout with r rows and c columns.
public GridLayout(int rows, int cols, int hg,
    int vg)
  A GridLayout with r rows, c columns, and
  horizontal and vertical gaps of hg and vg.

METHODS

public int getColumns()
public int getHgap()
public int getRows()
public int getVgap()
  = the number of columns, horizontal gap,
  number of rows, and vertical gap.
public void setColumns(int x)
public void setHgap(int x)
public void setRows(int x)
public void setVgap(int x)
  Set the number of columns, horizontal
  gap, number of rows, vertical gap to x.
public String toString()
  = this GridLayout's String representation.

D.2.2.21   CLASS **Label**

public class Label extends Component
    implements Accessible
  A graphical label containing text.

FIELDS

public static final int LEFT
public static final int CENTER
public static final int RIGHT
  Constants: the alignment of the text.

CONSTRUCTORS

public Label()
public Label(String s)
  A Label with left-justified text "" (or s).

public Label(String s, int al)
  A Label with text s and alignment al (one
  of the class constants).

METHODS

public int getAlignment()
public String getText()
  = this Label's alignment and text.

public synchronized void setAlignment(int al)
  Set this Label's alignment to al (one of the
  class constants).

public void setText(String s)
  Set this Label's text to s.

INHERITED FROM Component (in D.2.2.9,
  p. 255) : 165

D.2.2.22   CLASS **Menu**

public class Menu extends MenuItem
    implements MenuContainer, Accessible
  A drop-down menu in a menu bar (option-
  ally, can be "torn off").

CONSTRUCTORS

public Menu()
  A Menu named "". Cannot be torn off.

public Menu(String s)
  A Menu named s. Cannot be torn off.

public Menu(String s, boolean b)
  A Menu named s. Can be torn off iff b.

METHODS

public MenuItem add(MenuItem mi)
  Append mi to this Menu and return mi

(Remove mi from another menu if it is in
one.)

public void add(String s)
  Append a MenuItem named s to this Menu.

public void addSeparator()
  Append a separator line to this Menu.

public MenuItem getItem(int ind)
  = item this[ind].

public int getItemCount()
  = the number of items in this Menu.

public void insert(MenuItem mi, int ind)
  Insert mi (or a MenuItem named s) at
  this[ind], shifting this[ind..] to make room.

public void insert(String s, int ind)
  Insert mi (or a MenuItem named s) at
  this[ind], shifting this[in..] to make room.

public void insertSeparator(int ind)
  Insert a separator at this[ind], shifting
  this[ind..] to make room.

public boolean isTearOff()
  = "this Menu can be torn off".

public void remove(int ind)
  Remove this[ind], shifting this[ind+1..] to
  fill the hole.

public void remove(MenuComponent it)
  Remove it from this Menu.

public void removeAll()
  Empty this Menu.

INHERITED FROM MenuItem (in D.2.2.25,
  p. 263) : 22

INHERITED FROM MenuComponent (in
  D.2.2.24, p. 263) : dispatchEvent,
  getAccessibleContext, getFont, getName,
  getParent, getPeer, getTreeLock,
  paramString, postEvent, processEvent,
  removeNotify, setFont, setName, toString

D.2.2.23   CLASS **MenuBar**

public class MenuBar extends
    MenuComponent implements
    MenuContainer, Accessible
  A menu bar. See Frame.setMenuBar.

CONSTRUCTORS

public MenuBar()
  An empty MenuBar.

METHODS

public Menu add(Menu m)

Append m to this MenuBar.

public void deleteShortcut(MenuShortcut s)
Delete s.

public Menu getHelpMenu()
= this MenuBar's help menu.

public Menu getMenu(int ind)
= this[ind].

public int getMenuCount()
= this MenuBar's number of menus.

public MenuItem
getShortcutMenuItem(MenuShortcut s)
= the MenuItem associated with s (null if
none).

public void remove(int ind)
Remove this[ind], shifting this[ind+1..] to
fill the hole.

public void remove(MenuComponent m)
Remove m from this MenuBar.

public void setHelpMenu(Menu m)
Set this MenuBar's help menu to m.

public synchronized Enumeration shortcuts()
= the shortcuts in this MenuBar.

INHERITED FROM MenuComponent (in
D.2.2.24, p. 263) : dispatchEvent,
getAccessibleContext, getFont, getName,
getParent, getPeer, getTreeLock,
paramString, postEvent, processEvent,
removeNotify, setFont, setName, toString

D.2.2.24   CLASS **MenuComponent**

public abstract class MenuComponent
extends Object implements Serializable
A menu-related component. Subclasses include Menu, MenuItem, and MenuBar.

CONSTRUCTORS

public MenuComponent()
An empty MenuComponent.

METHODS

public Font getFont()
public String getName()
public MenuContainer getParent()
= this MenuComponent's font (null if
none), name, and parent.

public void setFont(Font s)
public void setName(String s)
Set this MenuComponent's font and name
to s.

public String toString()
= this MenuComponent's String representation.

D.2.2.25   CLASS **MenuItem**

public class MenuItem extends
MenuComponent implements
Accessible
An item in a menu. Each MenuItem is ei-
ther *enabled* or *disabled* –disabled Menu-
Items cannot be selected.

CONSTRUCTORS

public MenuItem()
An empty, enabled MenuItem with no keyboard shortcut.

public MenuItem(String s)
public MenuItem(String s, MenuShortcut sh)
A MenuItem with label s and no keyboard
shortcut (or shortcut sh). Disabled iff s is
"-" (indicates a separator).

METHODS

public synchronized void
addActionListener(ActionListener l)
Register l to respond to this MenuItem's
action events.

public void deleteShortcut()
Delete this MenuItem's keyboard shortcut.

public String getLabel()
public MenuShortcut getShortcut()
= this MenuItem's label and keyboard
shortcut (null if none).

public boolean isEnabled()
= "this MenuItem is enabled".

public synchronized void
removeActionListener(ActionListener l)
Deregister l: it will no longer respond to
this MenuItem's events.

public synchronized void setEnabled(boolean
b)
Set this MenuItem's enabled attribute to
b.

public synchronized void setLabel(String l)
Set this MenuItem's label to l (use null for
no label).

public void setShortcut(MenuShortcut sh)
Set this MenuItem's keyboard shortcut to
sh.

INHERITED FROM MenuComponent (in
D.2.2.24, p. 263) : dispatchEvent,
getAccessibleContext, getFont, getName,
getParent, getPeer, getTreeLock,
paramString, postEvent, processEvent,
removeNotify, setFont, setName, toString

D.2.2.26   CLASS Panel

public class Panel extends Container
    implements Accessible
    A simple container. Add Components to it
    using inherited Container.add methods.

CONSTRUCTORS

public Panel()
public Panel(LayoutManager m)
    An empty Panel with FlowLayout layout
    manager (or m).

INHERITED FROM Container (in D.2.2.10,
p. 256) : 52
INHERITED FROM Component (in D.2.2.9,
p. 255) : 165

D.2.2.27   CLASS Point

public class Point extends Point2D
    implements Serializable
    A coordinate (x, y).

FIELDS

public int x
public int y
    The horizontal and vertical coordinates.

CONSTRUCTORS

public Point()
    A Point (0, 0).
public Point(int x, int y)
public Point(Point p)
    A Point (x,y) or (p.x,p.y).

METHODS

public boolean equals(Object b)
    = "b and this Point represent the same
    point (x,y)".
public Point getLocation()
    = a copy of this Point.
public double getX()
public double getY()

= this Point's x and y coordinate.
public void move(int x, int y)
public void setLocation(double x, double y)
public void setLocation(int x, int y)
public void setLocation(Point p)
    Set this Point to (x,y) or (p.x,p.y).
public String toString()
    = this Point's String representation.
public void translate(int x, int y)
    Set this Point to (this.x + x, this.y + y).

INHERITED FROM Point2D : clone, distance,
distanceSq, equals, getX, getY, hashCode,
setLocation

D.2.2.28   CLASS Polygon

public class Polygon extends Object
    implements Shape, Serializable
    A polygon.

FIELDS

public int npoints
    This Polygon's number of points.
public int xpoints
public int ypoints
    x and y coordinate lists.

CONSTRUCTORS

public Polygon()
    A Polygon with no points.
public Polygon(int[] xpoints, int[] ypoints, int
    n)
    A Polygon with n points, which are de-
    scribed by xpoints and ypoints. Throw a
    NegativeArraySizeException if n <0.

METHODS

public void addPoint(int x, int y)
    Append (x,y) to this Polygon.
public boolean contains(double x, double y)
    = "(x, y) is inside this Polygon".
public boolean contains(double x, double y,
    double w, double h)
    = "the rectangle at location (x,y) with
    width w and height h is inside this Poly-
    gon".
public boolean contains(int x, int y)
public boolean contains(Point p)
    = "(x, y) or p is inside this Polygon".
public Rectangle getBounds()

= the smallest rectangle that encloses this Polygon.

public boolean intersects(double x, double y, double w, double h)
= "The interior of this Polygon intersects the interior of the rectangle with top-left corner (x, y), width w, and height h".

public void translate(int x, int y)
Add (x, y) to each point of this Polygon.

D.2.2.29   CLASS **PopupMenu**

public class PopupMenu extends Menu
A menu that can be "popped up".

CONSTRUCTORS

public PopupMenu()
public PopupMenu(String s)
A popup menu with title "" or s.

METHODS

public void show(Component origin, int x, int y)
Pop up this PopupMenu at location (x,y). Throw a RuntimeException if this Popup-Menu's parent is not itself showing.

INHERITED FROM Menu (in D.2.2.22, p. 262) : 17
INHERITED FROM MenuItem (in D.2.2.25, p. 263) : 22
INHERITED FROM MenuComponent (in D.2.2.24, p. 263) : dispatchEvent, getAccessibleContext, getFont, getName, getParent, getPeer, getTreeLock, paramString, postEvent, processEvent, removeNotify, setFont, setName, toString

D.2.2.30   CLASS **Rectangle**

public class Rectangle extends Rectangle2D
implements Shape, Serializable
A rectangular area described by its top-left point (x,y), width, and height.

FIELDS

public int x
public int y
public int width
public int height
This Rectangle's x and y coordinates,

width, and height.

CONSTRUCTORS

public Rectangle(int x, int y, int w, int h)
A Rectangle with top-left corner (x,y), width w, and height h.

public Rectangle(Point p, Dimension d)
A Rectangle with top-left corner p and width and height given by d.

public Rectangle(Rectangle r)
A Rectangle with the same attributes as r.

METHODS

public void add(int x, int y)
public void add(Point p)
public void add(Rectangle r)
Change this Rectangle to the smallest one that contains it and (x,y), p, or r.

public boolean contains(int x, int y)
= "this Rectangle contains point (x,y)".

public boolean contains(int x, int y, int w, int h)
= "this Rectangle entirely contains the Rectangle at location (x,y) with width w and height h".

public boolean contains(Point p)
public boolean contains(Rectangle r)
= "this Rectangle contains p or r".

public boolean equals(Object b)
= "this Rectangle and b are the same".

public double getHeight()
public Point getLocation()
public Dimension getSize()
public double getWidth()
public double getX()
public double getY()
= this Rectangle's height, location (top-left corner), size, width, X-coordinate, and Y-coordinate.

public Rectangle intersection(Rectangle r)
= the intersection of this Rectangle and r.

public boolean intersects(Rectangle r)
= "this Rectangle and r intersect".

public boolean isEmpty()
= "this Rectangle is empty (has a non-positive width or height)".

public void setBounds(int x, int y, int w, int h)
Set this Rectangle to have location (x,y), width w, and height h.

public void setBounds(Rectangle r)

Set this Rectangle to match r.

public void setLocation(int x, int y)
public void setLocation(Point p)
Set this Rectangle's location to (x,y) or p.

public void setRect(double x, double y,
double w, double h)
Set this Rectangle to have location (x,y),
width w, and height h.

public void setSize(Dimension d)
public void setSize(int w, int h)
Set this Rectangle's width and height to w
and h or to d.width and d.height.

public String toString()
= this Rectangle's String representation.

public void translate(int x, int y)
Set this Rectangle's location to (getX()+x,
getY()+y).

public Rectangle union(Rectangle r)
= the smallest rectangle that contains this
Rectangle and r.

INHERITED FROM Rectangle2D : 22
INHERITED FROM RectangularShape : 30

D.2.2.31   CLASS **Scrollbar**

public class Scrollbar extends Component
implements Adjustable, Accessible
A horizontal or vertical scrollbar. Its state
is determined by four properties: value
(the location of the thumb along the
scrollbar), extent (visible range), range of
values, and orientation (one of the class
constants HORIZONTAL and VERTICAL).

FIELDS

public static final int HORIZONTAL
public static final int VERTICAL
Possible orientations of this Scrollbar.

CONSTRUCTORS

public Scrollbar()
A vertical Scrollbar with value 0, extent
10, and range 0..100.

public Scrollbar(int b)
public Scrollbar(int b, int v, int ex, int min,
int max)
A Scrollbar with orientation b, value 0 or
v, extent 10 or ex, and range 0..100 or
min..max. Throw an IllegalArgumentException if b is not one of the class constants.

METHODS

public synchronized void addAdjustmentLis-
tener(AdjustmentListener
l)
Register l to respond to this ScrollBar's adjustment events.

public int getMaximum()
public int getMinimum()
= this ScrollBar's max or min value.

public int getOrientation()
public int getValue()
public int getVisibleAmount()
= this Scrollbar's orientation, value, and
extent.

public synchronized void removeAdjust-
mentListener(AdjustmentListener
l)
Deregister l: it will no longer respond to
this JScrollBar's events.

public void setMaximum(int m)
public void setMinimum(int m)
Set this ScrollBar's max or min value to m.

public void setOrientation(int b)
public void setValue(int b)
Set this Scrollbar's orientation (one of class
constants HORIZONTAL and VERTICAL)
or value to b.

public void setValues(int v, int ex, int min,
int max)
Set this Scrollbar's value, extent, and
range to v, ex, and min..max.

public void setVisibleAmount(int ex)
Set this Scrollbar's extent to ex.

INHERITED FROM Component (in D.2.2.9,
p. 255) : 165

D.2.2.32   CLASS **TextArea**

public class TextArea extends
TextComponent
A region of editable text.

FIELDS

public static final int SCROLLBARS_BOTH
public static final int
SCROLLBARS_VERTICAL_ONLY
public static final int
SCROLLBARS_HORIZONTAL_ONLY
public static final int SCROLLBARS_NONE
Constants: existence of horizontal and vertical scrollbars.

CONSTRUCTORS

public TextArea()
  A TextArea with text "" and both scroll-bars.
public TextArea(int r, int c)
  An empty TextArea with r rows, c columns, and both scrollbars.
public TextArea(String s)
  A TextArea with text s and both scroll-bars.
public TextArea(String s, int r, int c)
  A TextArea with text s, r rows, c columns, and both scrollbars.
public TextArea(String s, int r, int c, int scr)
  A TextArea with text s, r rows, c columns, and scrollbar visibility given by scr (one of the class constants).

METHODS

public void append(String s)
  Append s to this TextArea.
public int getColumns()
public int getRows()
  = this TextArea's number of columns and rows.
public void insert(String s, int pos)
  Insert text s at this[pos], shifting this[pos..] to make room.
public void replaceRange(String s, int start, int end)
  Replace text this[start..end-1] with s.
public void setColumns(int x)
public void setRows(int x)
  Set this TextArea's number of columns and rows to x.

INHERITED FROM TextComponent (in D.2.2.33, p. 267) : 23
INHERITED FROM Component (in D.2.2.9, p. 255) : 165

D.2.2.33   CLASS **TextComponent**

public class TextComponent extends
  Component implements Accessible
  A component that contains editable text.

METHODS

public synchronized void
  addTextListener(TextListener l)
  Register l to respond to this TextCompo-nent's text events.
public synchronized int getCaretPosition()
  = the position of the text-insertion caret.
public synchronized String getSelectedText()
  = this TextComponent's selected text.
public synchronized int getSelectionEnd()
public synchronized int getSelectionStart()
  = the end index and start index of this TextComponent's selected text.
public synchronized String getText()
  = this TextComponent's text.
public boolean isEditable()
  = "this text is editable".
public synchronized void
  removeTextListener(TextListener l)
  Deregister l: it will no longer respond to this TextComponent's events.
public synchronized void select(int beg, int end)
  Select the text this[beg..end-1] –all the rest is deselected.
public synchronized void selectAll()
  Select all the text.
public synchronized void setCaretPosition(int p)
  Set the position of the text-insertion caret to p.
public synchronized void setEditable(boolean b)
  Make this text editable iff b.
public synchronized void setSelectionEnd(int ind)
public synchronized void setSelectionStart(int ind)
  Set this TextComponent's selection end and selection start to ind.
public synchronized void setText(String t)
  Set this TextComponent's text to t.

INHERITED FROM Component (in D.2.2.9, p. 255) : 165

D.2.2.34   CLASS **TextField**

public class TextField extends
  TextComponent
  A single line of editable text.

CONSTRUCTORS

public TextField()
public TextField(int c)

public TextField(String s)
public TextField(String s, int c)
　　A TextField with text s ("" if missing) that
　　is wide enough to hold, on the average, c
　　characters (0 if missing).

METHODS

public synchronized void
　　addActionListener(ActionListener l)
　　Register l to respond to this TextField's
　　action events.
public int getColumns()
　　= this TextField's number of columns.
public synchronized void
　　removeActionListener(ActionListener l)
　　Deregister l: it will no longer respond to
　　this TextFields's events.
public synchronized void setColumns(int c)
　　Set this TextField's number of columns to
　　c.
public void setText(String s)
　　Change this TextField's text to s.

INHERITED FROM TextComponent (in
　　D.2.2.33, p. 267) : 23
INHERITED FROM Component (in D.2.2.9,
　　p. 255) : 165

D.2.2.35   CLASS **Window**

public class Window extends Container
　　implements Accessible
　　A window with no borders and no menu
　　bar.

CONSTRUCTORS

public Window(Frame w)
public Window(Window w)
　　A Window with layout manager Border-
　　Layout and owner w. Initially not visible.

METHODS

public synchronized void
　　addWindowListener(WindowListener l)
　　Register l to respond to this Window's win-
　　dow events.
public Locale getLocale()
public Window getOwner()
　　= this Window's Locale and owner.
public void hide()
　　Hide this Window (use show to make it

visible).
public void pack()
　　Lay out this Window to fit the preferred
　　size, then validate it.
public synchronized void
　　removeWindowListener(WindowListener
　　l)
　　Deregister l: it will no longer respond to
　　this Window's events.
public void setCursor(Cursor c)
　　Set this Window's cursor to c.
public void show()
　　Make this Window visible and bring it to
　　the front.
public void toBack()
public void toFront()
　　Send this Window to the back or front.

INHERITED FROM Container (in D.2.2.10,
　　p. 256) : 52
INHERITED FROM Component (in D.2.2.9,
　　p. 255) : 165

D.3   Package java.awt.event

Package Contents　　　　　　　　　*Page*

Interfaces

An entity that responds to MouseMotionEvents.

An entity that responds to TextEvents.
An entity that responds to WindowEvents.

Classes
An event.

D.3.1   INTERFACES

D.3.1.1   INTERFACE **ActionListener**

public interface ActionListener implements EventListener
An entity that responds to ActionEvents. Implement this interface to have a class respond to ActionEvents for a Component. See Component.addComponentListener.

METHODS

public void actionPerformed(ActionEvent e)
Called when e happens in a Component this ActionListener is registered with.

D.3.1.2   INTERFACE **AdjustmentListener**

public interface AdjustmentListener implements EventListener
An entity that responds to AdjustmentEvents. Implement this interface to have a class respond to AdjustmentEvents for a Component.

METHODS

public void adjustmentValueChanged(AdjustmentEvent e)
Called when e happens in a Component this AdjustmentListener is registered with.

D.3.1.3   INTERFACE **ComponentListener**

public interface ComponentListener implements EventListener
An entity that responds to ComponentEvents. Implement this interface to have a class respond to ComponentEvents for a Component. See Component.addComponentListener.

METHODS

public void componentHidden(ComponentEvent e)
public void componentMoved(ComponentEvent e)
public void componentResized(ComponentEvent e)
public void componentShown(ComponentEvent e)
Called when e happens in a Component this ComponentListener is registered with.

D.3.1.4   INTERFACE **ContainerListener**

public interface ContainerListener implements EventListener
An entity that responds to ContainerEvents. Implement this interface to have a class respond to ContainerEvents for a Component. See Component.addContainerListener.

METHODS

public void componentAdded(ContainerEvent e)
public void componentRemoved(ContainerEvent e)
Called when e happens in a Component this ContainerListener is registered with.

D.3.1.5   INTERFACE **ItemListener**

public interface ItemListener implements EventListener
An entity that responds to ItemEvents. Implement this interface to have a class respond to ItemEvents for a Component. See Component.addItemListener.

METHODS

public void itemStateChanged(ItemEvent e)
  Called when e happens in a Component
  this ItemListener is registered with.

D.3.1.6   INTERFACE **KeyListener**

public interface KeyListener implements
    EventListener
  An entity that responds to KeyEvents. Implement this interface to have a class respond to KeyEvents for a Component. See Component.addKeyListener.

METHODS

public void keyPressed(KeyEvent e)
public void keyReleased(KeyEvent e)
public void keyTyped(KeyEvent e)
  Called when e happens in a Component
  this KeyListener is registered with.

D.3.1.7   INTERFACE **MouseListener**

public interface MouseListener implements
    EventListener
  An entity that responds to MouseEvents. Implement this interface to have a class respond to MouseEvents for a Component. See Component.addMouseListener.

METHODS

public void mouseClicked(MouseEvent e)
public void mouseEntered(MouseEvent e)
public void mouseExited(MouseEvent e)
public void mousePressed(MouseEvent e)
public void mouseReleased(MouseEvent e)
  Called when e happens in a Component
  this MouseListener is registered with.

D.3.1.8   INTERFACE **MouseMotionListener**

public interface MouseMotionListener
    implements EventListener
  An entity that responds to MouseMotionEvents. Implement this interface to have a class respond to MouseMotionEvents for a Component. See Component. addMouseMotionListener.

METHODS

public void mouseDragged(MouseEvent e)
public void mouseMoved(MouseEvent e)
  Called when e happens in a Component this MouseMotionListener is registered with.

D.3.1.9   INTERFACE **TextListener**

public interface TextListener implements
    EventListener
  An entity that responds to TextEvents. Implement this interface to have a class respond to TextEvents for a Component. See Component.addTextListener.

METHODS

public void textValueChanged(TextEvent e)
  Called when e happens in a Component
  this TextListener is registered with.

D.3.1.10   INTERFACE **WindowListener**

public interface WindowListener implements
    EventListener
  An entity that responds to WindowEvents. Implement this interface to have a class respond to WindowEvents for a Component. See Component.addWindowListener.

METHODS

public void windowActivated(WindowEvent e)
public void windowClosed(WindowEvent e)
public void windowClosing(WindowEvent e)
public void windowDeactivated(WindowEvent
    e)
public void windowDeiconified(WindowEvent
    e)
public void windowIconified(WindowEvent e)
public void windowOpened(WindowEvent e)
  Called when e happens in a Component
  this WindowListener is registered with.

D.3.2   CLASSES

D.3.2.1   CLASS **ActionEvent**

public class ActionEvent extends AWTEvent

An event. Every ActionListener attached to a Component receives this event through method ActionListener.actionPerformed.

FIELDS

public static final int SHIFT_MASK
public static final int CTRL_MASK
public static final int META_MASK
public static final int ALT_MASK
  Constants: keyboard modifiers

public static final int ACTION_FIRST
public static final int ACTION_LAST
  Constants: action events have numbers in the range ACTION_FIRST..ACTION_LAST.

public static final int ACTION_PERFORMED
  Constant: means that an action occurred.

CONSTRUCTORS

public ActionEvent(Object s, int i, String c)
  An ActionEvent with id i belonging to component s with command name c.

METHODS

public String getActionCommand()
  = the command name of this ActionEvent.

public int getModifiers()
  = the modifier keys that were pressed when this ActionEvent was generated.

INHERITED FROM AWTEvent (in D.2.2.1, p. 252) : consume, finalize, getID, isConsumed, paramString, toString

INHERITED FROM EventObject : getSource, toString

D.4 Package java.io

A writer for a String.

A character stream writer.

D.4.1   INTERFACES

D.4.1.1   INTERFACE **DataInput**

public interface DataInput
A reader for primitive-type binary input.

METHODS
public boolean readBoolean()
public byte readByte()
public char readChar()
public double readDouble()
public float readFloat()
Read and return a value written by the corresponding method DataOutput.write....
public void readFully(byte[] b)
public void readFully(byte[] b, int off, int len)
Read b.length bytes (or len bytes) and store them into b (or in b[off..]. (Wait until enough bytes can be read.) Throw a NullPointerException if b is null.
public int readInt()
Read and return a value written by method DataOutput.writeInt.
public String readLine()
Read and return the next line of text (null if there are no more lines). Do not include the line terminator.
public long readLong()
Read and return a value written by method DataOutput.writeInt.
public short readShort()
public int readUnsignedByte()
public int readUnsignedShort()
Read and return a value written by the corresponding method DataOutput.write....
public int skipBytes(int n)
Skip up to n bytes and return the number of bytes skipped.

D.4.1.2   INTERFACE **DataOutput**

public interface DataOutput

A writer for primitive-type binary input, always associated with an output stream.

METHODS
public void write(byte[] b)
public void write(byte[] b, int off, int len)
Write b (or b[off..off+len-1]). Throw a NullPointerException if b = null.
public void writeBoolean(boolean x)
Write x.
public void writeByte(int x)
Write the low-order byte of x to the output stream.
public void writeBytes(String x)
public void writeChar(int x)
public void writeChars(String x)
public void writeDouble(double x)
public void writeFloat(float x)
public void writeInt(int x)
public void writeLong(long x)
Write x.
public void writeShort(int x)
Write x as a short.

D.4.1.3   INTERFACE **FileFilter**

public interface FileFilter
A filter for files.

METHODS
public boolean accept(File f)
= "this FileFilter accepts f".

D.4.1.4   INTERFACE **FilenameFilter**

public interface FilenameFilter
A filter for file names.

METHODS
public boolean accept(File dir, String f)
= "this FilenameFilter accepts f (in folder dir)".

D.4.2 Classes

D.4.2.1 Class BufferedInputStream

public class BufferedInputStream extends FilterInputStream
A buffered input stream, useful for restarting input.

Constructors

public BufferedInputStream(InputStream in)
public BufferedInputStream(InputStream in, int s)
A BufferedInputStream "wrapped around" in (with buffer size s).

Methods

public synchronized int available()
= the number of bytes that can be read.

public void close()
Close this BufferedInputStream.

public synchronized void mark(int lim)
Set the mark. Method reset() will reposition at the current mark if fewer than lim bytes have been read.

public boolean markSupported()
= "methods mark and reset are supported".

public synchronized int read()
= the next byte of data (-1 if at eos).

public synchronized int read(byte[] b, int off, int len)
Read and store up to len bytes into b[off..]. Return the number of bytes read (or -1 if the first read indicates an eos).

public synchronized void reset()
Move the input position to the mark set by method mark. Throw an IOException is there is no mark or if too many bytes were read since method mark was called (see method mark).

public synchronized long skip(long n)
Skip up to n bytes. Return the number of bytes skipped.

Inherited from FilterInputStream :
available, close, mark, markSupported, read, reset, skip

Inherited from InputStream (in D.4.2.11, p. 277) : available, close, mark, markSupported, read, reset, skip

D.4.2.2 Class BufferedReader

public class BufferedReader extends Reader
Reader for a character input stream, buffering for efficiency.

Constructors

public BufferedReader(Reader in)
public BufferedReader(Reader in, int s)
A BufferedReader "wrapped around" in (with buffer size s).

Methods

public void close()
Close this BufferedReader.

public void mark(int lim)
Set the mark. Method reset() will reposition at the current mark, if fewer than lim characters have been read.

public boolean markSupported()
= "methods mark and reset are supported".

public int read()
= the next character (-1 if at eos).

public int read(char[] cbuf, int off, int len)
Read and store up to len bytes into b[off..]. Return the number of bytes read (or -1 if the first read indicates an eos).

public String readLine()
Read a line of text (terminated by '\n', '\r', or "\n\r"). Return null if at eos.

public void reset()
Move the input position to the mark set by method mark. Throw an IOException if there is no mark or if too many characters were read since method mark was called.

public long skip(long n)
Skip up to n characters. Return the number of characters skipped.

Inherited from Reader : close, mark, markSupported, read, ready, reset, skip

D.4.2.3 Class DataInputStream

public class DataInputStream extends FilterInputStream implements DataInput
A reader for primitive values written by DataOutputStream.

CONSTRUCTORS

public DataInputStream(InputStream in)
   A DataInputStream reading from in.

METHODS

public final int read(byte[] b)
public final int read(byte[] b, int off, int len)
   Read up to b.length bytes into b (or up to len bytes into b[off..]) and return the number read (-1 if this stream has no bytes).
public final boolean readBoolean()
public final byte readByte()
public final char readChar()
public final double readDouble()
public final float readFloat()
   Read and return a value written by the corresponding method DataOutput.write...
public final void readFully(byte[] b)
public final void readFully(byte[] b, int off, int len)
   Read bytes from this stream into b (or into b[off..off+len-1]). Throw an EOFException if there is not enough input.
public final int readInt()
   Read and return a value written by method DataOutput.writeInt.
public final String readLine()
   Deprecated: Use method readLine of class BufferedReader. Convert a program that uses DataInputStream to BufferedReader by replacing code of the form:
      DataInputStream d=
         new DataInputStream(in);
   by
      BufferedReader d=
         new BufferedReader(
            new InputStreamReader(in));
public final long readLong()
public final short readShort()
public final int readUnsignedByte()
public final int readUnsignedShort()
   Read and return a value written by the corresponding method DataOutput.write...
public final int skipBytes(int n)
   Skip up to n bytes and return the number of bytes skipped.

INHERITED FROM FilterInputStream :
   available, close, mark, markSupported, read, reset, skip
INHERITED FROM InputStream (in D.4.2.11, p. 277) : available, close, mark,
markSupported, read, reset, skip

D.4.2.4   CLASS **DataOutputStream**

public class DataOutputStream extends FilterOutputStream implements DataOutput
   An instance has methods for writing primitive-type values to a binary stream, to be read using class DataInputStream. Generally, the write methods throw an IOException if an I/O error occurs.

CONSTRUCTORS

public DataOutputStream(OutputStream out)
   An instance to write data to underlying output stream out.

METHODS

public void flush()
   Flush this output stream.
public final int size()
   = the number of bytes written to this output stream so far.
public synchronized void write(byte[] b, int off, int len)
   Write bytes b[off..off+len-1] to the underlying output stream.
public synchronized void write(int b)
   Write the low-order 8 bits of b to the underlying output stream.
public final void writeBoolean(boolean x)
public final void writeByte(int x)
   Write x to the output stream.
public final void writeBytes(String s)
   Write the low-order byte of each character of s to the underlying output stream.
public final void writeChar(int x)
public final void writeChars(String x)
public final void writeDouble(double x)
public final void writeFloat(float x)
public final void writeInt(int x)
public final void writeLong(long x)
public final void writeShort(int v)
   Write x to the output stream.
public final void writeUTF(String str)
   Write str to the underlying output stream using the Java-modified UTF-8 encoding.

INHERITED FROM FilterOutputStream :
   close, flush, write

INHERITED FROM OutputStream (in
D.4.2.14, p. 278) : close, flush, write

D.4.2.5 CLASS **File**

public class File extends Object implements
Serializable, Comparable
A file or directory path on the system. A
directory path may be absolute or relative
to the current directory.

FIELDS
public static final char separatorChar
The character that separates directory
names in paths in the current operating
system. In UNIX, this character is '/', in
Windows, '\'.
public static final String separator
A 1-char **String** containing separatorChar.
public static final char pathSeparatorChar
The character that separates paths in the
current operating system. In UNIX, this
character is ':', in Windows, ';'.
public static final String pathSeparator
A 1-char **String** containing pathSeparator-
Char.

CONSTRUCTORS
public File(File d, String c)
public File(String p)
public File(String d, String c)
File with pathname d, catenated with c (if
present).

METHODS
public int compareTo(File p)
public int compareTo(Object p)
= an integer that is >0, zero, or <0 depending on whether the pathname of this
File is greater than, equal to, or less than
p's pathname.
public boolean createNewFile()
Create an empty file for this **File** and return the value of "the file did not exist
and was created". Will not overwrite an
existing file.
public boolean delete()
Delete the file or non-empty directory and
return the value of "the deletion was successful".
public boolean equals(Object b)

= "b's pathname is the same as this File's
pathname".
public boolean exists()
= "this File is a real file on the system".
public File getAbsoluteFile()
= new File(getAbsolutePath()).
public String getAbsolutePath()
= the absolute pathname of this pathname.
public String getName()
= the last name in the pathname of the
File ("" if this pathname is empty).
public String getParent()
= all but the last name in the pathname
of the File (null if this pathname is empty).
public String getPath()
= the pathname corresponding to this
File, with each name separated by separatorChar.
public boolean isAbsolute()
= "this abstract pathname is absolute".
public boolean isDirectory()
= "exists() and this File is a directory".
public boolean isFile()
= "exists() and this File is not a directory".
public long lastModified()
= the number of milliseconds since
00:00:00 GMT, 1 January 1970 that this
file was last modified.
public long length()
= the number of bytes in this File.
public String[] list()
public File[] listFiles()
= the names of or Files for all files and
directories in this directory (null if this File
is not a directory).
public boolean mkdir()
Create the directory represented by this
File and return the value of "the file did
not exist and was created".
public boolean setReadOnly()
Make this file/directory read-only. Return
true iff successful.
public String toString()
= this File's String representation.

D.4.2.6 CLASS **FileDescriptor**

public final class FileDescriptor extends
    Object
  A system-dependent file handle. Used to
  create a FileInputStream or FileOutput-
  Stream.

METHODS

public boolean valid()
  = "this file descriptor is a valid I/O connection".

D.4.2.7 CLASS **FileInputStream**

public class FileInputStream extends
    InputStream
  A stream of bytes read from a file.

CONSTRUCTORS

public FileInputStream(File f)
public FileInputStream(String f)
  A FileInputStream reading from file f.

METHODS

public native int available()
  = the number of bytes that can be read.
public native void close()
  Close this FileInputStream.
protected void finalize()
  Ensure that method close is called when
  there are no more references to this FileInputStream. Throw an IOException if an
  I/O error occurs.
public native int read()
  = the next byte of data (-1 if at end of
  stream). Pauses until a byte is available.
public int read(byte[] b)
public int read(byte[] b, int off, int len)
  Read and store as many bytes as possible into b (or b[off..off+len-1]). Return the
  number of bytes read (or -1 if the first read
  indicates end of stream). (Pauses until a
  byte is available.)
public native long skip(long n)
  Skip up to n bytes. Return the number of
  bytes skipped.

INHERITED FROM InputStream (in D.4.2.11,
  p. 277) : available, close, mark,
  markSupported, read, reset, skip

D.4.2.8 CLASS **FileOutputStream**

public class FileOutputStream extends
    OutputStream
  A stream of bytes written to a file.

CONSTRUCTORS

public FileOutputStream(File f)
public FileOutputStream(String f)
public FileOutputStream(String f, boolean b)
  A FileOutputStream writing to file f (or appending if b is true).

METHODS

public native void close()
  Close this FileOutputStream
protected void finalize()
  Clean up the connection to the file and
  ensure that method close is called when
  there are no more references to this
  stream.
public void write(byte[] b)
public void write(byte[] b, int off, int len)
  Write b[0..] (or b[off..off+len-1]) to this
  FileOutputStream.
public native void write(int b)
  Write b to this FileOutputStream.

INHERITED FROM OutputStream (in
  D.4.2.14, p. 278) : close, flush, write

D.4.2.9 CLASS **FileReader**

public class FileReader extends
    InputStreamReader
  A character-file reader.

CONSTRUCTORS

public FileReader(File f)
public FileReader(FileDescriptor f)
public FileReader(String f)
  A FileReader reading from f. Throw a
  FileNotFoundException if f is not found.

INHERITED FROM InputStreamReader (in
  D.4.2.12, p. 277) : close, getEncoding,
  read, ready
INHERITED FROM Reader : close, mark,
  markSupported, read, ready, reset, skip

D.4.2.10   CLASS **FileWriter**

public class FileWriter extends
  OutputStreamWriter
  A character-file writer.

CONSTRUCTORS

public FileWriter(File f)
public FileWriter(FileDescriptor f)
  A FileWriter writing to f.
public FileWriter(String f)
public FileWriter(String f, boolean b)
  A FileWriter writing to a file named f (or
  appending if b is true).

INHERITED FROM OutputStreamWriter :
  close, flush, getEncoding, write
INHERITED FROM Writer (in D.4.2.20,
  p. 280) : close, flush, write

D.4.2.11   CLASS **InputStream**

public abstract class InputStream extends
  Object
  A generic byte input stream.

CONSTRUCTORS

public InputStream()

METHODS

public int available()
  = the number of bytes that can be read.
public void close()
  Close this InputStream.
public synchronized void mark(int lim)
  Set the mark. Method reset() will reposition at the current mark if fewer than lim
  bytes have been read.
public boolean markSupported()
  = "methods mark and reset are supported".
public abstract int read()
  = the next byte of data (-1 if at end of
  stream). Pauses until a byte is available.
public int read(byte[] b)
public int read(byte[] b, int off, int len)
  Read and store as many bytes as possible into b (or b[off..off+len-1]). Return the
  number of bytes read (or -1 if the first read
  indicates end of stream). Pauses until a
  byte is available.

public synchronized void reset()
  Move the input position to the mark set
  by method mark. Throw an IOException if
  there is no mark or if too many bytes were
  read since method mark was called.
public long skip(long n)
  Skip up to n bytes. Return the number of
  bytes skipped.

D.4.2.12   CLASS **InputStreamReader**

public class InputStreamReader extends
  Reader
  Reader to turn a byte stream into a
  character stream. Usually wrapped in a
  BufferedReader.

CONSTRUCTORS

public InputStreamReader(InputStream in)
  An InputStreamReader to translate bytes
  read from in into characters.

METHODS

public void close()
  Close this InputStreamReader.
public int read()
  = the next byte of data (-1 if at end of
  stream). Pauses until a byte is available.
public int read(char[] b, int off, int len)
  Read and store as many bytes as possible
  into b[off..off+len-1]). Return the number
  of bytes read (or -1 if the first read indicates end of stream). Pauses until a byte
  is available.

INHERITED FROM Reader : close, mark,
  markSupported, read, ready, reset, skip

D.4.2.13   CLASS **IOException**

public class IOException extends Exception
  An error related to I/O.

CONSTRUCTORS

public IOException()
public IOException(String s)
  An IOException with no message or with
  message s.

INHERITED FROM Exception (in D.5.2.7,

p. 285) :

INHERITED FROM Throwable (in D.5.2.23, p. 294) : fillInStackTrace, getLocalizedMessage, getMessage, printStackTrace, toString

D.4.2.14   CLASS **OutputStream**

public abstract class OutputStream extends Object
  A generic byte output stream.

CONSTRUCTORS
public OutputStream()

METHODS
public void close()
  Close this OutputStream.
public void flush()
  Write out any buffered bytes.
public void write(byte[] b)
public void write(byte[] b, int off, int len)
  Write b[..] (or b[off..off+len-1]).
public abstract void write(int b)
  Write b.

D.4.2.15   CLASS **PrintStream**

public class PrintStream extends FilterOutputStream
  A character writer. For example, System.out is a PrintStream.

CONSTRUCTORS
public PrintStream(OutputStream out)
public PrintStream(OutputStream out, boolean b)
  A PrintStream that prints to out (with automatic flushing iff b is true.)

METHODS
public void close()
  Flush and close this PrintStream.
public void flush()
  Write out any buffered characters.
public void print(boolean x)
  Write String.valueOf(x).
public void print(char x)
public void print(char[] x)
  Write x.

public void print(double x)
public void print(float x)
public void print(int x)
public void print(long x)
public void print(Object x)
  Write String.valueOf(x).
public void print(String x)
  Write x to this stream (or "null" if x is null).
public void println()
  Terminate the current line.
public void println(boolean x)
  Write String.valueOf(x) and terminate the line.
public void println(char x)
public void println(char[] x)
  Write x and terminate the line.
public void println(double x)
public void println(float x)
public void println(int x)
public void println(long x)
public void println(Object x)
  Write String.valueOf(x) and terminate the line.
public void println(String x)
  Write x (or "null" if x is null) and terminate the line.
public void write(byte[] buf, int off, int len)
public void write(int b)
  Write b (or b[off..off+len-1]).

INHERITED FROM FilterOutputStream : close, flush, write
INHERITED FROM OutputStream (in D.4.2.14, p. 278) : close, flush, write

D.4.2.16   CLASS **PrintWriter**

public class PrintWriter extends Writer
  A character writer, like PrintStream but without byte-related methods.

CONSTRUCTORS
public PrintWriter(OutputStream out)
public PrintWriter(OutputStream out, boolean b)
public PrintWriter(Writer out)
public PrintWriter(Writer out, boolean b)
  A PrintWriter that prints to out (with automatic flushing iff b is true.)

METHODS

public void close()
Close this PrintStream.

public void flush()
Write any buffered characters.

public void print(boolean x)
Write String.valueOf(x).

public void print(char x)
public void print(char[] x)
Write x.

public void print(double x)
public void print(float x)
public void print(int x)
public void print(long x)
public void print(Object x)
Write String.valueOf(x).

public void print(String x)
Write x to this stream (or "null" if x is null).

public void println()
Terminate the current line using line.separator.

public void println(boolean x)
Write String.valueOf(x) and terminate the line using line.separator.

public void println(char x)
public void println(char[] x)
Write x and terminate the line using line.separator.

public void println(double x)
public void println(float x)
public void println(int x)
public void println(long x)
public void println(Object x)
Write String.valueOf(x) and terminate the line using line.separator.

public void println(String x)
Write x (or "null" if x is null) and terminate the line using line.separator.

protected void setError()
Indicate that an error has occurred.

public void write(char[] s)
public void write(char[] s, int off, int len)
Write s[..] (or s[off..off+len-1]).

public void write(int s)
public void write(String s)
Write s.

public void write(String s, int off, int len)
Write s[..] (or s[off..off+len-1]).

INHERITED FROM Writer (in D.4.2.20, p. 280) : close, flush, write

D.4.2.17 CLASS **StreamTokenizer**

public class StreamTokenizer extends Object
An input stream parser. Turns Strings and numbers into "tokens".

FIELDS

public int ttype
The type of the last-read token:
1. TT_WORD: a non-number.
2. TT_NUMBER: a number.
3. TT_EOF: there was no token, the end of the input was reached.
4. TT_EOL: there was no token, the end of the line was reached. (See method eollsSignificant).

public static final int TT_EOF
public static final int TT_EOL
Constants: eos or end of line was just read.

public static final int TT_NUMBER
public static final int TT_WORD
Constants: a number or word token was just read.

public String sval
The word token just read. (Only valid if ttype = TT_WORD.)

public double nval
The number token just read. (Only valid if ttype = TT_NUMBER.)

CONSTRUCTORS

public StreamTokenizer(InputStream s)
public StreamTokenizer(Reader s)
A StreamTokenizer for s.

METHODS

public void eollsSignificant(boolean flag)
Treat ends of line as tokens iff flag.

public int lineno()
= the current line number.

public int nextToken()
Find the next token of this input stream, store it in ttype, set fields nval or sval accordingly, and return ttype.

public void ordinaryChar(int ch)
public void ordinaryChars(int low, int hi)
Treat character ch (or chars in the range low..hi) as single-character tokens.

public void parseNumbers()
Treat numbers as something different from words.

public void pushBack()
 Figuratively, push the value in field **ttype** back into the input stream, so that next call **nextToken()** will return the same value.

public void resetSyntax()
 Treat all characters, including newlines and numbers, as single-character tokens.

public String toString()
 = the current token's **String** representation.

public void whitespaceChars(int low, int hi)
 Treat all characters in the range **low..hi** as token separators.

public void wordChars(int low, int hi)
 Treat all characters in the range **low..hi** as letters.

D.4.2.18   CLASS **StringReader**

public class StringReader extends Reader
 A reader for a String.

CONSTRUCTORS

public StringReader(String s)
 A StringReader for **s**.

METHODS

public void close()
 Close this **StringReader**.

public void mark(int lim)
 Set the mark. Method **reset()** will reposition at the current mark if fewer than **lim** bytes have been read.

public boolean markSupported()
 = "methods **mark** and **reset** are supported" (they are).

public int read()
 Read and return one character (or -1 if no more).

public int read(char[] b, int off, int len)
 Read and store up to **len** bytes into **b[off..]**. Return the number of bytes read (or -1 if the first read indicates an end of stream).

public boolean ready()
 = "this stream is ready to be read".

public void reset()
 Move the input position to the mark set by method **mark**. Throw an **IOException** if there is no mark or if too many bytes were

read since method **mark** was called.

public long skip(long ns)
 Skip up to **n** bytes. Return the number of bytes skipped.

INHERITED FROM Reader : close, mark, markSupported, read, ready, reset, skip

D.4.2.19   CLASS **StringWriter**

public class StringWriter extends Writer
 A writer for a String.

CONSTRUCTORS

public StringWriter()
public StringWriter(int s)
 A StringWriter of default size (or of size **s**).

METHODS

public void close()
 Close this **StringWriter**. (Methods **toString** and **getBuffer** will still work.)

public void flush()
 Flush this **StringWriter**.

public StringBuffer getBuffer()
 = this **StringWriter**'s contents. WARNING: this is a shallow copy. If you change it, the **StringWriter** will change.

public String toString()
 = this **StringWriter**'s contents.

public void write(char[] b, int off, int len)
 Write b[off..off+len-1].

public void write(int x)
public void write(String x)
 Write **x**.

public void write(String b, int off, int len)
 Write b[off..off+len-1].

INHERITED FROM Writer (in D.4.2.20, p. 280) : close, flush, write

D.4.2.20   CLASS **Writer**

public abstract class Writer extends Object
 A character stream writer.

CONSTRUCTORS

protected Writer()
protected Writer(Object lock)
 Constructor: Critical sections synchronize on the writer itself (or on **lock**, if present).

METHODS

public abstract void close()
    Flush and close this Writer.
public abstract void flush()
    Write any buffered characters.
public void write(char[] b)
public abstract void write(char[] b, int off, int len)
public void write(int b)
public void write(String b)
public void write(String b, int off, int len)
    Write b (or b[off..off+len-1]).

D.5 Package java.lang

D.5.1 INTERFACES

D.5.1.1 INTERFACE **Cloneable**

public interface Cloneable
    A copyable object. Implement this interface if a class can be cloned with method

Object.clone.

D.5.1.2   INTERFACE **Comparable**

public interface Comparable
   Something that can be compared.

METHODS

public int compareTo(Object b)
   >0, $= 0$, or <0 depending on whether this
   object is greater than, equal to, or less
   than b.

D.5.1.3   INTERFACE **Runnable**

public interface Runnable
   Something that can be executed by a
   thread.

METHODS

public void run()
   Begin execution. Called when the imple-
   mentor's Thread is started.

D.5.2   CLASSES

D.5.2.1   CLASS **Boolean**

public final class Boolean extends Object
      implements Serializable
   A "wrapper" for a boolean value.

FIELDS

public static final Boolean TRUE
public static final Boolean FALSE
   Objects that wrap true and false.

CONSTRUCTORS

public Boolean(boolean v)
   A Boolean wrapper for v.
public Boolean(String s)
   A wrapper for the boolean value "s != null
   && s.toLowerCase().equals("true")".

METHODS

public boolean booleanValue()
   = this Boolean's wrapped value.
public boolean equals(Object b)

= "b != null and b's wrapped value is the
same as this Boolean's wrapped value".
public String toString()
   = this Boolean's String representation.
public static Boolean valueOf(String s)
   = "s != null && s.toLowerCase().
equals("true")".

D.5.2.2   CLASS **Byte**

public final class Byte extends Number
      implements Comparable
   A "wrapper" for a byte value.

FIELDS

public static final byte MIN_VALUE
public static final byte MAX_VALUE
   The smallest and largest values of type
   byte.

CONSTRUCTORS

public Byte(byte b)
   A Byte wrapping b.
public Byte(String s)
   A Byte wrapping the value in s.

METHODS

public byte byteValue()
   = this Byte's wrapped value.
public int compareTo(Byte b)
public int compareTo(Object b)
   >0, $= 0$, or <0 depending on whether this
   Byte is greater than, equal to, or less than
   b. Throw a ClassCastException if b is not
   a Byte.
public double doubleValue()
   = this Byte's wrapped value.
public boolean equals(Object b)
   = "b != null and b's wrapped value is the
   same as this Byte's wrapped value".
public float floatValue()
public int intValue()
public long longValue()
   = this Byte's wrapped value.
public static byte parseByte(String s)
   = the value in s. Throw a NumberFormat-
   Exception if s does not represent a byte.
public short shortValue()
   = this Byte's wrapped value.
public String toString()

= this Byte's String representation.

public static String toString(byte b)
= a String representing value b (in decimal).

public static Byte valueOf(String s)
= a Byte wrapping the value in s. Throw a NumberFormatException if s does not represent a byte.

INHERITED FROM Number (in D.5.2.14, p. 288) : byteValue, doubleValue, floatValue, intValue, longValue, shortValue

D.5.2.3   CLASS **Character**

public final class Character extends Object
implements Serializable, Comparable
A "wrapper" for a char value.

FIELDS

public static final char MIN_VALUE
public static final char MAX_VALUE
The smallest and largest value of type char.

CONSTRUCTORS

public Character(char c)
A Character wrapping c.

METHODS

public char charValue()
= this Character's wrapped value.

public int compareTo(Character b)
public int compareTo(Object b)
>0, = 0, or <0 depending on whether this Character is greater than, equal to, or less than b. Throw a ClassCastException if b is not a Character.

public boolean equals(Object b)
= "b != null and wraps the same char as this Character".

public static boolean isDefined(char ch)
= "ch is a defined Unicode character".

public static boolean isDigit(char ch)
public static boolean isLetter(char ch)
public static boolean isLetterOrDigit(char ch)
public static boolean isLowerCase(char ch)
= "ch is what the method name says".

public static boolean isSpaceChar(char ch)
= "ch is a Unicode space character".

public static boolean isTitleCase(char ch)

public static boolean isUpperCase(char ch)
public static boolean isWhitespace(char ch)
= "ch is what the method name says".

public static char toLowerCase(char ch)
= the lowercase version of ch (or ch if there is no lowercase version).

public String toString()
= this Character's String representation.

public static char toTitleCase(char ch)
= the titlecase equivalent of ch (or ch if there is no titlecase equivalent).

public static char toUpperCase(char ch)
= the uppercase version of ch (or ch if there is no uppercase version).

D.5.2.4   CLASS **Class**

public final class Class extends Object
implements Serializable
A Java representation of a type: a class (including an array), an interface, a primitive type, or void.

METHODS

public static Class forName(String s)
= the object representing the type named s.

public native Class getComponentType()
= T if this Class represents T[] (null if this class does not represent an array).

public native Class[] getInterfaces()
The interfaces that are implemented or extended by this Class.

public native String getName()
= the full name of the type represented by this Class.

public native Class getSuperclass()
= the superclass of the type represented by this Class. (null if this instance represents a non-class type, or Object.)

public native boolean isArray()
= "this Class represents an array".

public native boolean isInstance(Object b)
= "b is an instance of the type represented by this Class".

public native boolean isInterface()
= "this Class represents an interface".

public native boolean isPrimitive()
= "this Class represents a primitive type or void".

public Object newInstance()
    = a new instance of the type that this
    Class represents. Uses the constructor
    with 0 arguments.
public String toString()
    = this Class'es String representation.

D.5.2.5   CLASS **Double**

public final class Double extends Number
        implements Comparable
    A "wrapper" for a double value.

FIELDS

public static final double
    POSITIVE_INFINITY
public static final double
    NEGATIVE_INFINITY
public static final double NaN
    Positive and negative infinities and Not-a-
    Number (NaN).
public static final double MAX_VALUE
public static final double MIN_VALUE
    The largest and smallest positive double
    values.

CONSTRUCTORS

public Double(double v)
    A Double wrapping v.
public Double(String s)
    A Double wrapping the value in s. Uses
    method valueOf.

METHODS

public byte byteValue()
    = this Double's value.
public int compareTo(Double d)
public int compareTo(Object d)
    >0, = 0, or <0 depending on whether this
    Double is greater than, equal to, or less
    than d. Throw a ClassCastException if d is
    not a Double.
public double doubleValue()
    = this Double's value.
public boolean equals(Object b)
    = "b != null and b's wrapped value is the
    same as this Double's wrapped value".
public float floatValue()
public int intValue()
    = this Double's value.

public boolean isInfinite()
    = "this Double's value is positive or nega-
    tive infinity".
public static boolean isInfinite(double v)
    = "v is positive or negative infinity".
public boolean isNaN()
    = "this Double's value is Not a Number
    (NaN)".
public static boolean isNaN(double v)
    = "v is Not a Number (NaN)".
public long longValue()
    = this Double's value.
public static double parseDouble(String s)
    = the value in s. Throw a NumberFormat-
    Exception if s does not represent a double.
    Surrounding whitespace is allowed.
public short shortValue()
    = this Double's value.
public String toString()
    = this Double's String representation.
public static String toString(double d)
    = d's String representation.
public static Double valueOf(String s)
    = a Double wrapping the value in s. Throw
    a NumberFormatException if s does not
    represent a double. Surrounding white-
    space is allowed.

INHERITED FROM Number (in D.5.2.14,
    p. 288) : byteValue, doubleValue,
    floatValue, intValue, longValue, shortValue

D.5.2.6   CLASS **Error**

public class Error extends Throwable
    An abnormal, serious, unrecoverable er-
    ror.

CONSTRUCTORS

public Error()
public Error(String s)
    An Error with no message or with message
    s.

INHERITED FROM Throwable (in D.5.2.23,
    p. 294) : fillInStackTrace,
    getLocalizedMessage, getMessage,
    printStackTrace, toString

D.5.2.7 CLASS Exception

public class Exception extends Throwable
  An error that is not necessarily serious and
  therefore recoverable.

CONSTRUCTORS

public Exception()
public Exception(String s)
  An Exception with no message or with
  message s.

INHERITED FROM Throwable (in D.5.2.23,
  p. 294) : fillInStackTrace,
  getLocalizedMessage, getMessage,
  printStackTrace, toString

D.5.2.8 CLASS Float

public final class Float extends Number
      implements Comparable
  A "wrapper" for a float value.

FIELDS

public static final float POSITIVE_INFINITY
public static final float NEGATIVE_INFINITY
public static final float NaN
  Positive and negative infinities and Not-a-
  Number (NaN).

public static final float MAX_VALUE
public static final float MIN_VALUE
  The largest and smallest positive float values.

CONSTRUCTORS

public Float(double v)
public Float(float v)
  A Float wrapping v.

public Float(String s)
  A Float wrapping the value in s. Uses
  method valueOf.

METHODS

public byte byteValue()
  = this Float's value.

public int compareTo(Float f)
public int compareTo(Object f)
  >0, = 0, or <0 depending on whether this
  Float is greater than, equal to, or less than
  f. Throw a ClassCastException if f is not a
  Float.

public double doubleValue()
  = this Float's value.

public boolean equals(Object b)
  = "b != null and b's wrapped value is the
  same as this Float's wrapped value".

public float floatValue()
public int intValue()
  = this Float's value.

public boolean isInfinite()
  = "this Float's value is positive or negative
  infinity".

public static boolean isInfinite(float v)
  = "v is positive or negative infinity".

public boolean isNaN()
  = "this Float's value is Not a Number
  (NaN)".

public static boolean isNaN(float v)
  = "v is Not a Number (NaN)".

public long longValue()
  = this Float's value.

public static float parseFloat(String s)
  = the value in s. Throw a NumberFormat-
  Exception if s does not represent a float.
  Surrounding whitespace is allowed.

public short shortValue()
  = this Float's value.

public String toString()
  = this Float's String representation.

public static String toString(float f)
  = f's String representation.

public static Float valueOf(String s)
  = a Float wrapping the value in s. Throw a
  NumberFormatException if s does not represent a float. Surrounding whitespace is
  allowed.

INHERITED FROM Number (in D.5.2.14,
  p. 288) : byteValue, doubleValue,
  floatValue, intValue, longValue, shortValue

D.5.2.9 CLASS IndexOutOfBound-
            sException

public class IndexOutOfBoundsException
      extends RuntimeException
  An error indicating that an index (e.g. of
  an array) is out of range.

CONSTRUCTORS

public IndexOutOfBoundsException()
public IndexOutOfBoundsException(String s)

An IndexOutOfBoundsException with no message or with message s.

INHERITED FROM RuntimeException (in D.5.2.16, p. 288) :

INHERITED FROM Exception (in D.5.2.7, p. 285) :

INHERITED FROM Throwable (in D.5.2.23, p. 294) : fillInStackTrace, getLocalizedMessage, getMessage, printStackTrace, toString

D.5.2.10   CLASS Integer

public final class Integer extends Number
    implements Comparable
A "wrapper" for an int value.

FIELDS

public static final int MIN_VALUE
public static final int MAX_VALUE
    The largest and smallest int values.

CONSTRUCTORS

public Integer(int v)
    An Integer wrapping v.

public Integer(String s)
    An Integer wrapping the value in s. Uses method valueOf.

METHODS

public byte byteValue()
    = this Integer's value.

public int compareTo(Integer i)
public int compareTo(Object i)
    >0, = 0, or <0 depending on whether this Integer is greater than, equal to, or less than i. Throw a ClassCastException if i is not an Integer.

public double doubleValue()
    = this Integer's value.

public boolean equals(Object b)
    = "b != null and b's wrapped value is the same as this Integer's wrapped value".

public float floatValue()
public int intValue()
public long longValue()
    = this Integer's value.

public static int parseInt(String s)
    = the value in s. Throw a NumberFormat-Exception if s does not represent an int.

Surrounding whitespace is allowed.

public short shortValue()
    = this Integer's value.

public String toString()
    = this Integer's String representation.

public static String toString(int i)
    = i's String representation.

public static Integer valueOf(String s)
    = an Integer wrapping the value in s. Throw a NumberFormatException if s does not represent a double. Surrounding whitespace is allowed.

INHERITED FROM Number (in D.5.2.14, p. 288) : byteValue, doubleValue, floatValue, intValue, longValue, shortValue

D.5.2.11   CLASS Long

public final class Long extends Number
    implements Comparable
A "wrapper" for a long value.

FIELDS

public static final long MIN_VALUE
public static final long MAX_VALUE
    The largest and smallest long values.

CONSTRUCTORS

public Long(long v)
    A Long wrapping v.

public Long(String s)
    A Long wrapping the value in s. Uses method valueOf.

METHODS

public byte byteValue()
    = this Long's value.

public int compareTo(Long i)
public int compareTo(Object i)
    >0, = 0, or <0 depending on whether this Long is greater than, equal to, or less than i. Throw a ClassCastException if i is not a Long.

public double doubleValue()
    = this Long's value.

public boolean equals(Object b)
    = "b != null and b's wrapped value is the same as this Long's wrapped value".

public float floatValue()
public int intValue()

public long longValue()
= this Long's value.

public static long parseLong(String s)
= the value in s. Throw a NumberFormat-
Exception if s does not represent a long.
Surrounding whitespace is allowed.

public short shortValue()
= this Long's value.

public String toString()
= this Long's String representation.

public static String toString(long i)
= i's String representation.

public static Long valueOf(String s)
= a Long wrapping the value in s. Throw a
NumberFormatException if s does not represent a long. Surrounding whitespace is
allowed.

INHERITED FROM Number (in D.5.2.14,
p. 288) : byteValue, doubleValue,
floatValue, intValue, longValue, shortValue

D.5.2.12   CLASS Math

public final class Math extends Object
Contains static constants and functions
related to mathematical operations.
Many of these functions deal with infinity, -infinity, and NaN (not a number). To
save space, we have eliminated these from
the specification.

FIELDS

public static final double E
The closest double to e, the base of the
natural logarithm.

public static final double PI
The closest double to pi, the ratio of the
circumference of a circle to its diameter.

METHODS

public static double abs(double a)
public static float abs(float a)
public static int abs(int a)
public static long abs(long a)
= the absolute value of a.

public static double acos(double a)
public static double asin(double a)
= arc cosine and arc sine of a (given in
radians).

public static double atan(double a)
= arc tangent of a (given in radians).

public static double atan2(double a, double b)
= theta in the polar-coordinates representation (r,theta) of rectangular coordinates
(b,a).

public static double ceil(double a)
= the smallest integer not less than a.

public static double cos(double a)
= cosine of a (where a is in radians).

public static double exp(double a)
= E raised to the power a.

public static double floor(double a)
= the largest integer not greater than a.

public static double log(double a)
= the natural logarithm (base E) of a.

public static double max(double a, double b)
public static float max(float a, float b)
public static int max(int a, int b)
public static long max(long a, long b)
= the larger of a and b.

public static double min(double a, double b)
public static float min(float a, float b)
public static int min(int a, int b)
public static long min(long a, long b)
= the smaller of a and b.

public static double pow(double a, double b)
= a raised to the power b.

public static double random()
= a random value r, $0 <= r < 1$.

public static double rint(double a)
= the integer closest to a. (If a is equidistant from two integers, return the even
one.)

public static long round(double a)
public static int round(float a)
= the closest integer to a.

public static double sin(double a)
= sine of a (where a is in radians).

public static double sqrt(double a)
= the positive square root of a.

public static double tan(double a)
= tangent of a (where a is in radians).

public static double toDegrees(double a)
= angle a, converted from radians to degrees.

public static double toRadians(double a)
= angle a, converted from degrees to radians.

D.5.2.13 Class NullPointerException

public class NullPointerException extends
    RuntimeException
    An error indicating that null is used where
    the name of an object is required. For ex-
    ample, if String s is null, s.length() throws
    a NullPointerException.

CONSTRUCTORS
public NullPointerException()
public NullPointerException(String s)
    A NullPointerException with no message or
    with message s.

INHERITED FROM RuntimeException (in
    D.5.2.16, p. 288) :
INHERITED FROM Exception (in D.5.2.7,
    p. 285) :
INHERITED FROM Throwable (in D.5.2.23,
    p. 294) : fillInStackTrace,
    getLocalizedMessage, getMessage,
    printStackTrace, toString

D.5.2.14   Class Number

public abstract class Number extends Object
    implements Serializable
    The superclass of the wrapper classes
    (e.g. Byte).

CONSTRUCTORS
public Number()

METHODS
public byte byteValue()
public abstract double doubleValue()
public abstract float floatValue()
public abstract int intValue()
public abstract long longValue()
public short shortValue()
    = this Number's value.

D.5.2.15   Class Object

public class Object
    The root of the class hierarchy: the su-
    perest class of all. All classes (including
    arrays) that do not extend another class
    automatically extend Object.

CONSTRUCTORS
public Object()

METHODS
protected native Object clone()
    = a copy of this object. Creates a new in-
    stance of class Object and copies its fields
    –contents of the fields are not cloned.
public boolean equals(Object b)
    = "this object is equal to b". In class Ob-
    ject, x.equals(y) is equivalent to x == y,
    but subclasses can override equals to com-
    pare fields.
protected void finalize()
    Override finalize in order to dispose of sys-
    tem resources or perform other cleanup.
    Called by the garbage collector.
protected native int hashCode()
    = a hash code value for this object.
public final native void notify()
public final native void notifyAll()
    Wake up an arbitrary thread (or all
    threads) waiting on this object's monitor
    (see method wait). The awakened thread
    will wait until the current thread releases
    the lock on this Object.
public String toString()
    = this Object's String representation. Sub-
    classes can override equals to produce a
    less shallow copy.
public final void wait()
    Equivalent to the call wait(0).
public final native void wait(long t)
    Make the current thread wait until an-
    other thread either calls notify for this Ob-
    ject or for t milliseconds to elapse. The
    awakened thread will wait until the cur-
    rent thread releases the lock on this Ob-
    ject.

D.5.2.16   Class RuntimeException

public class RuntimeException extends
    Exception
    An error that occurred during program
    execution. These need not be declared in
    throws clauses, whereas all other Excep-
    tions must be.

CONSTRUCTORS

public RuntimeException()
public RuntimeException(String s)
　A RuntimeException with no message or
　with message s.

INHERITED FROM Exception (in D.5.2.7,
　p. 285) :

INHERITED FROM Throwable (in D.5.2.23,
　p. 294) : fillInStackTrace,
　getLocalizedMessage, getMessage,
　printStackTrace, toString

D.5.2.17   CLASS Short

public final class Short extends Number
　implements Comparable
　A "wrapper" for a short value.

FIELDS

public static final short MIN_VALUE
public static final short MAX_VALUE
　The largest and smallest int values.

CONSTRUCTORS

public Short(short v)
　A Short wrapping v.

public Short(String s)
　A Short wrapping the value in s. Uses
　method parseShort.

METHODS

public byte byteValue()
　= this Short's value.

public int compareTo(Object i)
public int compareTo(Short i)
　>0, = 0, or <0 depending on whether this
　Short is greater than, equal to, or less than
　i. Throw a ClassCastException if i is not a
　Short.

public double doubleValue()
　= this Short's value.

public boolean equals(Object b)
　= "b != null and b's wrapped value is the
　same as this Short's wrapped value".

public float floatValue()
public int intValue()
public long longValue()
　= this Short's value.

public static short parseShort(String s)
　= the value in s. Throw a NumberFormat-
　Exception if s does not represent a short.

Surrounding whitespace is not allowed.

public short shortValue()
　= this Short's value.

public String toString()
　= this Short's String representation.

public static String toString(short s)
　= s's String representation.

public static Short valueOf(String s)
　= a Short wrapping the value in s. Throw a
　NumberFormatException if s does not rep-
　resent a double. Surrounding whitespace is
　not allowed.

INHERITED FROM Number (in D.5.2.14,
　p. 288) : byteValue, doubleValue,
　floatValue, intValue, longValue, shortValue

D.5.2.18   CLASS StrictMath

public final class StrictMath extends Object
　Contains static constants and functions
　related to math operations. The algo-
　rithms in this class are taken from netlib,
　the Freely Distributable Math Library.
　For full details, see the SUN API spec.
　　Many of these functions deal with infin-
　ity, -infinity, and NaN (not a number). To
　save space, we have eliminated these from
　the specification.

FIELDS

public static final double E
　The closest double to e, the base of the
　natural logarithm.

public static final double PI
　The closest double to pi, the ratio of the
　circumference of a circle to its diameter.

METHODS

public static double abs(double a)
public static float abs(float a)
public static int abs(int a)
public static long abs(long a)
　= the absolute value of a.

public static native double acos(double a)
public static native double asin(double a)
　= arc cosine and arc sine of angle a (where
　a is in radians).

public static native double atan(double a)
　= arc tangent of a (where a is in radians).

public static native double atan2(double a,

double b)
= theta in the polar-coordinates representation (r,theta) of rectangular coordinates (b,a).

public static native double ceil(double a)
= the smallest integer not less than a.

public static native double cos(double a)
= cosine of a (where a is in radians).

public static native double exp(double a)
= E raised to the power a.

public static native double floor(double a)
= the largest integer not greater than a.

public static native double log(double a)
= the natural logarithm (base E) of a.

public static double max(double a, double b)
public static float max(float a, float b)
public static int max(int a, int b)
public static long max(long a, long b)
= the larger of a and b.

public static double min(double a, double b)
public static float min(float a, float b)
public static int min(int a, int b)
public static long min(long a, long b)
= the smaller of a and b.

public static native double pow(double a,
    double b)
= a raised to the power b.

public static double random()
= a random value r, 0 <= r <1.

public static native double rint(double a)
= the integer closest to a. (If a is equidistant from two integers, return the even one.)

public static long round(double a)
public static int round(float a)
= the closest integer to a.

public static native double sin(double a)
= sine of a (where a is in radians).

public static native double sqrt(double a)
= the positive square root of a.

public static native double tan(double a)
= tangent of a (where a is in radians).

public static double toDegrees(double a)
= angle a, converted from radians to degrees.

public static double toRadians(double a)
= angle a, converted from degrees to radians.

D.5.2.19   CLASS String

public final class String extends Object
        implements Serializable, Comparable
    An immutable string of characters. Class StringBuffer supports mutable strings.

CONSTRUCTORS
public String()
    A String representing "".
public String(char[] v)
public String(char[] v, int off, int len)
    A String representing the sequence of characters in v or in v[off..off+len-1]. Throw a NullPointerException if v == null.
public String(String s)
public String(StringBuffer s)
    A String representing the sequence of characters in s.

METHODS
public char charAt(int index)
    = the character this[index].
public int compareTo(Object s)
public int compareTo(String s)
    >0, = 0, or <0 depending on whether this String is greater than, equal to, or less than s. Throw a ClassCastException if s is not a String.
public int compareToIgnoreCase(String s)
    >0, = 0, or <0 depending on whether this String is greater than, equal to, or less than s, ignoring case.
public String concat(String str)
    = a copy of this String with the characters of str appended to it.
public boolean endsWith(String s)
    = "s is a suffix of this String".
public boolean equals(Object b)
    = "b != null and b's character sequence is the same as this String's".
public boolean equalsIgnoreCase(String s)
    = "this String and s are equal, ignoring case considerations".
public int indexOf(int s)
public int indexOf(int s, int fr)
public int indexOf(String s)
public int indexOf(String s, int fr)
    = index of the first occurrence of s in this[0..] or in this[fr..] (-1 if s is not in this String).

public native String intern()
= a String equal to this one, but taken from a list of existing Strings. If this String was not already in that list, it is placed there. See the Sun APIs for more detail.

public int lastIndexOf(int ch)
= index of the last occurrence of ch in this String (-1 if ch is not found).

public int lastIndexOf(int ch, int fr)
= index of the last occurrence of ch in this[0..fr] (-1 if ch is not found).

public int lastIndexOf(String s)
public int lastIndexOf(String s, int f)
= index of the last occurrence of s in this[0..] or in this[f..] (-1 if no such occurrence). For s equal to "", the result is this.length(). Throw a NullPointerException if s == null.

public int length()
= this String's length.

public boolean regionMatches(boolean b, int f, String s, int of, int len)
public boolean regionMatches(int f, String s, int of, int len)
= "this[f..f+len-1] is equal to s[of..of+len-1], ignoring case iff b is true". Throw a NullPointerException if s == null.

public String replace(char oldC, char newC)
= a copy of this String with all occurrences of oldC replaced by newC.

public boolean startsWith(String s)
= "s is a prefix of this String".

public boolean startsWith(String s, int toff)
= "s is a prefix of this[toff..]" (false if this[toff..] has an illegal index).

public String substring(int f)
= substring this[f..].

public String substring(int beg, int end)
= substring this[beg..end-1]. Throw an IndexOutOfBoundsException if the following is false: 0 <= beg <= end <= this.length.

public char[] toCharArray()
= the sequence of characters in this String.

public String toLowerCase()
= a copy of this String with uppercase letters translated to lowercase.

public String toString()
= this String (not a copy).

public String toUpperCase()
= a copy of this String with lowercase letters translated to uppercase.

public String trim()
= a copy of this String but with white-space removed from the ends. Whitespace consists of blanks, tabs, newlines, and carriage returns.

public static String valueOf(boolean x)
public static String valueOf(char x)
= x's String representation.

public static String valueOf(char[] x)
public static String valueOf(char[] x, int f, int len)
= the String representation of x[0..] or of x[f..f+len-1].

public static String valueOf(double x)
public static String valueOf(float x)
public static String valueOf(int x)
public static String valueOf(long x)
= x's String representation.

public static String valueOf(Object b)
= b's String representation. Return "null" if b == null.

D.5.2.20 CLASS **StringBuffer**

public final class StringBuffer extends Object implements Serializable
A mutable string of characters.

CONSTRUCTORS

public StringBuffer()
A StringBuffer representing "".

public StringBuffer(String s)
A StringBuffer representing the sequence of characters in s.

METHODS

public StringBuffer append(boolean x)
public synchronized StringBuffer append(char x)
Append x's String representation of x to this StringBuffer and return this StringBuffer.

public synchronized StringBuffer append(char[] x)
Append the characaters of x to this StringBuffer and return this StringBuffer.

public StringBuffer append(double x)
public StringBuffer append(float x)
public StringBuffer append(int x)
public StringBuffer append(long x)
public synchronized StringBuffer

append(Object x)

Append x's String representation of x to this StringBuffer and return this String-Buffer.

public synchronized StringBuffer
    append(String x)

Append x's String representation to this StringBuffer and return this StringBuffer.

public synchronized char charAt(int i)
    = the character this[i].

public synchronized StringBuffer delete(int beg, int end)

Delete characters this[beg..end-1] from this instance and return this StringBuffer.

public synchronized StringBuffer
    deleteCharAt(int ind)

Delete character this[ind] from this String-Buffer and return this StringBuffer.

public StringBuffer insert(int off, boolean x)

public synchronized StringBuffer insert(int off, char x)

public synchronized StringBuffer insert(int off, char[] x)

public StringBuffer insert(int off, double x)

public StringBuffer insert(int off, float x)

public StringBuffer insert(int off, int x)

public StringBuffer insert(int off, long x)

public synchronized StringBuffer insert(int off, Object x)

public synchronized StringBuffer insert(int off, String x)

Insert the String representation of x at this[off] (shifting this[off..] to make room) and return this StringBuffer. If off = this.length(), append the characters.

public int length()
    = this StringBuffer's length.

public synchronized StringBuffer replace(int beg, int end, String str)

Replace characters this[beg .. min(this.length, end)-1] of this String-Buffer by the characters of str and return this StringBuffer.

public synchronized StringBuffer reverse()

Reverse the sequence of characters in this StringBuffer and return this StringBuffer.

public synchronized void setCharAt(int ind, char ch)

Execute this[ind]= ch;.

public synchronized void setLength(int len)

Set this StringBuffer's length to len, truncating existing characters or appending

the null character if len is greater or less than the current length. Throw an Index-OutOfBoundsException if len <0.

public String substring(int beg)
    = a String containing the characters in this[beg..].

public synchronized String substring(int beg, int end)
    = a String containing the characters in this[beg..end-1].

public String toString()
    = this StringBuffer's String representation.

D.5.2.21 CLASS **System**

public final class System extends Object

The underlying operating system. We specify only some of the things in this class: standard input, standard output, and error output streams; a method for quickly copying a portion of an array; and methods for terminating execution and invoking the garbage collector.

FIELDS

public static final InputStream in

The "standard" input stream, which typically corresponds to keyboard input.

public static final PrintStream out

The "standard" output stream, which typically corresponds to Java console. See class PrintStream for methods related to printing.

public static final PrintStream err

The "standard" error output stream, which typically corresponds to Java console. It is used to display error messages.

METHODS

public static native void arraycopy(Object src, int soff, Object dst, int doff, int len)

Copy src[soff..soff+len-1] to dst[doff .. doff+len-1]. It works even if src == dst, by copying first to a temporary array and then to dst.

Throw a NullPointerException if src or dst is null.

Throw an ArrayStoreException if either src or dst is not an array or src and dst have different types.

Throw an ArrayStoreException if an element of src cannot be converted to the component type of dst; previous array elements will already have been copied.

public static native long currentTimeMillis()
= the number of milliseconds since midnight on 1 January 1970.

public static void exit(int status)
Terminate the Java Virtual Machine. status = 0 means normal termination; status != 0, something bothersome happened.

public static void gc()
Ask the garbage collector to collect discarded objects in order to free up memory.

public static void setErr(PrintStream st)
public static void setIn(InputStream st)
public static void setOut(PrintStream st)
Change the "standard" error (or input or output) stream to st. Throw a SecurityException if it can't be done.

D.5.2.22   CLASS **Thread**

public class Thread extends Object
        implements Runnable
A thread of execution. Several execution threads can be running at the same time.

Each thread has a priority, which describes how important it is. Higher-priority threads get more CPU time.

A *daemon* thread is a background thread: when there are no non-daemon threads running, the Java Virtual Machine quits.

FIELDS
public static final int MIN_PRIORITY
public static final int NORM_PRIORITY
public static final int MAX_PRIORITY
Minimum, default, and maximum Thread priorities.

CONSTRUCTORS
public Thread()
A new Thread with no target object.

public Thread(Runnable target)
A new Thread associated with target; target.run is called when this Thread starts.

METHODS
public static native Thread currentThread()
= the currently-executing Thread.

public static void dumpStack()
Print a stack trace of the current thread.

public final String getName()
public final int getPriority()
= this Thread's name and priority.

public void interrupt()
Interrupt this Thread.

public static boolean interrupted()
= "this Thread was interrupted". Side effect: un-interrupts this thread.

public final native boolean isAlive()
= "this Thread has been started and has not died".

public final boolean isDaemon()
= "this Thread is a daemon".

public boolean isInterrupted()
= "this Thread was interrupted".

public void run()
Call this Thread's run method for the associated Runnable object. (Do nothing if not associated with anything.) Override this method.

public final void setDaemon(boolean b)
Make this Thread a daemon iff b. Throw an IllegalThreadStateException if called while this Thread is active.

public final void setName(String name)
Set this Thread's name to name.

public final void setPriority(int p)
Set this Thread's priority to p. Throw an IllegalArgumentException if p is not in the range MIN_PRIORITY..MAX_PRIORITY.

public static native void sleep(long m)
public static void sleep(long m, int n)
Pause the current thread for m milliseconds (and n nanoseconds). Throw an InterruptedException if another thread interrupts the sleeping thread.

public native synchronized void start()
Call this Thread's run method to start the new Thread. Throw an IllegalThreadStateException if this Thread was already started.

public String toString()
= this Thread's String representation.

public static native void yield()
Pause the executing Thread, allowing another Thread to execute.

D.5.2.23   CLASS **Throwable**

public class Throwable extends Object
    implements Serializable
    The superclass of any object that can be thrown by a throw statement or the Java Virtual Machine.

CONSTRUCTORS
public Throwable()
public Throwable(String s)
    A Throwable with no message or with message s.

METHODS
public native Throwable fillInStackTrace()
    Overwrite the original stack trace with the current one.
public String getMessage()
    = this Throwable's message.
public void printStackTrace()
    Print the stack trace in existence when this Throwable was created.
public String toString()
    = this Throwable's String representation.

D.5.2.24   CLASS **Void**

public final class Void extends Object
    Nothing. Nada. Not even a black hole. (Okay, it's a "wrapper" for a value of primitive type void. But just try and access that value: you can't. See?)

FIELDS
public static final Class TYPE
    = the object that represents primitive type void.

D.6   **Package java.text**

Package Contents   *Page*

Classes

Used by Format and its subclasses to keep track of the current position during parsing.

D.6.1   CLASSES

D.6.1.1   CLASS **NumberFormat**

public abstract class NumberFormat extends Format
    The interface for formatting and parsing numbers and finding out which locales have number formats. See the Program-Live Lab "Formatting in locales" in Lesson "Primitive types" for info on using this interface.

FIELDS
public static final int INTEGER_FIELD
public static final int FRACTION_FIELD
    Use these as an argument in creating a FieldPosition (in package java.text) to indicate whether the integer or fraction part of number is to be returned.

CONSTRUCTORS
public NumberFormat()

METHODS
public Object clone()
    = a clone of this instance.
public boolean equals(Object b)
    = "this instance equals b".
public final String format(double n)
    = number n in String form.
public abstract StringBuffer format(double n, StringBuffer toAppendTo, FieldPosition pos)
    See the Java API spec for details.
public final String format(long n)
    = number n in String form.
public abstract StringBuffer format(long n, StringBuffer toAppendTo, FieldPosition pos)
    See the Java API spec for details.
public final StringBuffer format(Object obj, StringBuffer toAppendTo, FieldPosition pos)
    See the Java API spec for details.
public static Locale[] getAvailableLocales()

= the Locales that have NumberFormats.

public static final NumberFormat
    getCurrencyInstance()
public static NumberFormat
    getCurrencyInstance(Locale loc)
    = a currency format for the default locale
    or for locale loc.

public static final NumberFormat
    getInstance()
public static NumberFormat
    getInstance(Locale loc)
    = the default number format for the de-
    fault locale or locale loc.

public int getMaximumFractionDigits()
public int getMaximumIntegerDigits()
    = the maximum number of digits allowed
    in the fraction part or integer part of a
    number.

public int getMinimumFractionDigits()
public int getMinimumIntegerDigits()
    = the minimum number of digits allowed
    in the fraction part or integer part of a
    number.

public static final NumberFormat
    getNumberInstance()
public static NumberFormat
    getNumberInstance(Locale loc)
    = a general-purpose number format for
    the default locale or for locale loc.

public static final NumberFormat
    getPercentInstance()
public static NumberFormat
    getPercentInstance(Locale loc)
    = a percentage format for the default lo-
    cale or for locale loc.

public static final NumberFormat
    getScientificInstance()
public static NumberFormat
    getScientificInstance(Locale loc)
    = a scientific format for the default locale
    or for locale loc.

public boolean isGroupingUsed()
    = "grouping is used in this instance" (e.g.
    2345 might appear as 2,345).

public boolean isParseIntegerOnly()
    = "this instance will parse numbers as in-
    tegers only".

public Number parse(String s)
    Parse s and return the parsed number (or
    part of it); the result is a Long (if possible)
    or a Double.

public abstract Number parse(String s,

ParsePosition p)
    Parse s[p..], change p to the index of the
    char following the parsed number, and re-
    turn the parsed number (or part of it); the
    result is a Long (if possible) or a Double.
    If nothing can be parsed, p is unchanged.

public final Object parseObject(String s,
    ParsePosition p)
    Parse s[p..], set p to the index of the first
    unparsed character in s, and return the
    parsed number. Return null if there is an
    error.

public void setGroupingUsed(boolean b)
    Hereafter, grouping will be used in this
    format iff b. See method isGroupingUsed.

public void setMaximumFractionDigits(int n)
public void setMaximumIntegerDigits(int n)
    Set the maximum number of digits al-
    lowed in the fraction part (or integer part)
    of a number to max(0,n). If this number is
    less than minimumFractionDigits (minimu-
    mIntegerDigits), set the latter to this num-
    ber also.

public void setMinimumFractionDigits(int n)
public void setMinimumIntegerDigits(int n)
    Set the minimum number of digits al-
    lowed in the fraction part (integer part)
    of a number to max(0,n). If this number is
    larger than maximumFractionDigits (max-
    imumIntegerDigits), set the latter to this
    number also.

public void setParseIntegerOnly(boolean b)
    After this call, numbers should be parsed
    as integers only iff b.

INHERITED FROM Format : clone, format,
parseObject

D.6.1.2 CLASS **ParsePosition**

public class ParsePosition extends Object
    Used by Format and its subclasses to keep
    track of the current position during pars-
    ing.

CONSTRUCTORS

public ParsePosition(int i)
    An instance with initial index i.

METHODS

public boolean equals(Object b)
    = "this instance equals b".

public int getErrorIndex()
> = the index at which an error occurred (-1 if the error index was not set).

public int getIndex()
> = the current parse position.

public void setErrorIndex(int ei)
> Set the index at which a parse error occurred.

public void setIndex(int i)
> Set the current parse position to i.

public String toString()
> = a string representation of this instance.

D.7   Package java.util

D.7.1   INTERFACES

D.7.1.1   INTERFACE **Collection**

public interface Collection
> A (possibly ordered) group of elements. Subclasses decide whether duplicate elements are allowed and whether null is allowed.
>
> It is standard for subclasses to provide both a constructor with no parameters

and one that has a parameter Collection c that copies elements from c into itself.

METHODS

public boolean add(Object b)
Try to add b to this Collection and return the value of "b was added". Subclasses may disallow duplicate elements or disallow certain values such as null.

Throw a ClassCastException if b's class is the wrong type. Throw an IllegalArgumentException if b is disallowed.

public boolean addAll(Collection c)
Add to this Collection every element in c and return the value of "at least one element was added".

public void clear()
Remove every element from this Collection.

public boolean contains(Object b)
= "this Collection contains b".

public boolean containsAll(Collection c)
= "this Collection contains every element in c".

public boolean equals(Object obj)
= "this Collection's are the same as obj's elements". If a subclass is a List or a Set, see those APIs for further specifications.

public boolean isEmpty()
= "this Collection is empty".

public Iterator iterator()
= an iterator for this Collection.

public boolean remove(Object obj)
Remove b from this Collection and return the value of "b was removed". (If there are several copies, remove only one. If there are no copies of b, return false.)

public boolean removeAll(Collection c)
Remove from this Collection every element in c and return the value of "at least one element was removed".

public boolean retainAll(Collection c)
Remove from this Collection every element that is not in c and return the value of "at least one element was removed".

public int size()
= this Collection's number of elements.

public Object[] toArray()
= a new array containing the elements in this Collection.

public Object[] toArray(Object[] b)
= an array that contains this Collection's elements. If b isn't big enough, allocate, fill, and return a new array. If b is big enough, fill b and return it; also, if b[this.size()] exists, set it to null.

Throw an ArrayStoreException if the base type of b is not a superclass of the class of every element in this Collection.

D.7.1.2   INTERFACE **Comparator**

public interface Comparator
An item comparer. Should be an equivalence relation: reflexive, symmetric, and transitive.

METHODS

public int compare(Object o1, Object o2)
>0, $= 0$, or <0, depending on whether o1 is greater than, equal to, or less than o2. Must be reflexive, symmetric, and transitive.

public boolean equals(Object b)
= "b equals this Comparator": both Comparator's compare methods must provide exactly the same answers.

D.7.1.3   INTERFACE **Enumeration**

public interface Enumeration
Attached to a Collection, much like a secretary is attached to a professor: an Enumeration has access to the contents of its Collection. An Enumeration returns the elements of its Collection one at a time, *in any order*. Use Iterator if you are using Java 1.2 or higher.

METHODS

public boolean hasMoreElements()
= "this Enumeration has elements that have not yet been returned by method nextElement".

public Object nextElement()
= the next element in this Enumeration's Collection. Throw a NoSuchElementException if this Enumeration's Collection has no more elements.

D.7.1.4 INTERFACE **Iterator**

public interface Iterator
Attached to a Collection, much like a secretary is attached to a professor: an Iterator has access to the contents of its Collection. An Iterator returns the elements of its Collection one at a time. Do not modify this Iterator's Collection while this this Iterator is in use: behaviour is unpredictable.

METHODS

public boolean hasNext()
= "this Iterator has elements that have not yet been returned by method next".

public Object next()
= the next element in this Iterator's Collection. Throw a NoSuchElementException if this Iterator's Collection has no more elements.

public void remove()
Remove from this Iterator's Collection the last element just returned by method next. If called more than once per call to next, behavior is unpredictable. Throw an UnsupportedOperationException if remove is not supported by this Iterator. Throw an IllegalStateException if there is no element to remove.

D.7.1.5 INTERFACE **List**

public interface List implements Collection
An ordered list of elements. Subclasses decide whether to allow null elements. They should throw an UnsupportedOperationException in any unimplemented methods.

METHODS

public void add(int ind, Object elem)
Insert elem at position this[ind], shifting this[ind..] to make room.

public boolean add(Object b)
Try to append b to this List and return the value of "b was added". Subclasses may disallow duplicate elements or disallow certain values such as null.

Throw a ClassCastException if b's class is the wrong type. Throw an IllegalArgumentException if b is disallowed.

public boolean addAll(Collection c)
Append to this List every element in c (using c's Iterator) and return the value of "at least one element was added".

public boolean addAll(int ind, Collection c)
Insert c's elements at position this[ind], shifting this[ind..] to make room, and return the value of "at least one element was added".

public void clear()
Remove every element from this List.

public boolean contains(Object b)
= "this List contains b".

public boolean containsAll(Collection c)
= "this List contains every element in c".

public boolean equals(Object b)
= "b is a List, and this List's elements are the same as b's elements, in the same order".

public Object get(int ind)
= element this[ind].

public int indexOf(Object b)
= the index of the first occurrence of b in this List (-1 if none).

public boolean isEmpty()
= "this List is empty".

public Iterator iterator()
= an Iterator for this List, returning the elements in order.

public int lastIndexOf(Object b)
= the index of the last occurrence of b in this List (-1 if none).

public ListIterator listIterator()
public ListIterator listIterator(int ind)
= an iterator for this List (operating only on this[ind..]).

public Object remove(int ind)
Remove element this[ind], shifting this[ind+1..] to fill the hole.

public boolean remove(Object b)
Remove b from this List and return the value of "b was removed". (If there are several copies, remove the first. If there are no copies of b, return false.)

public boolean removeAll(Collection c)
Remove from this List every element in c and return the value of "at least one element was removed".

public boolean retainAll(Collection c)
Remove from this List every element that is not in c and return the value of "at least one element was removed".

public Object set(int ind, Object elem)
 Replace element this[ind] with elem and return the old value of this[ind].

public int size()
 = this List's number of elements.

public List subList(int from, int to)
 = this[from..to-1]. Changing either the returned List or this List affects the other
 List!

public Object[] toArray()
 = a new array containing the elements in
 this List, in order.

public Object[] toArray(Object[] b)
 = an array that contains this List's elements. If b isn't big enough, allocate, fill,
 and return a new array. If b is big enough,
 fill b and return it; also, if b[this.size()] exists, set it to null.

 Throw an ArrayStoreException if the
 base type of b is not a superclass of the
 class of every element in this List.

D.7.1.6 INTERFACE **ListIterator**

public interface ListIterator implements
 Iterator
 Attached to a List, much like a secretary is
 attached to a professor: an ListIterator has
 access to the contents of its List. A ListIterator returns the elements of its List one at
 a time and can travel in either direction.
 Supports removal of elements. An element
 is *following* if it occurs after the current
 point in the List. An element is *preceding*
 if it occurs before the current point in the
 List. Do not modify this ListIterator's List
 while this ListIterator is in use: behaviour
 would be unpredictable.

METHODS
public void add(Object b)
 Insert b into this List: this List behaves as
 if b had just been returned by next.

public boolean hasNext()
public boolean hasPrevious()
 = "this List has following or previous elements".

public Object next()
 = the following element in this ListIterator's List. Throw a NoSuchElementException if this ListIterator's List has no more

elements.

public int nextIndex()
 = the index of the following element (the
 list size if the ListIterator is at the end of
 its List).

public Object previous()
 = the preceding element in this ListIterator's List. Throw a NoSuchElementException if this ListIterator's List has no preceding elements.

public int previousIndex()
 = the index of the following element (the
 list size if the ListIterator is at the beginning of its List).

public void remove()
 Remove from this ListIterator's List the element just returned by method next or previous. Call only once per call to method
 next or previous! Throw an Unsupported-
 OperationException if remove is not supported by this ListIterator. Throw an IllegalStateException if there is no element to
 remove.

public void set(Object b)
 Replace the element just returned by next
 or previous with b.

D.7.1.7 INTERFACE **Map**

public interface Map
 A function that maps keys to values. For
 each key k, the map contains at most one
 pair (k,v).
 Do not change key state while using a
 map: behaviour for any method that uses
 method equals to compare keys would be
 unpredictable.
 It is standard for subclasses to provide
 both a constructor with no parameters
 and one that has a parameter Map m that
 copies elements from m into itself.
 Generally methods throw a ClassCast-
 Exception if a parameter is of the wrong
 type for this Map and throw a NullPointerException if a key (or value) is null and
 this Map disallows null keys (or values).

METHODS
public void clear()
 Remove all key-value pairs from this Map.
public boolean containsKey(Object k)

"this Map contains a key-value pair (k,v) (for some k)".

public boolean containsValue(Object v)
= "this Map contains a key-value pair (k,v) (for some v)".

public Set entrySet()
= the key-value pairs (Map.Entrys) in this Map. Changing either the returned Set or this Map affects the other! Do not change this Map while using an Iterator over the Set, except through that Iterator's operations.

public boolean equals(Object b)
= "b is a Map that contains the same Map.Entry key-value pairs as this Map".

public Object get(Object k)
= v in the key-value pair (k,v) (null if no such pair).

public boolean isEmpty()
= "this Map contains no key-value pairs".

public Set keySet()
= the keys in this Map. Changing either the returned Set or this Map affects the other! Do not change this Map while using an Iterator over the Set, except through that Iterator's operations.

public Object put(Object k, Object v)
Add the key-value pair (k,v) to this Map and return the old value that was associated with k (null if none).

public void putAll(Map t)
Add all key-value pairs (k,v) in t to this Map (replace old pairs if they exist).

public Object remove(Object k)
Remove the key-value pair (k,v) (if it exists) and return the old value associated with k (null if none).

public int size()
= this Map's number of key-value pairs.

public Collection values()
= the values in this Map. Changing either the returned Collection or this Map affects the other! Do not change this Map while using an Iterator over the Collection, except through that Iterator's operations.

D.7.1.8   INTERFACE **Map.Entry**

public static interface Map.Entry
A key-value pair in a Map. Warning: an Entry is *not* directly inside a Map. Instead, Entrys are created as needed by an Iterator of the Set returned by Map.entrySet.

METHODS

public boolean equals(Object b)
= "b is an Entry that represents the same key-value pair as this Entry".

public Object getKey()
public Object getValue()
= this Entry's key or value.

public Object setValue(Object v)
Replace this Entry's value with v and return the old value.

D.7.1.9   INTERFACE **Set**

public interface Set implements Collection
An unordered list of unique elements –a mathematical set. Subclasses decide whether to allow null elements. They should throw an UnsupportedOperationException in any unimplemented methods.

METHODS

public boolean add(Object b)
Try to insert b into this Set and return the value of "b was added". Duplicate elements are disallowed. Subclasses may also disallow null. Throw a ClassCastException if b's class is the wrong type. Throw an IllegalArgumentException if b is disallowed.

public boolean addAll(Collection c)
Make this Set the union of this Set and c and return the value of "at least one element was added".

public void clear()
Remove every element from this Set.

public boolean contains(Object b)
= "this Set contains b".

public boolean containsAll(Collection c)
= "this Set is a superset of c".

public boolean equals(Object b)
= "b is a Set, and this Set and b are subsets of each other".

public boolean isEmpty()
= "this Set is empty".

public Iterator iterator()
= an Iterator for this Set.

public boolean remove(Object b)

Remove b from this Set and return the value of "b was removed". If there are no copies of b, return false.

public boolean removeAll(Collection c)
 Remove from this Set all elements that are in c and return the value of "at least one element was removed".

public boolean retainAll(Collection c)
 Remove from this Set all elements that are not in c and return the value of "at least one element was removed".

public int size()
 = this Set's number of elements.

public Object[] toArray()
 = a new array containing the elements in this Set.

public Object[] toArray(Object[] b)
 = an array that contains this Set's elements. If b isn't big enough, allocate, fill, and return a new array. If b is big enough, fill b and return it; also, if b[this.size()] exists, set it to null.

 Throw an ArrayStoreException if the base type of b is not a superclass of the class of every element in this Set.

D.7.2 CLASSES

D.7.2.1 CLASS **AbstractCollection**

public abstract class AbstractCollection
 extends Object implements Collection
 A (possibly ordered) group of elements. Subclasses decide whether duplicate elements are allowed. It is standard for subclasses to provide both a constructor with no parameters and one that has a parameter Collection c that copies elements from c into itself. Some methods simply throw an UnsupportedOperationException.

CONSTRUCTORS

protected AbstractCollection()
 An empty AbstractCollection.

METHODS

public boolean add(Object b)
 Throw an UnsupportedOperationException. See Collection.add(Object).

public boolean addAll(Collection c)

Add to this AbstractCollection every element in c and return the value of "at least one element was added".

public void clear()
 Remove every element from this AbstractCollection.

public boolean contains(Object b)
 = "this AbstractCollection contains b".

public boolean containsAll(Collection c)
 = "this AbstractCollection contains every element in c".

public boolean isEmpty()
 = "this AbstractCollection is empty".

public abstract Iterator iterator()
 = an iterator for this AbstractCollection.

public boolean remove(Object b)
 Remove b from this AbstractCollection and return the value of "b was removed". (If there are several copies, remove the first. If there are no copies of b, return false.)

public boolean removeAll(Collection c)
 Remove from this AbstractCollection every element in c and return the value of "at least one element was removed".

public boolean retainAll(Collection c)
 Remove from this AbstractCollection every element that is not in c and return the value of "at least one element was removed".

public abstract int size()
 = this AbstractCollection's number of elements.

public Object[] toArray()
 = a new array containing the elements in this AbstractCollection. Uses an iterator for this AbstractCollection.

public Object[] toArray(Object[] b)
 = an array that contains this AbstractCollection's elements. If b isn't big enough, allocate, fill, and return a new array. If b is big enough, fill b and return it; also, if b[this.size()] exists, set it to null.

 Throw an ArrayStoreException if the base type of b is not a superclass of the class of every element in this AbstractCollection.

public String toString()
 = this AbstractCollection's String representation.

D.7.2.2 CLASS **AbstractList**

public abstract class AbstractList extends
  AbstractCollection implements List
A basic implementation of interface List.
Some methods simply throw an UnsupportedOperationException. Methods that
insert require method add to be implemented, Methods that remove require
method remove to be implemented.

CONSTRUCTORS

protected AbstractList()
  An empty AbstractCollection.

METHODS

public void add(int index, Object element)
  Throw an UnsupportedOperationException. See List.add(int,Object).

public boolean add(Object b)
  Try to append b to this AbstractList and
  return the value of "b was added". Subclasses may disallow duplicate elements or
  disallow certain values such as null.
    Throw a ClassCastException if b's class
  is the wrong type. Throw an IllegalArgumentException if b is disallowed.

public boolean addAll(int ind, Collection c)
  Insert c's elements at position this[ind],
  shifting this[ind..] to make room.

public void clear()
  Remove every element from this AbstractList.

public boolean equals(Object b)
  = "b is a List, and this AbstractList's elements are the same as b's elements, in the
  same order".

public abstract Object get(int index)
  = element this[ind].

public int indexOf(Object b)
  = the index of the first occurrence of b in
  this AbstractList (-1 if none).

public Iterator iterator()
  = an iterator for this AbstractList.

public int lastIndexOf(Object b)
  = the index of the last occurrence of b in
  this AbstractList (-1 if none).

public ListIterator listIterator()
public ListIterator listIterator(int ind)
  = an iterator for this AbstractList (operating on this[0..] or this[ind..]).

public Object remove(int ind)
  Throw an UnsupportedOperationException. See List.remove(int).

protected void removeRange(int from, int to)
  Remove this[from..to-1] from this list,
  shifting this[to..] to fill the big hole. This
  implementation uses a list iterator and
  calls its method remove once for each element being removed. If remove requires
  linear time, this implementation requires
  quadratic time. Override it to get better
  performance.

public Object set(int ind, Object elem)
  Throw an UnsupportedOperationException. See List.set(int,Object).

public List subList(int from, int to)
  = this[from..to-1]. Changing either the returned List or this AbstractList affects the
  other List!

INHERITED FROM AbstractCollection (in
  D.7.2.1, p. 301) : add, addAll, clear,
  contains, containsAll, isEmpty, iterator,
  remove, removeAll, retainAll, size, toArray,
  toString

D.7.2.3 CLASS **AbstractMap**

public abstract class AbstractMap extends
  Object implements Map
A basic implementation of interface Map.
Some methods currently throw an UnsupportedOperationException. Methods that
insert require method add to be implemented, Methods that remove require
method remove to be implemented.
  It is standard for subclasses to provide
both a constructor with no parameters
and one that has a parameter AbstractMap
m that copies elements from m into itself.
  Generally methods throw a ClassCastException if a parameter is of the wrong
type for this Map and throw a NullPointerException if a key (or value) is null and
this Map disallows null keys (or values).

CONSTRUCTORS

protected AbstractMap()

METHODS

public void clear()
  Remove all key-value pairs from this AbstractMap.

public boolean containsKey(Object key)
"this Map contains a key-value pair (k,v) (for some k)". Running time: linear.

public boolean containsValue(Object v)
= "this Map contains a key-value pair (k,v) (for some k)". Running time: linear.

public abstract Set entrySet()
= the key-value pairs (Map.Entrys) in this Map. Changing either the returned Set or this Map affects the other! Do not change this Map while using an Iterator over the Set, except through that Iterator's operations.

public boolean equals(Object b)
= "b is a Map that contains the same Map.Entry key-value pairs as this Map".

public Object get(Object k)
= v in the key-value pair (k,v) (null if no such pair). Running time: linear.

public boolean isEmpty()
= "this Map contains no key-value pairs".

public Set keySet()
= the keys in this Map. Changing either the returned Set or this Map affects the other! Do not change this Map while using an Iterator over the Set, except through that Iterator's operations.

public Object put(Object k, Object v)
Throw an UnsupportedOperationException. See Map.put(Object,Object).

public void putAll(Map t)
Add all key-value pairs (k,v) in t to this Map (replace old pairs if they exist).

public Object remove(Object k)
Remove the key-value pair (k,v) (if it exists) and return v (or null). Running time: linear.

public int size()
= this AbstractMap's number of key-value pairs.

public String toString()
= this AbstractMap's String representation.

public Collection values()
= the values in this Map. Changing either the returned Collection or this Map affects the other! Do not change this Map while using an Iterator over the Collection, except through that Iterator's operations.

D.7.2.4 CLASS AbstractSequentialList

public abstract class AbstractSequentialList extends AbstractList
A basic implementation of AbstractList. Requires only method ListIterator to be implemented.

CONSTRUCTORS

protected AbstractSequentialList()
An empty AbstractSequentialList.

METHODS

public void add(int ind, Object elem)
Insert elem at position this[ind], shifting this[ind..] to make room.

public boolean addAll(int index, Collection c)
Insert c's elements at position this[ind], shifting this[ind..] to make room, and return the value of "at least one element was added".

public Object get(int ind)
= element this[ind].

public Iterator iterator()

public abstract ListIterator listIterator(int ind)
= an iterator for this AbstractSequentialList (operating on this[0..] or this[ind..]).

public Object remove(int ind)
Remove and return element this[ind], shifting this[ind+1..] to fill the hole.

public Object set(int ind, Object elem)
Replace this[ind] by elem and return the old value in this[ind].

INHERITED FROM AbstractList (in D.7.2.2, p. 302) : 16

INHERITED FROM AbstractCollection (in D.7.2.1, p. 301) : add, addAll, clear, contains, containsAll, isEmpty, iterator, remove, removeAll, retainAll, size, toArray, toString

D.7.2.5 CLASS AbstractSet

public abstract class AbstractSet extends AbstractCollection implements Set
A basic implementation of interface Set. Some methods currently throw an UnsupportedOperationException. Methods that insert require method add to be imple-

mented, Methods that remove require method remove to be implemented.

CONSTRUCTORS

protected AbstractSet()
An empty AbstractSet.

METHODS

public boolean equals(Object b)
= "b is a Set, and this Set and b are subsets of each other".

public boolean removeAll(Collection c)
Remove from this Set all elements that are in c and return the value of "at least one element was removed".

INHERITED FROM AbstractCollection (in D.7.2.1, p. 301) : add, addAll, clear, contains, containsAll, isEmpty, iterator, remove, removeAll, retainAll, size, toArray, toString

D.7.2.6 CLASS ArrayList

public class ArrayList extends AbstractList
implements List, Cloneable, Serializable
A resizable list, much like Vector but not synchronized.

CONSTRUCTORS

public ArrayList()
An empty ArrayList with initial capacity 10 and capacity increment 1.

public ArrayList(Collection c)
An ArrayList containing every element in c. The capacity is 1.1 * c.size().

public ArrayList(int c)
An empty ArrayList with initial capacity c and capacity increment 1. Throw an IllegalArgumentException if c <0.

METHODS

public void add(int ind, Object b)
Insert b at position this[ind], shifting this[ind..] to make room.

public boolean add(Object b)
Append b to this ArrayList and return true.

public boolean addAll(Collection c)
Append to this List every element in c and return the value of "at least one element was added".

public boolean addAll(int ind, Collection c)
Insert c's elements at position this[ind], shifting this[ind..] to make room, and return the value of "at least one element was added".

public void clear()
Remove every element from this ArrayList.

public Object clone()
= a shallow copy of this ArrayList.

public boolean contains(Object b)
= "this ArrayList contains b".

public void ensureCapacity(int m)
Make sure that this ArrayList can hold at least m elements.

public Object get(int ind)
= element this[ind].

public int indexOf(Object elem)
= the index of the first occurrence of b in this ArrayList (-1 if none).

public boolean isEmpty()
= "this ArrayList is empty".

public int lastIndexOf(Object b)
= the index of the last occurrence of b in this ArrayList (-1 if none).

public Object remove(int ind)
Remove element this[ind], shifting this[ind+1..] to fill the hole.

protected void removeRange(int from, int to)
Remove elements this[from..to-1] from this ArrayList, shifting this[to..] to fill the big hole.

public Object set(int ind, Object elem)
Replace element this[ind] with elem and return the old value of this[ind].

public int size()
= this ArrayList's number of elements.

public Object[] toArray()
= a new array containing the elements in this ArrayList, in order.

public Object[] toArray(Object[] b)
= an array that contains this ArrayList's elements. If b isn't big enough, allocate, fill, and return a new array. If b is big enough, fill b and return it; also, if b[this.size()] exists, set it to null.
Throw an ArrayStoreException if the base type of b is not a superclass of the class of every element in this ArrayList.

INHERITED FROM AbstractList (in D.7.2.2, p. 302) : 16

INHERITED FROM AbstractCollection (in D.7.2.1, p. 301) : add, addAll, clear, contains, containsAll, isEmpty, iterator, remove, removeAll, retainAll, size, toArray, toString

D.7.2.7 CLASS **Arrays**

public class Arrays extends Object
Static methods for array manipulation. Sort methods are either *stable* (order of equal keys is maintained) or *unstable*.

METHODS

public static List asList(Object[] a)
= a List containing the same elements as a. Changing the List changes a as well!

public static int binarySearch(byte[] a, byte key)

public static int binarySearch(char[] a, char key)

public static int binarySearch(double[] a, double key)

public static int binarySearch(float[] a, float key)

public static int binarySearch(int[] a, int key)

public static int binarySearch(long[] a, long key)
= an index of key in b, or an index i that satisfies this[i] <this[i+1] if key is not in b. A binary search is used. Array b must be sorted (in ascending order). See Program-Live for a better binary search algorithm.

public static int binarySearch(Object[] a, Object key)
= an index of key in b, or an index i that satisfies this[i] <this[i+1] if key is not in b. A binary search is used. Array b must be sorted (in ascending order). Array elements must implement interface Compa-rable. See ProgramLive for a better binary search algorithm.

public static int binarySearch(Object[] a, Object key, Comparator c)
= an index of key in b, or an index i that satisfies this[i] <this[i+1] if key is not in b. A binary search is used, using c to de-termine element order. Array b must be sorted (in ascending order). See Program-Live for a better binary search algorithm.

public static int binarySearch(short[] a, short key)

= an index of key in b, or an index i that satisfies this[i] <this[i+1] if key is not in b. A binary search is used. Array b must be sorted (in ascending order). See Program-Live for a better binary search algorithm.

public static boolean equals(boolean[] a, boolean[] a2)

public static boolean equals(byte[] a, byte[] a2)

public static boolean equals(char[] a, char[] a2)

public static boolean equals(double[] a, double[] a2)

public static boolean equals(float[] a, float[] a2)

public static boolean equals(int[] a, int[] a2)

public static boolean equals(long[] a, long[] a2)

public static boolean equals(Object[] a, Object[] a2)

public static boolean equals(short[] a, short[] a2)
= "a == a2: a contains the same elements as a2 in the same order".

public static void fill(boolean[] a, boolean v)

public static void fill(boolean[] a, int from, int to, boolean v)

public static void fill(byte[] a, byte v)

public static void fill(byte[] a, int from, int to, byte v)

public static void fill(char[] a, char v)

public static void fill(char[] a, int from, int to, char v)

public static void fill(double[] a, double v)

public static void fill(double[] a, int from, int to, double v)

public static void fill(float[] a, float v)

public static void fill(float[] a, int from, int to, float v)

public static void fill(int[] a, int v)

public static void fill(int[] a, int from, int to, int v)

public static void fill(long[] a, int from, int to, long v)

public static void fill(long[] a, long v)

public static void fill(Object[] a, int from, int to, Object v)

public static void fill(Object[] a, Object v)

public static void fill(short[] a, int from, int to, short v)

public static void fill(short[] a, short v)
Assign v to each location in a (or to each location in a[from..to-1].

public static void sort(byte[] a)
public static void sort(byte[] a, int from, int
    to)
public static void sort(char[] a)
public static void sort(char[] a, int from, int
    to)
public static void sort(double[] a)
public static void sort(double[] a, int from, int
    to)
public static void sort(float[] a)
public static void sort(float[] a, int from, int
    to)
public static void sort(int[] a)
public static void sort(int[] a, int from, int to)
public static void sort(long[] a)
public static void sort(long[] a, int from, int
    to)
> Sort a (or a[from..to-1]. Uses Quick sort. It
> is unstable and has average running time
> $O(n*\log(n))$.

public static void sort(Object[] a)
> Sort a (or a[from..to-1]. Uses a stable
> merge sort and has average running time
> $O(n*\log(n))$ (near $O(n)$ if a is almost
> sorted). Array elements must implement
> interface Comparable.

public static void sort(Object[] a, Comparator
    c)
> Sort a (or a[from..to-1] using c. Uses a sta-
> ble merge sort and has average running
> time $O(n*\log(n))$ (near $O(n)$ if a is almost
> sorted).

public static void sort(Object[] a, int from,
    int to)
> Sort a (or a[from..to-1]. Uses a stable
> merge sort and has average running time
> $O(n*\log(n))$ (near $O(n)$ if a is almost
> sorted). Array elements must implement
> interface Comparable.

public static void sort(Object[] a, int from,
    int to, Comparator c)
> Sort a (or a[from..to-1] using c. Uses a sta-
> ble merge sort and has average running
> time $O(n*\log(n))$ (near $O(n)$ if a is almost
> sorted).

public static void sort(short[] a)
public static void sort(short[] a, int from, int
    to)
> Sort a (or a[from..to-1]. Uses Quick sort. It
> is unstable and has average running time
> $O(n*\log(n))$.

D.7.2.8   CLASS **Calendar**

public abstract class Calendar extends
    Object implements Serializable,
    Cloneable
> A calendar representing a time; also used
> to manipulate Dates.

CONSTRUCTORS

protected Calendar()
> A Calendar with the default time zone and
> locale.

protected Calendar(TimeZone tz, Locale loc)
> A Calendar with time zone tz and locale
> loc.

METHODS

public boolean after(Object b)
public boolean before(Object b)
> = "b instanceof Calendar and this Calen-
> dar's current time comes after (before) b's
> time".

public Object clone()
> = a copy of this Calendar.

public boolean equals(Object b)
> = "this Calender is the same as b, includ-
> ing date, time, and time zone".

public static synchronized Locale[]
    getAvailableLocales()
> = the Locales that have Calendars.

public static synchronized Calendar
    getInstance()
public static synchronized Calendar
    getInstance(Locale loc)
public static synchronized Calendar
    getInstance(TimeZone z)
public static synchronized Calendar
    getInstance(TimeZone z, Locale loc)
> = a GregorianCalendar calendar for the
> current time zone and locale (or time zone
> z and locale loc) representing the current
> date and time.

public final Date getTime()
> = this Calendar's current date and time.

protected long getTimeInMillis()
> = this Calendar's current time in millisec-
> onds since midnight on 1 January 1970.

public TimeZone getTimeZone()
> = this Calendar's time zone

public final void setTime(Date d)
> Set this Calendar's current date and time

to d.

public void setTimeInMillis(long m)
Set this Calendar's current time to m.

public void setTimeZone(TimeZone z)
Set this Calendar's time zone to z.

public String toString()
= this Calendar's String representation.

D.7.2.9   CLASS **Date**

public class Date extends Object implements
Serializable, Cloneable, Comparable
A date and time, in milliseconds since 1
Jan 1970, 00:00:00 GMT.

CONSTRUCTORS

public Date()
public Date(long d)
A Date containing the current time (or
d, the number of milliseconds since 1 Jan
1970).

METHODS

public boolean after(Date d)
public boolean before(Date d)
= "this Date comes after or before d".

public Object clone()
= a copy of this Date.

public int compareTo(Date d)
public int compareTo(Object d)
>0, = 0, or <0, depending on whether this
Date is after, the same as, or before d.

public boolean equals(Object b)
= "b != null and is a Date that has the
same time as this Date".

public long getTime()
= this Date time, in milliseconds since 1
Jan 1970.

public void setTime(long t)
Set this Date's time to t, a number of milliseconds since 1 Jan 1970.

public String toString()
= this Date's String representation.

D.7.2.10   CLASS **Dictionary**

public abstract class Dictionary extends
Object
A function that maps keys to values. For

each key k, the map contains at most one
pair (k,v). Use interface Map if you are
using Java 1.2 or higher.

CONSTRUCTORS

public Dictionary()
An empty Dictionary.

METHODS

public abstract Enumeration elements()
= the values in this Dictionary.

public abstract Object get(Object k)
= v in the key-value pair (k,v) (null if no
such pair).

public abstract boolean isEmpty()
= "this Dictionary contains no key-value
pairs".

public abstract Enumeration keys()
= the keys in this Dictionary.

public abstract Object put(Object k, Object
v)
Add the key-value pair (k,v) to this Dictionary and return the old v value (null if
none).

public abstract Object remove(Object k)
Remove the key-value pair (k,v) (if it exists) and return the old value associated
with k (null if none).

public abstract int size()
= this Dictionary's number of key-value
pairs.

D.7.2.11   CLASS **LinkedList**

public class LinkedList extends
AbstractSequentialList implements
List, Cloneable, Serializable
A linked list of elements. Modifying this
LinkedList while an iterator is being used
throws a ConcurrentModificationException.

CONSTRUCTORS

public LinkedList()
An empty LinkedList.

public LinkedList(Collection c)
A LinkedList containing c's elements.

METHODS

public void add(int ind, Object elem)
Insert elem at position this[ind], shifting

this[ind..] to make room.

public boolean add(Object b)
  Append b to this LinkedList and return true.

public boolean addAll(Collection c)
public boolean addAll(int ind, Collection c)
  Append every element in c (using c's Iterator) to this List (or insert them at position this[ind], shifting this[ind..] to make room) and return the value of "at least one element was added".

public void addFirst(Object b)
public void addLast(Object b)
  Prepend (append) b to this List.

public void clear()
  Remove every element from this LinkedList.

public Object clone()
  = a shallow copy of this LinkedList.

public boolean contains(Object b)
  = "b is in this LinkedList".

public Object get(int index)
  = element this[ind].

public Object getFirst()
public Object getLast()
  = This LinkedList's first (or last) element. Throw a NoSuchElementException if none.

public int indexOf(Object b)
public int lastIndexOf(Object b)
  = the index of the first (last) occurrence of b in this List (-1 if none).

public ListIterator listIterator(int ind)
  = an iterator for this List, operating only on this[ind..].

public Object remove(int ind)
  Remove element this[ind], shifting this[ind+1..] to fill the hole.

public boolean remove(Object b)
  Remove the first occurrence of b from this LinkedList (if it exists) and return the value of "b was removed".

public Object removeFirst()
public Object removeLast()
  Remove and return this LinkedList's first (last) element. Throw a NoSuchElementException if none.

public Object set(int ind, Object elem)
  Replace element this[ind] with elem and return the old value of this[ind].

public int size()
  = this LinkedList's number of elements.

public Object[] toArray()
  = a new array containing the elements in this List, in order.

public Object[] toArray(Object[] b)
  = an array that contains this List's elements. If b isn't big enough, allocate, fill, and return a new array. If b is big enough, fill b and return it; also, if b[this.size()] exists, set it to null.
  Throw an ArrayStoreException if the base type of b is not a superclass of the class of every element in this List.

INHERITED FROM AbstractSequentialList (in D.7.2.4, p. 303) : add, addAll, get, iterator, listIterator, remove, set

INHERITED FROM AbstractList (in D.7.2.2, p. 302) : 16

INHERITED FROM AbstractCollection (in D.7.2.1, p. 301) : add, addAll, clear, contains, containsAll, isEmpty, iterator, remove, removeAll, retainAll, size, toArray, toString

D.7.2.12   CLASS Locale

public final class Locale extends Object
    implements Cloneable, Serializable
  A region, language, or culture, such as English. Among other things, it provides methods (or classes that provide methods) for formatting decimal numbers, currencies, and percentages the way they do it in that Locale. The ProgramLive lab "Formatting in locales" in lesson "Primitive types" explains the basics of using locales.

FIELDS

public static final Locale ENGLISH
public static final Locale FRENCH
public static final Locale GERMAN
public static final Locale ITALIAN
public static final Locale JAPANESE
public static final Locale KOREAN
public static final Locale CHINESE
public static final Locale
      SIMPLIFIED_CHINESE
public static final Locale
      TRADITIONAL_CHINESE
public static final Locale FRANCE
public static final Locale GERMANY
public static final Locale ITALY
public static final Locale JAPAN

public static final Locale KOREA
public static final Locale CHINA
public static final Locale PRC
public static final Locale TAIWAN
public static final Locale UK
public static final Locale US
public static final Locale CANADA
public static final Locale CANADA_FRENCH
  Constant locales.

METHODS

public boolean equals(Object b)
  = "this Locale equals b –b is a locale with identical language, country, and variant".

public static Locale[] getAvailableLocales()
  = all available locales.

public String getCountry()
  = the ISO 2-letter country code for this Locale ("" if none).

public static Locale getDefault()
  = the default locale.

public final String getDisplayCountry()
public String getDisplayCountry(Locale d)
  = a real name (such as England) for this Locale's (or d's) country ("" if none).

public final String getDisplayLanguage()
public String getDisplayLanguage(Locale inL)
  = a real name (such as "English") for this Locale's (or inL's) language ("" if none).

public final String getDisplayName()
public String getDisplayName(Locale inL)
  = a real name for this Locale (or inL's) ("" if none).

public String getISO3Country()
public String getISO3Language()
  = the ISO 3-letter country or language code for this Locale ("" if none).

public static String[] getISOCountries()
  = 2-letter country codes defined in ISO 3166.

public static String[] getISOLanguages()
  = 2-letter language codes defined in ISO 639.

public String getLanguage()
  = the 2-letter language code for this Locale ("" if none).

public static synchronized void
    setDefault(Locale loc)
  Set the default locale to loc. Throw a SecurityException if this operation is not allowed. Throw a NullPointerException if loc

= null.

public final String toString()
  = this Locale's String representation.

D.7.2.13 CLASS **Random**

public class Random extends Object
        implements Serializable
  A generator for a stream of pseudorandom numbers.

CONSTRUCTORS

public Random()
public Random(long s)
  A Random with seed is based on the current time (or s).

METHODS

protected synchronized int next(int b)
  = the next pseudorandom number. If $1 <= b <= 32$, then the low-order b bits of the result will be (approximately) independently chosen bit values, each of which is equally likely to be 0 and 1.

public boolean nextBoolean()
public double nextDouble()
public float nextFloat()
public int nextInt()
public int nextInt(int n)
public long nextLong()
  = this Random's next pseudorandom value (in the range 0..n-1).

public synchronized void setSeed(long s)
  Set the seed of this Random using s.

D.7.2.14 CLASS **StringTokenizer**

public class StringTokenizer extends Object
        implements Enumeration
  A String parser. Turns embedded substrings and numbers into "tokens".

CONSTRUCTORS

public StringTokenizer(String s)
  A StringTokenizer for s, using space, tab, newline, carriage-return, and form-feed as delimiters. Delimiters are not returned as tokens.

public StringTokenizer(String s, String delim)
public StringTokenizer(String s, String delim,

boolean b)

A StringTokenizer for s. Uses the characters in delim as delimiters, which are not returned as tokens (or are are returned as tokens iff b.)

METHODS

public int countTokens()

= the number of tokens left in this StringTokenizer's String.

public boolean hasMoreElements()
public boolean hasMoreTokens()

= "more tokens are available in this StringTokenizer's String".

public Object nextElement()
public String nextToken()

= the next token from this StringTokenizer. Throw a NoSuchElementException if at the end of this StringTokenizer's String.

public String nextToken(String delim)

Change the delimiters to the characters in delim and return the next token in this StringTokenizer's String. Throw a NoSuchElementException if at the end of this StringTokenizer's String.

D.7.2.15 CLASS **Vector**

public class Vector extends AbstractList
    implements List, Cloneable, Serializable
A resizable list, much like ArrayList but synchronized.

CONSTRUCTORS

public Vector()

An empty Vector with initial capacity 10 and capacity increment 1.

public Vector(Collection c)

A Vector containing every element in c. The capacity is 1.1 * c.size().

public Vector(int c)
public Vector(int c, int i)

An empty Vector with initial capacity 10 (or c) and capacity increment 0 (or i). Throw an IllegalArgumentException if c <0.

METHODS

public void add(int ind, Object b)

Insert b at position this[ind], shifting this[ind..] to make room.

public synchronized boolean add(Object b)

Append b to this Vector and return true.

public synchronized boolean
    addAll(Collection c)

Append to this Vector every element in c (using c's Iterator) and return the value of "at least one element was added".

public synchronized boolean addAll(int ind,
    Collection c)

Insert c's elements at position this[ind], shifting this[ind..] to make room, and return the value of "at least one element was added".

public synchronized void addElement(Object b)

Append b to this Vector.

public int capacity()

= this Vector's capacity.

public void clear()

Remove all elements from this Vector.

public synchronized Object clone()

= a shallow copy of this Vector.

public boolean contains(Object b)

= "b is an element of this Vector".

public synchronized boolean
    containsAll(Collection c)

= "this Vector contains all of c's elements".

public synchronized void copyInto(Object[] b)

Copy this Vector's elements into b. Throw an IndexOutOfBoundsException if b is not big enough.

public synchronized Object elementAt(int ind)

= this[ind].

public Enumeration elements()

= the elements of this Vector.

public synchronized void ensureCapacity(int m)

Make sure that this Vector can hold at least m elements.

public synchronized boolean equals(Object b)

= "b is a List, and this Vector's elements are the same as b's elements, in the same order".

public synchronized Object firstElement()

= this[0]. Throw a NoSuchElementException if this Vector is empty.

public synchronized Object get(int ind)

= element this[ind].

public int indexOf(Object b)

public synchronized int indexOf(Object b, int ind)
= the index of the first occurrence of b in this Vector (or in this[ind..]) (-1 if none).

public synchronized void insertElementAt(Object b, int ind)
Insert elem at position this[ind], shifting this[ind..] to make room. Append if ind = size().

public boolean isEmpty()
= "this Vector is empty".

public synchronized Object lastElement()
= this[this.size()-1]. Throw a NoSuchElementException if this Vector is empty.

public int lastIndexOf(Object b)

public synchronized int lastIndexOf(Object b, int ind)
= the index of the first occurrence of b in this Vector (or in this[0..ind]) (-1 if none).

public synchronized Object remove(int ind)
Remove element this[ind], shifting this[ind+1..] to fill the hole.

public boolean remove(Object b)
Remove the first occurrence of b (if present) and return the value of "an element was removed".

public synchronized boolean removeAll(Collection c)
Remove from this Vector every element in c and return the value of "at least one element was removed".

public synchronized void removeAllElements()
Remove every element from this Vector.

public synchronized boolean removeElement(Object b)
Remove the first occurrence of b from this Vector and return the value of "an element was removed".

public synchronized void removeElementAt(int ind)
Remove element this[ind], shifting this[ind+1..] to fill the hole.

protected void removeRange(int from, int to)
Remove elements this[from..to-1], shifting elements this[to..] to fill the big hole.

public synchronized boolean retainAll(Collection c)
Remove from this Vector every element that is not in c and return the value of "at least one element was removed".

public synchronized Object set(int ind, Object b)
Replace element this[ind] with elem and return the old value of this[ind].

public synchronized void setElementAt(Object b, int ind)
Change element this[ind] to b.

public synchronized void setSize(int s)
Set this Vector's size to s —add nulls if the size is increased, or delete elements from the end if decreased. Throw an ArrayIndexOutOfBoundsException if s <0.

public int size()
= this Vector's number of elements.

public List subList(int from, int to)
= the sublist this[from..to-1]. Any future changes to the result will cause a change in this Vector!

public synchronized Object[] toArray()
= a new array containing the elements in this Vector, in order.

public synchronized Object[] toArray(Object[] b)
= an array that contains this Vector's elements. If b isn't big enough, allocate, fill, and return a new array. If b is big enough, fill b and return it; also, if b[this.size()] exists, set it to null.

Throw an ArrayStoreException if the base type of the b (in the method call) is not a superclass of the class of every element in this Vector.

public synchronized String toString()
= this Vector's String representation.

INHERITED FROM AbstractList (in D.7.2.2, p. 302) : 16

INHERITED FROM AbstractCollection (in D.7.2.1, p. 301) : add, addAll, clear, contains, containsAll, isEmpty, iterator, remove, removeAll, retainAll, size, toArray, toString

D.8 Package javax.swing

Package Contents   *Page*

Interfaces

D.8.1   INTERFACES

D.8.1.1   INTERFACE   **ListSelectionModel**

public interface ListSelectionModel
   Describes the state of the selections in a list of selectable values.

FIELDS

public static final int SINGLE_SELECTION
   Allow only one item selection at a time.

public static final int
   SINGLE_INTERVAL_SELECTION
   Allow selection of a contiguous range.

public static final int
   MULTIPLE_INTERVAL_SELECTION

Allow any selections.

METHODS

public void addListSelectionLis-
    tener(ListSelectionListener
    l)
Register l to respond to this ListSelection-
Model's selection events.

public void addSelectionInterval(int from, int
    to)
Add this[from..to] to the selection.

public void clearSelection()
Deselect everything.

public int getMaxSelectionIndex()
public int getMinSelectionIndex()
= the highest and lowest selected index
(-1 if none).

public int getSelectionMode()
= the selection mode (one of the class constants).

public boolean isSelectedIndex(int ind)
= "this[ind] is selected".

public boolean isSelectionEmpty()
= "nothing is selected".

public void removeListSelectionLis-
    tener(ListSelectionListener
    l)
Deregister l: it will no longer respond to
this ListSelectionModel's events.

public void removeSelectionInterval(int from,
    int to)
Deselect this[from..to].

public void setSelectionInterval(int from, int
    to)
Change the selection to this[from..to].

public void setSelectionMode(int m)
Set the selection mode to m (one of the
class constants).

D.8.1.2 INTERFACE SwingConstants

public interface SwingConstants
    Constants used in javax.swing.

FIELDS

public static final int CENTER
public static final int TOP
public static final int LEFT
public static final int BOTTOM
public static final int RIGHT

Constants: location in a box.

public static final int NORTH
public static final int NORTH_EAST
public static final int EAST
public static final int SOUTH_EAST
public static final int SOUTH
public static final int SOUTH_WEST
public static final int WEST
public static final int NORTH_WEST
    Constants: compass directions.

public static final int HORIZONTAL
public static final int VERTICAL
    Constants: scrollbar and slider orienta-
    tions.

public static final int LEADING
public static final int TRAILING
    Constants: whether left edge is leading or
    trailing.

D.8.1.3 INTERFACE WindowConstants

public interface WindowConstants
    Window-closing constants.

FIELDS

public static final int
    DO_NOTHING_ON_CLOSE
public static final int HIDE_ON_CLOSE
public static final int DISPOSE_ON_CLOSE
    Constants: what should happen when a
    window closes.

D.8.2 CLASSES

D.8.2.1 CLASS AbstractButton

public abstract class AbstractButton extends
    JComponent implements
    ItemSelectable, SwingConstants
    A labeled clickable/selectable button or
    menu item. Extend this class to further
    specify button or menu item behavior.

CONSTRUCTORS

public AbstractButton()

METHODS

public void addActionListener(ActionListener
    l)

Register l to receive events from this AbstractButton.

public void
    addChangeListener(ChangeListener l)
Register l to respond to this AbstractButton's change events.

public void addItemListener(ItemListener l)
Register l to receive events from this AbstractButton.

public Action getAction()
= this AbstractButton's action (null if none).

public String getActionCommand()
= this AbstractButton's action command (null if none).

public String getText()
= this AbstractButton's text.

public boolean isSelected()
= "this AbstractButton is selected".

public void
    removeActionListener(ActionListener l)
Deregister l, so that it no longer receives events from this AbstractButton.

public void
    removeChangeListener(ChangeListener l)
Deregister l: it will no longer respond to this AbstractButton's events.

public void removeItemListener(ItemListener l)
Deregister l, so that it no longer receives events from this AbstractButton.

public void setAction(Action s)
Set this AbstractButton's action to s.

public void setActionCommand(String s)
Set this AbstractButton's action command to s.

public void setEnabled(boolean b)
Make this AbstractButton respond to user input iff b.

public void setSelected(boolean b)
Select this AbstractButton iff b.

public void setText(String s)
Set this AbstractButton's text to s.

INHERITED FROM JComponent (in D.8.2.9, p. 317) : 134

INHERITED FROM Container (in D.2.2.10, p. 256) : 52

INHERITED FROM Component (in D.2.2.9, p. 255) : 165

D.8.2.2   CLASS Box

public class Box extends Container
    implements Accessible
A container associated with a BoxLayout layout manager.

CONSTRUCTORS

public Box(int axis)
A Box that lays out its components along the axis (one of BoxLayout.X_AXIS and BoxLayout.Y_AXIS).

METHODS

public static Component createGlue()
= a blank Component useful for spacing: it expands to fill space between adjacent components.

public static Box createHorizontalBox()
= a Box that lays out its components horizontally.

public static Component
    createHorizontalGlue()
= a blank Component useful for horizontal or vertical spacing: it expands to fill space between adjacent components.

public static Component
    createHorizontalStrut(int w)
= a blank horizontal Component of height 0 and width w, useful for spacing.

public static Component
    createRigidArea(Dimension d)
= a blank Component of size d, useful for spacing.

public static Box createVerticalBox()
= a Box that lays out its components vertically.

public static Component createVerticalGlue()
= a blank Component useful for horizontal or vertical spacing: it expands to fill space between adjacent components.

public static Component
    createVerticalStrut(int h)
= a blank vertical Component of height h and width 0, useful for spacing.

INHERITED FROM Container (in D.2.2.10, p. 256) : 52

INHERITED FROM Component (in D.2.2.9, p. 255) : 165

D.8.2.3   CLASS **BoxLayout**

public class BoxLayout extends Object
   implements LayoutManager2,
   Serializable
   Controls the layout of a container either
   horizontally or vertically with no wrapping.

FIELDS
public static final int X_AXIS
public static final int Y_AXIS
   Constants: how to lay out components:
   left-right (X) or top-bottom (Y).

CONSTRUCTORS
public BoxLayout(Container c, int ax)
   A BoxLayout for c that lays out components horizontally or vertically, depending
   on ax (one of the class constants).

D.8.2.4   CLASS **JApplet**

public class JApplet extends Applet
   implements Accessible,
   RootPaneContainer
   A program embedded in a web page. Add
   components to a JApplet's content pane:
   japp.getContentPane().add(comp);
   Simlarly, use the content pane for setting layout managers, adding and removing components, etc.

CONSTRUCTORS
public JApplet()
   An empty JApplet.

METHODS
public Container getContentPane()
   = this JApplet's content pane.
public JMenuBar getJMenuBar()
   = this JApplet's menu bar.
public void setJMenuBar(JMenuBar mb)
   Set this JApplet's menubar to mb.

INHERITED FROM Applet (in D.1.1.1,
   p. 249) : 24
INHERITED FROM Panel (in D.2.2.26,
   p. 264) : addNotify, getAccessibleContext
INHERITED FROM Container (in D.2.2.10,
   p. 256) : 52

INHERITED FROM Component (in D.2.2.9,
   p. 255) : 165

D.8.2.5   CLASS **JButton**

public class JButton extends
   AbstractButton implements Accessible
   A labeled clickable button.

CONSTRUCTORS
public JButton()
public JButton(String s)
   An instance with an empty text label (or
   with label s).

INHERITED FROM AbstractButton (in
   D.8.2.1, p. 313) : 75
INHERITED FROM JComponent (in D.8.2.9,
   p. 317) : 134
INHERITED FROM Container (in D.2.2.10,
   p. 256) : 52
INHERITED FROM Component (in D.2.2.9,
   p. 255) : 165

D.8.2.6   CLASS **JCheckBox**

public class JCheckBox extends
   JToggleButton implements Accessible
   A checkable component. Clicking toggles
   between on (checked) and off (unchecked).
   See CheckboxGroup.

CONSTRUCTORS
public JCheckBox()
public JCheckBox(String s)
   An unchecked JCheckBox with no text label or with text label s.
public JCheckBox(String s, boolean b)
   A JCheckBox with text label s that is
   checked iff b.

INHERITED FROM JToggleButton (in
   D.8.2.29, p. 328) : getAccessibleContext,
   getUIClassID, paramString, updateUI
INHERITED FROM AbstractButton (in
   D.8.2.1, p. 313) : 75
INHERITED FROM JComponent (in D.8.2.9,
   p. 317) : 134
INHERITED FROM Container (in D.2.2.10,
   p. 256) : 52
INHERITED FROM Component (in D.2.2.9,
   p. 255) : 165

D.8.2.7 CLASS
JCheckBoxMenuItem

public class JCheckBoxMenuItem extends
    JMenuItem implements
    SwingConstants, Accessible
A checkable item in a menu.

CONSTRUCTORS

public JCheckBoxMenuItem()
public JCheckBoxMenuItem(String s)
    An unchecked JCheckBoxMenuItem with
    no text label or with text label s.
public JCheckBoxMenuItem(String s, boolean
    b)
    A JCheckBoxMenuItem with text label s
    that is checked iff b.

METHODS

public boolean getState()
    = "this JCheckBoxMenuItem is checked".
public synchronized void setState(boolean b)
    Check this JCheckBoxMenuItem iff b.

INHERITED FROM JMenuItem (in D.8.2.17,
    p. 322) : 31
INHERITED FROM AbstractButton (in
    D.8.2.1, p. 313) : 75
INHERITED FROM JComponent (in D.8.2.9,
    p. 317) : 134
INHERITED FROM Container (in D.2.2.10,
    p. 256) : 52
INHERITED FROM Component (in D.2.2.9,
    p. 255) : 165

D.8.2.8 CLASS **JComboBox**

public class JComboBox extends
    JComponent implements
    ItemSelectable, ListDataListener,
    ActionListener, Accessible
A component with a button or text field
and a drop-down list. The user can select
a value from the drop-down list. If the instance is editable, it has a text field for
user input.

CONSTRUCTORS

public JComboBox()
    An instance with no elements.
public JComboBox(Object[] items)

public JComboBox(Vector items)
    An instance with the elements of items,
    with the first one selected.

METHODS

public void addActionListener(ActionListener
    l)
    Register l to receive an action event when
    the user finishes making a selection.
public void addItem(Object obj)
    Append item obj to this list.
public void addItemListener(ItemListener l)
    Register l to receive an event when the
    selected item changes.
public Action getAction()
    = the Action for this ActionEvent source
    (null if none).
public String getActionCommand()
    = the action command that is included in
    the event sent to action listeners.
public Object getItemAt(int ind)
    = item this[ind] (null if none).
public int getItemCount()
    = the number of items in this.
public int getMaximumRowCount()
    = the maximum number of items to dis-
    play without a scrollbar.
public int getSelectedIndex()
    = the index of the first selected item (-1
    if no item is selected).
public Object getSelectedItem()
public Object[] getSelectedObjects()
    = the first selected item or an array of
    selected items.
public void hidePopup()
    Hide this JComboBox's popup window.
public void insertItemAt(Object obj, int ind)
    Insert item obj at this[ind], shifting
    this[ind..] to make room.
public boolean isEditable()
    = "this JComboBox is editable".
public boolean isLightWeightPopupEnabled()
    = "lightweight (all-Java) popups are in
    use".
public boolean isPopupVisible()
    = "the popup is visible".
public void
    removeActionListener(ActionListener l)
    Deregister l as an action listener.
public void removeAllItems()

Remove all items from the item list.

public void removeItem(Object b)
public void removeItemAt(int ind)
Remove item b or this[ind] from the item list.

public void removeItemListener(ItemListener l)
Deregister l as an item-change listener.

public void setAction(Action a)
Set the Action for the ActionEvent source to a.

public void setActionCommand(String s)
Set to s the action command to be included in the event sent to action listeners.

public void setEditable(boolean b)
Set this JComboBox to editable iff b.

public void setEnabled(boolean b)
Enable this JComboBox so that items can be selected iff b.

public void setLightWeightPopupEnabled(boolean b)
When displaying the popup, choose to use a lightweight popup iff b. Disable use of lightweight if some components are heavyweight.

public void setMaximumRowCount(int r)
Set the maximum number of rows to display to r. (A scrollbar is used if neccessary.)

public void setPopupVisible(boolean b)
Set the visibility of the popup to b.

public void setSelectedIndex(int ind)
public void setSelectedItem(Object obj)
Select item this[ind] or item obj if it is in the list.

public void showPopup()
Display this JComboBox's popup window.

INHERITED FROM JComponent (in D.8.2.9, p. 317) : 134
INHERITED FROM Container (in D.2.2.10, p. 256) : 52
INHERITED FROM Component (in D.2.2.9, p. 255) : 165

D.8.2.9   CLASS **JComponent**

public abstract class JComponent extends Container implements Serializable
Superclass of Swing components (except JFrame, JDialog, and JApplet).

CONSTRUCTORS

public JComponent()
A JComponent with no layout manager.

METHODS

public boolean contains(int x, int y)
= "this JComponent contains point (x,y)".

public int getHeight()
public int getWidth()
= the height and width of this component.

public int getX()
public int getY()
= the x- and y-coordinates of the top-left corner of this component.

public void paint(Graphics g)
Paint this JComponent using g. Never call this method: call repaint instead.

public void reshape(int x, int y, int w, int h)
Move this component to (x,y) and resize it to width w and height h.

public void setBackground(Color b)
= this JComponent's background color.

public void setEnabled(boolean b)
Make this JComponent respond to user events iff b.

public void setFont(Font f)
Set this JComponent's font to f (to the parent's font, if f is null).

public void setForeground(Color c)
Set JComponent's foreground color to c.

public void setVisible(boolean b)
Make this JComponent visible iff b.

INHERITED FROM Container (in D.2.2.10, p. 256) : 52
INHERITED FROM Component (in D.2.2.9, p. 255) : 165

D.8.2.10   CLASS **JDialog**

public class JDialog extends Dialog implements WindowConstants, Accessible, RootPaneContainer
A customizable dialog window. It can be *modal* (execution pauses while it is open) or non-modal. A dialog window may be "owned" by another window –when a window is destroyed or inconified, all owned dialogs are destroyed or iconified as well. Use the content pane to add and remove a component, change layout managers, etc.,

as in:
> dialog.getContentPane().add(child);

CONSTRUCTORS

public JDialog()
public JDialog(Dialog w)
public JDialog(Dialog w, boolean m)
> A non-modal JDialog with no title and no owner or owner w. Modal iff m.

public JDialog(Dialog w, String s)
public JDialog(Dialog w, String s, boolean m)
> A JDialog with title s owned by w. Modal iff m.

public JDialog(Frame w)
public JDialog(Frame w, boolean m)
> A JDialog with no title owned by w. Modal iff m.

public JDialog(Frame w, String s)
public JDialog(Frame w, String s, boolean m)
> A JDialog with title s owned by w. Modal iff m.

METHODS

public Container getContentPane()
> = this JDialog's content pane.

public int getDefaultCloseOperation()
> = the operation that occurs when the user initiates a close –see method setDefault-CloseOperation.

public JMenuBar getJMenuBar()
> = this JDialog's menu bar.

public void setDefaultCloseOperation(int operation)
> Set the operation that will happen when the user initiates a "close" on this dialog. Choices are (default is HIDE_ON-_CLOSE):
> DO_NOTHING_ON_CLOSE: nothing – force the program to handle the operation in method windowClosing of a WindowListener.
> HIDE_ON_CLOSE: call registered WindowListeners and hide the dialog.
> DISPOSE_ON_CLOSE: call registered WindowListeners and dispose of the dialog.

public void setJMenuBar(JMenuBar mb)
> Set this JDialog's menu bar to mb.

INHERITED FROM Dialog : addNotify, dispose, getAccessibleContext, getTitle, hide, isModal, isResizable, paramString, setModal, setResizable, setTitle, show

INHERITED FROM Window (in D.2.2.35, p. 268) : 27
INHERITED FROM Container (in D.2.2.10, p. 256) : 52
INHERITED FROM Component (in D.2.2.9, p. 255) : 165

D.8.2.11   CLASS **JFileChooser**

public class JFileChooser extends
> JComponent implements Accessible
> A window prompting the user to select a file.

FIELDS

public static final int OPEN_DIALOG
public static final int SAVE_DIALOG
public static final int CUSTOM_DIALOG
> Constants: dialog types.

public static final int CANCEL_OPTION
public static final int APPROVE_OPTION
public static final int ERROR_OPTION
> Constants: dialog results.

public static final int FILES_ONLY
public static final int DIRECTORIES_ONLY
public static final int
> FILES_AND_DIRECTORIES
> Constants: what type of directory contents to display.

public static final String
> CANCEL_SELECTION
public static final String
> APPROVE_SELECTION
> Constants: the button selection.

CONSTRUCTORS

public JFileChooser()
> A JFileChooser with current directory set to the user's home directory.

public JFileChooser(File x)
public JFileChooser(String x)
> A JFileChooser with current directory x.

METHODS

public void addActionListener(ActionListener l)
> Register l to respond to this JFileChooser's action events.

public void changeToParentDirectory()
> Set this JFileChooser's current directory to its parent.

public void ensureFileIsVisible(File f)
Ensure that f is not hidden.

public boolean getControlButtonsAreShown()
= "this JFileChooser's accept and cancel buttons are shown".

public File getCurrentDirectory()

public String getDialogTitle()

public int getDialogType()
= this JFileChooser's directory, title, or type (OPEN_DIALOG, SAVE_DIALOG, or CUSTOM_DIALOG).

public int getFileSelectionMode()
= the file content selection mode (FILES_ONLY, DIRECTORIES_ONLY, or FILES_AND_DIRECTORIES).

public String getName(File f)
= the name of file f.

public File getSelectedFile()
= this JFileChooser's selected file.

public File[] getSelectedFiles()
= this JFileChooser's selected files.

public boolean isMultiSelectionEnabled()
= "multiple files can be selected".

public void
removeActionListener(ActionListener l)
Deregister l: it will no longer respond to this JFileChooser's events.

public void
setControlButtonsAreShown(boolean b)
Show this JFileChooser's accept and cancel buttons iff b.

public void setCurrentDirectory(File dir)
Set this JFileChooser's current directory to dir (to the user's home directory if null).

public void setDialogTitle(String s)
Set this JFileChooser's title to s.

public void setDialogType(int d)
Set this JFileChooser's type to d (OPEN-_DIALOG, SAVE_DIALOG, or CUSTOM-_DIALOG).

public void setFileSelectionMode(int m)
Set this to select file types based on m (FILES_ONLY, DIRECTORIES_ONLY, or FILES_AND_DIRECTORIES).

public void setMultiSelectionEnabled(boolean b)
Enable multiple file selections iff b.

public void setSelectedFile(File f)
Set this JFileChooser's selected file to f. Ensure that the current directory is f's parent directory.

public void setSelectedFiles(File[] sf)
Set this JFileChooser's list of selected files to sf.

public int showOpenDialog(Component p)

public int showSaveDialog(Component p)
Show a dialog with owner p prompting the user to open or save a file. Return the appropriate JFileChooser dialog result codes.

INHERITED FROM JComponent (in D.8.2.9, p. 317) : 134

INHERITED FROM Container (in D.2.2.10, p. 256) : 52

INHERITED FROM Component (in D.2.2.9, p. 255) : 165

D.8.2.12   CLASS **JFrame**

public class JFrame extends Frame
implements WindowConstants,
Accessible, RootPaneContainer
A window with a border and title. Use the content pane to add and remove a component, change layout managers, etc., as in:
window.getContentPane().add(child);

FIELDS

public static final int EXIT_ON_CLOSE
The exit-application default window close operation. For applications only.

CONSTRUCTORS

public JFrame()

public JFrame(String s)
An empty JFrame with no title (or title s), not yet visible on the screen.

METHODS

public Container getContentPane()
= this JFrame's content pane.

public int getDefaultCloseOperation()
= the operation that occurs when the user initiates a "close" (see method setDefault-CloseOperation).

public JMenuBar getJMenuBar()
= this JFrame's menu bar (null if none).

public void setDefaultCloseOperation(int op)
Set to op the operation that happens when the user initiates a "close". Choices are (default is HIDE_ON_CLOSE):
DO_NOTHING_ON_CLOSE: let the program handle it in method **windowClosing**

of a registered WindowListener.
    HIDE_ON_CLOSE: call registered WindowListeners and hide the frame.
    DISPOSE_ON_CLOSE: call registered WindowListeners and dispose of the frame.
    EXIT_ON_CLOSE (defined in JFrame): call System.exit.

public void setJMenuBar(JMenuBar mb)
    Set this JFrame's JMenuBar to mb.

INHERITED FROM Frame (in D.2.2.16, p. 259) : 18
INHERITED FROM Window (in D.2.2.35, p. 268) : 27
INHERITED FROM Container (in D.2.2.10, p. 256) : 52
INHERITED FROM Component (in D.2.2.9, p. 255) : 165

D.8.2.13   CLASS **JLabel**

public class JLabel extends JComponent
        implements SwingConstants, Accessible
    A graphical label containing text. The text can be horizontally aligned in various ways. In the specs, parameter ha should be associated with one of the constants in interface SwingConstants: LEFT, CENTER, RIGHT, LEADING and TRAILING.
    For vertical alignment, parameter va should be one of the constants TOP, CENTER, and BOTTOM.

CONSTRUCTORS
public JLabel()
public JLabel(String s)
    A Label with left-justified text "" (or s).
public JLabel(String s, int ha)
    A JLabel with text "" (or s) justified according to ha.

METHODS
public int getHorizontalAlignment()
public String getText()
public int getVerticalAlignment()
    = this Label's horizontal alignment, text, and vertical alignment.
public void setHorizontalAlignment(int ha)
    Set this Label's horizontal alignment to ha (see the class spec for ha).
public void setText(String text)
    Set this Label's text to s ("" if s is null).

public void setVerticalAlignment(int va)
    Set this Label's vertical alignment to va (see the class spec for va).

INHERITED FROM JComponent (in D.8.2.9, p. 317) : 134
INHERITED FROM Container (in D.2.2.10, p. 256) : 52
INHERITED FROM Component (in D.2.2.9, p. 255) : 165

D.8.2.14   CLASS **JList**

public class JList extends JComponent
        implements Scrollable, Accessible
    A list of selectable items.

CONSTRUCTORS
public JList(Object[] d)
public JList(Vector d)
    A JList that contains d[..].

METHODS
public void addListSelectionListener(ListSelectionListener l)
    Register l to respond to this JList's selection events.
public void clearSelection()
    Deselect all selections.
public int getMaxSelectionIndex()
public int getMinSelectionIndex()
    = the largest and smallest index whose cell was selected.
public int getSelectedIndex()
    = smallest index of selected items (-1 if none).
public int[] getSelectedIndices()
    = indices of the selected items.
public Object getSelectedValue()
    = the selected item with smallest index (null if none).
public Object[] getSelectedValues()
    = the selected items.
public int getSelectionMode()
    = this JList's selection mode (see method setSelectionMode).
public boolean isSelectedIndex(int ind)
public boolean isSelectionEmpty()
    = "this[ind] was selected" and "nothing is selected".

public void removeListSelectionLis-
tener(ListSelectionListener
l)
Deregister l: it will no longer respond to
this JList's events.
public void removeSelectionInterval(int from,
int to)
Deselect items this[from..to].
public void setSelectedIndex(int ind)
public void setSelectedIndices(int[] in)
public void setSelectionInterval(int from, int
to)
Select item this[ind], or those with indices
in in, or this[from..to], clearing others.
public void setSelectionMode(int
selectionMode)
Set this JList's selection mode to a constant defined in class ListSelectionModel:
SINGLE_SELECTION: select only one
file at a time.
SINGLE_INTERVAL_SELECTION: selected files must be contiguous.
MULTIPLE_INTERVAL_SELECTION:
the default; any files can be selected.

INHERITED FROM JComponent (in D.8.2.9,
p. 317) : 134
INHERITED FROM Container (in D.2.2.10,
p. 256) : 52
INHERITED FROM Component (in D.2.2.9,
p. 255) : 165

D.8.2.15 CLASS JMenu

public class JMenu extends JMenuItem
implements Accessible, MenuElement
A drop-down menu in a menu bar (option-
ally, can be "torn off").

CONSTRUCTORS
public JMenu()
A JMenu named "". Cannot be torn off.
public JMenu(String s)
A JMenu named s. Cannot be torn off.
public JMenu(String s, boolean b)
A JMenu named s. Can be torn off iff b.

METHODS
public Component add(Component c)
Append c to this JMenu and return c.
public Component add(Component c, int ind)
Insert c at position this[ind], shifting

this[ind..] to make room. (Append if ind=-
1). Return c.
public JMenuItem add(JMenuItem mi)
Append mi to this JMenu and return mi.
public JMenuItem add(String s)
Append a new menu item with text s to
this JMenu and return the new item.
public void addMenuListener(MenuListener l)
Register l to respond to this JMenu's action events.
public void addSeparator()
Append a separator to this JMenu.
public JMenuItem getItem(int ind)
= menu item this[ind].
public int getItemCount()
= this JMenu's number of items.
public Component getMenuComponent(int n)
= component this[n].
public int getMenuComponentCount()
= the number of non-separators in this
JMenu.
public JPopupMenu getPopupMenu()
= the popup menu associated with this
menu.
public JMenuItem insert(JMenuItem mi, int
ind)
Insert mi at this[ind], shifting this[ind..] to
make room, and return mi.
public void insert(String s, int ind)
Insert a new menu item with text s at
this[ind], shifting this[ind..] to make room.
public void insertSeparator(int ind)
Insert a separator at this[ind], shifting
this[ind..] to make room.
public boolean isPopupMenuVisible()
= "this JMenu's popup menu is visible".
public boolean isSelected()
= "this JMenu is selected".
public void remove(Component c)
Remove menu item c or the item
at this[ind] from this JMenu. Shift
this[ind+1..] to fill the hole.
public void remove(int ind)
public void remove(JMenuItem c)
Remove menu item c or the item at
this[ind] from this JMenu.
public void removeAll()
Empty this JMenu.
public void
removeMenuListener(MenuListener l)

Deregister l: it will no longer respond to this JMenu's events.

public void setPopupMenuVisible(boolean b)
Make this JMenu's popup menu visible iff b.

public void setSelected(boolean b)
Select this JMenu iff b.

INHERITED FROM JMenuItem (in D.8.2.17, p. 322) : 31

INHERITED FROM AbstractButton (in D.8.2.1, p. 313) : 75

INHERITED FROM JComponent (in D.8.2.9, p. 317) : 134

INHERITED FROM Container (in D.2.2.10, p. 256) : 52

INHERITED FROM Component (in D.2.2.9, p. 255) : 165

D.8.2.16 CLASS JMenuBar

public class JMenuBar extends JComponent implements Accessible, MenuElement
A menu bar.

CONSTRUCTORS

public JMenuBar()
An empty JMenuBar.

METHODS

public JMenu add(JMenu c)
Append c to this JMenuBar.

public Component getComponentAtIndex(int ind)
= component this[ind].

public int getComponentIndex(Component c)
= the index of c in this[0..].

public JMenu getMenu(int ind)
= this[ind].

public int getMenuCount()
= the number of menus in this JMenuBar.

public boolean isSelected()
= "a component is selected".

public void setSelected(Component c)
Select c.

INHERITED FROM JComponent (in D.8.2.9, p. 317) : 134

INHERITED FROM Container (in D.2.2.10, p. 256) : 52

INHERITED FROM Component (in D.2.2.9,

p. 255) : 165

D.8.2.17 CLASS JMenuItem

public class JMenuItem extends AbstractButton implements Accessible, MenuElement
An item in a menu.

CONSTRUCTORS

public JMenuItem()
An empty MenuItem.

public JMenuItem(String s)

public JMenuItem(String s, int mn)
A MenuItem with text s and no keyboard shortcut (or keyboard shortcut mn).

METHODS

public KeyStroke getAccelerator()
= the KeyStroke for this menu item.

public boolean isArmed()
= "this menu item is armed".

public void setAccelerator(KeyStroke ks)
Set the key combination that invokes the menu item's action listeners to ks.

public void setArmed(boolean b)
Set the menu item to "armed" iff b – "armed" means that releasing the mouse over this item fires the menu's action event

public void setEnabled(boolean b)
Enable this item iff b.

INHERITED FROM AbstractButton (in D.8.2.1, p. 313) : 75

INHERITED FROM JComponent (in D.8.2.9, p. 317) : 134

INHERITED FROM Container (in D.2.2.10, p. 256) : 52

INHERITED FROM Component (in D.2.2.9, p. 255) : 165

D.8.2.18 CLASS JOptionPane

public class JOptionPane extends JComponent implements Accessible
A window asking the user for input (or alerting them). We present only methods that show a commonly used modal window, wait for the user to close it, and then return its results. Here are some of the parameters used.

Parameter pc: the parent component. The window is usually placed just below pc. If pc is null, the window is centered on the screen.

Parameter mt: the kind of window: ERROR_MESSAGE, INFORMATION_MESSAGE, WARNING_MESSAGE, QUESTION_MESSAGE, or PLAIN_MESSAGE.

Parameter ot: options to display in the window: YES_NO_OPTION or YES_NO_CANCEL_OPTION.

Returned value: YES_OPTION, NO_OPTION, CANCEL_OPTION, OK_OPTION, or CLOSED_OPTION.

FIELDS

public static final int DEFAULT_OPTION
public static final int YES_NO_OPTION
public static final int
    YES_NO_CANCEL_OPTION
public static final int OK_CANCEL_OPTION
    Constants: which options to display.

public static final int YES_OPTION
public static final int NO_OPTION
public static final int CANCEL_OPTION
public static final int OK_OPTION
public static final int CLOSED_OPTION
    Constants: dialog return values.

public static final int ERROR_MESSAGE
public static final int
    INFORMATION_MESSAGE
public static final int WARNING_MESSAGE
public static final int QUESTION_MESSAGE
public static final int PLAIN_MESSAGE
    Constants: dialog message types. Determines what the dialog box looks like.

METHODS

public static int
    showConfirmDialog(Component pc,
    Object m)
    Show a window with message m and title "Select an Option" (one of Yes, No, Cancel). Return answer selected by the user (one of the class dialog return values). See class spec for pc.

public static int
    showConfirmDialog(Component pc,
    Object m, String t, int ot)
    Show a window with message m and title t. Return answer selected by the user (one of the dialog return values). See class spec for pc and ot.

public static int
    showConfirmDialog(Component pc,
    Object m, String t, int ot, int mt)
    Show a window of type mt with message m, title t, and options ot; return selected option. See class spec for pc, mt, and ot.

public static String
    showInputDialog(Component pc, Object m)
    Show a window with message m. Return value entered by the user. See class spec for pc.

public static String
    showInputDialog(Component pc, Object m, String t, int mt)
    Show a window of type mt with title t and message m. Return value entered by the user. See class spec for pc and mt.

public static String showInputDialog(Object m)
    Show a window with message m. Return value entered by the user.

public static int
    showInternalConfirmDialog(Component pc, Object m)
    Show a YES_NO_CANCEL_OPTION window with title "Select an Option" and message m; return the option selected. See class spec for pc.

public static int
    showInternalConfirmDialog(Component pc, Object m, String t, int ot)
    Show an window with title t, message m, and choices given by ot; return the option selected. See class spec for pc and ot.

public static String
    showInternalInputDialog(Component pc, Object m)
    Show a QUESTION_MESSAGE window with title "Input" and message m; return answer entered by the user. See class spec for pc.

public static String
    showInternalInputDialog(Component pc, Object m, String t, int mt)
    Show a window with message type mt, title t, and message m; return answer entered by the user. See class spec for pc and mt.

public static void
    showInternalMessageDialog(Component pc, Object m)

Show an INFORMATION_MESSAGE window with title "Message" and message m. See class spec for pc.

public static void
showInternalMessageDialog(Component pc, Object m, String t, int mt)
Show a window of message type mt with title t and message m. See class spec for pc and mt.

public static void
showMessageDialog(Component pc, Object m)
Show a window with message m. See class spec for pc.

public static void
showMessageDialog(Component pc, Object m, String t, int mt)
Show a window of type mt with title t and message m. See class spec for pc and mt.

INHERITED FROM JComponent (in D.8.2.9, p. 317) : 134
INHERITED FROM Container (in D.2.2.10, p. 256) : 52
INHERITED FROM Component (in D.2.2.9, p. 255) : 165

D.8.2.19   CLASS **JPanel**

public class JPanel extends JComponent
implements Accessible
A simple container.

CONSTRUCTORS

public JPanel()
public JPanel(LayoutManager lm)
A JPanel with FlowLayout layout manager (or lm).

INHERITED FROM JComponent (in D.8.2.9, p. 317) : 134
INHERITED FROM Container (in D.2.2.10, p. 256) : 52
INHERITED FROM Component (in D.2.2.9, p. 255) : 165

D.8.2.20   CLASS **JPasswordField**

public class JPasswordField extends
JTextField
An editable line of hidden text.

CONSTRUCTORS

public JPasswordField(int c)
public JPasswordField(String s, int c)
A JPasswordField with no text (or text s) and c columns.

METHODS

public boolean echoCharIsSet()
= "this JPasswordField has an echo character" (echo char 0 stands for none).

public char getEchoChar()
= this JPasswordField's echo character (default '*').

public char[] getPassword()
= this JPasswordField's text. For more security, after use, set each char of the returned array to zero.

public void setEchoChar(char c)
Set this JPasswordField's echo character to c.

INHERITED FROM JTextField (in D.8.2.28, p. 327) : 26
INHERITED FROM JTextComponent : 66
INHERITED FROM JComponent (in D.8.2.9, p. 317) : 134
INHERITED FROM Container (in D.2.2.10, p. 256) : 52
INHERITED FROM Component (in D.2.2.9, p. 255) : 165

D.8.2.21   CLASS **JPopupMenu**

public class JPopupMenu extends
JComponent implements Accessible,
MenuElement
A popup menu that can appear anywhere. Used for the menu that appears when the user selects an item on the menu bar and for a "pull-right" menu.

CONSTRUCTORS

public JPopupMenu(String s)
A JPopupMenu with title s.

METHODS

public JMenuItem add(JMenuItem mi)
Append mi to this Menu and return mi.

public JMenuItem add(String s)
Append a new menu item with text s to this JMenu and return the new item.

public void addPopupMenuLis-
    tener(PopupMenuListener
    l)
    Register l to respond to this JPopupMenu's
    menu events.

public void addSeparator()
    Append a separator to this JPopupMenu.

public int getComponentIndex(Component c)
    = c's index in this JPopupMenu (-1 if
    none).

public String getLabel()
    = this JPopupMenu's text.

public void insert(Component comp, int ind)
    Insert comp at this[ind], shifting this[ind..]
    to make room.

public boolean isVisible()
    = "this JPopupMenu is visible".

public void remove(int ind)
    Remove menu item this[ind], shifting
    this[ind+1..] to fill the hole.

public void removePopupMenuLis-
    tener(PopupMenuListener
    l)
    Deregister l: it will no longer respond to
    this JPopupMenu's events.

public void setLabel(String s)
    Set this JPopupMenu's text label to s.

public void setVisible(boolean b)
    Make this JPopupMenu visible iff b.

INHERITED FROM JComponent (in D.8.2.9,
    p. 317) : 134
INHERITED FROM Container (in D.2.2.10,
    p. 256) : 52
INHERITED FROM Component (in D.2.2.9,
    p. 255) : 165

D.8.2.22   CLASS **JRadioButton**

public class JRadioButton extends
    JToggleButton implements Accessible
    A selectable button. See ButtonGroup.

CONSTRUCTORS
public JRadioButton()
public JRadioButton(String s)
    An unselected RadioButton with no text
    label or with text label s.

public JRadioButton(String text, boolean b)
    A RadioButton with text s that is selected
    iff b.

INHERITED FROM JToggleButton (in
    D.8.2.29, p. 328) : getAccessibleContext,
    getUIClassID, paramString, updateUI
INHERITED FROM AbstractButton (in
    D.8.2.1, p. 313) : 75
INHERITED FROM JComponent (in D.8.2.9,
    p. 317) : 134
INHERITED FROM Container (in D.2.2.10,
    p. 256) : 52
INHERITED FROM Component (in D.2.2.9,
    p. 255) : 165

D.8.2.23   CLASS **JRadioButtonMenuItem**

public class JRadioButtonMenuItem extends
    JMenuItem implements Accessible
    A selectable "button" in a menu. Use But-
    tonGroup to control the selection.

CONSTRUCTORS
public JRadioButtonMenuItem()
public JRadioButtonMenuItem(String s)
    An unselected JRadioButtonMenuItem
    with no text label or with text label s.

public JRadioButtonMenuItem(String s,
    boolean b)
    A JRadioButtonMenuItem with text label
    s that is selected iff b.

INHERITED FROM JMenuItem (in D.8.2.17,
    p. 322) : 31
INHERITED FROM AbstractButton (in
    D.8.2.1, p. 313) : 75
INHERITED FROM JComponent (in D.8.2.9,
    p. 317) : 134
INHERITED FROM Container (in D.2.2.10,
    p. 256) : 52
INHERITED FROM Component (in D.2.2.9,
    p. 255) : 165

D.8.2.24   CLASS **JScrollBar**

public class JScrollBar extends JComponent
    implements Adjustable, Accessible
    A horizontal or vertical scrollbar. Its
    state is determined by four proper-
    ties: value (the location of the thumb
    along the scrollbar), extent (the pro-
    portion of the viewable area to the
    entire document), range of values,

and orientation (one of the constants java.awt.Adjustable.HORIZONTAL and java.awt.Adjustable.VERTICAL).

CONSTRUCTORS

public JScrollBar()
A vertical scrollbar with value 0, visible amount (or extent) 10, and range 0..100.

public JScrollBar(int or)
A scrollbar with orientation or, value 0, extent 10, and range 0..100.

public JScrollBar(int or, int v, int ex, int min, int max)
A scrollbar with orientation or, value v, extent ex, and range min..max.

METHODS

public void addAdjustmentListener(AdjustmentListener l)
Register l to respond to this JScrollBar's adjustment events.

public int getMaximum()
public int getMinimum()
= this ScrollBar's maximum or minimum value.

public int getOrientation()
public int getValue()
public int getVisibleAmount()
= this JScrollBar's orientation, value, or extent.

public void removeAdjustmentListener(AdjustmentListener l)
Deregister l: it will no longer respond to this JScrollBar's events.

public void setMaximum(int m)
public void setMinimum(int m)
Set this ScrollBar's maximum or minimum value to m.

public void setOrientation(int x)
public void setValue(int x)
public void setVisibleAmount(int x)
Set this JScrollBar's orientation, value, or extent to x.

INHERITED FROM JComponent (in D.8.2.9, p. 317) : 134
INHERITED FROM Container (in D.2.2.10, p. 256) : 52
INHERITED FROM Component (in D.2.2.9, p. 255) : 165

D.8.2.25   CLASS **JScrollPane**

public class JScrollPane extends JComponent implements ScrollPaneConstants, Accessible
A scrollable component for a document with optional scrollbars and row and column headings.

CONSTRUCTORS

public JScrollPane(Component v)
A JScrollPane to display v; scrollbars appear when v's contents are larger than the view.

METHODS

public void setLayout(LayoutManager m)
Set the layout manager for this JScrollPane to m. Throw a ClassCastException if m is not a subclass of ScrollPaneLayout.

INHERITED FROM JComponent (in D.8.2.9, p. 317) : 134
INHERITED FROM Container (in D.2.2.10, p. 256) : 52
INHERITED FROM Component (in D.2.2.9, p. 255) : 165

D.8.2.26   CLASS **JSeparator**

public class JSeparator extends JComponent implements SwingConstants, Accessible
A menu item separator.

CONSTRUCTORS

public JSeparator()
A horizontal JSeparator.

public JSeparator(int or)
A JSeparator oriented according to or (one of SwingConstants.HORIZONTAL, SwingConstants.VERTICAL).

INHERITED FROM JComponent (in D.8.2.9, p. 317) : 134
INHERITED FROM Container (in D.2.2.10, p. 256) : 52
INHERITED FROM Component (in D.2.2.9, p. 255) : 165

D.8.2.27 CLASS **JTextArea**

public class JTextArea extends
   JTextComponent
   A multi-line region of editable text. Its
   row and column properties determine the
   size; if 0, the system determines the size.

CONSTRUCTORS

public JTextArea(int r, int c)
   An empty TextArea with r rows, c
   columns, and both scrollbars.
public JTextArea(String s)
   An instance with text s, 0 rows, and 0
   columns.
public JTextArea(String s, int r, int c)
   An instance with text s, r rows, and c
   columns.

METHODS

public void append(String s)
   Append s to this JTextArea.
public int getColumns()
public int getLineCount()
   = this JTextArea's number of columns or
   lines.
public int getLineEndOffset(int l)
   = the integer i such that this[i-1] is the last
   character on line l.
public int getLineOfOffset(int ind)
   = the line number corresponding to offset
   ind in this JTextArea.
public int getLineStartOffset(int l)
   = the integer i such that this[i] is the first
   character on line l.
public boolean getLineWrap()
   = "wrapping is in force".
public int getRows()
   = this JTextArea's number of rows.
public void insert(String s, int pos)
   Insert s at this[pos], shifting this[pos..] to
   make room.
public void replaceRange(String s, int start,
      int end)
   Replace this[start..end-1] by s.
public void setColumns(int c)
   Set this JTextArea's no. of columns to c.
public void setFont(Font f)
   Set this JTextArea's font to f.
public void setLineWrap(boolean wrap)

Wrap lines in this JTextArea iff wrap.
public void setRows(int r)
   Set this JTextArea's number of rows to r.

INHERITED FROM JTextComponent : 66
INHERITED FROM JComponent (in D.8.2.9,
   p. 317) : 134
INHERITED FROM Container (in D.2.2.10,
   p. 256) : 52
INHERITED FROM Component (in D.2.2.9,
   p. 255) : 165

D.8.2.28 CLASS **JTextField**

public class JTextField extends
   JTextComponent implements
   SwingConstants
   A single line of editable text. The no. of
   cols is used to calculate preferred size; if
   0, the system figures out the size.

CONSTRUCTORS

public JTextField()
   A 0-column empty JTextField.
public JTextField(int c)
   A c-column JTextField with text "".
public JTextField(String s)
   A JTextField with text s and as few
   columns as possible.
public JTextField(String s, int c)
   A c-column JTextField with text s.

METHODS

public synchronized void
      addActionListener(ActionListener l)
   Register l to respond to this JTextField's
   action events.
public int getColumns()
   = this JTextField's number of columns.
public int getHorizontalAlignment()
   = the horizontal alignment (constant in
   class SwingConstants: LEFT, CENTER,
   RIGHT, LEADING, TRAILING).
public synchronized void
      removeActionListener(ActionListener l)
   Deregister l: it will no longer respond to
   this JTextField's events.
public void setColumns(int c)
   Set this JTextField's number of cols to c.
public void setFont(Font f)
   Set this JTextField to f.

public void setHorizontalAlignment(int ha)
Set the horizontal alignment of the text to
ha –see the spec of getHorizontalAlignment
for values for ha.

INHERITED FROM JTextComponent : 66
INHERITED FROM JComponent (in D.8.2.9,
p. 317) : 134
INHERITED FROM Container (in D.2.2.10,
p. 256) : 52
INHERITED FROM Component (in D.2.2.9,
p. 255) : 165

D.8.2.29   CLASS **JToggleButton**

public class JToggleButton extends
AbstractButton implements Accessible
A selectable (on or off) button. Subclasses
are JRadioButton and JCheckBox.

CONSTRUCTORS

public JToggleButton(String s)
A JToggleButton labeled s.

public JToggleButton(String text, boolean b)
A JToggleButton labeled s that is selected
iff b.

INHERITED FROM AbstractButton (in
D.8.2.1, p. 313) : 75
INHERITED FROM JComponent (in D.8.2.9,
p. 317) : 134
INHERITED FROM Container (in D.2.2.10,
p. 256) : 52
INHERITED FROM Component (in D.2.2.9,
p. 255) : 165

D.8.2.30   CLASS **JWindow**

public class JWindow extends Window
implements Accessible,
RootPaneContainer
A window with no borders, buttons or
menubar. Use the content pane to add and
remove a component, change layout managers, etc., as in:
    window.getContentPane().add(child);

CONSTRUCTORS
public JWindow()
public JWindow(Frame w)
public JWindow(Window w)
A JWindow with layout manager Border-

Layout and no owner or owner w. Initially
not visible.

METHODS

public Container getContentPane()
= this JDialog's content pane.

INHERITED FROM Window (in D.2.2.35,
p. 268) : 27
INHERITED FROM Container (in D.2.2.10,
p. 256) : 52
INHERITED FROM Component (in D.2.2.9,
p. 255) : 165

Index